TEXTBOOK OF SUPPLY CHAIN MANAGEMENT

Second Revised & Enlarged Edition

Ashish Bhatnagar
MMS, Ph.D. (Lucknow University)
Professor & Head
Department of Business Administration
Dr. M.C. Saxena College of Engineering & Technology
Lucknow

Published by

Khushnuma Complex Basement
7, Meerabai Marg (Behind Jawahar Bhawan)
Lucknow 226 001 U.P. (INDIA)
Tel. : 91-522-2209542, 2209543, 2209544, 2209545
Fax : 0522-4045308
E-Mail : word-press@hotmail.com

First Edition 2009
Second Revised & Enlarged Edition 2010

Price: Rs. 225/-

ISBN 978-93-80257-10-5

Composed & Designed at :
Panacea Computers
3rd Floor, Agrawal Sabha Bhawan
Subhash Mohal, Sadar Cantt. Lucknow-226 002
Phone : 0522-2483312, 9452295008, 9335927082
E-mail : prasgupt@rediffmail.com

Printed at:
Salasar Imaging Systems
C-7/5, Lawrence Road Industrial Area
Delhi - 110 035
Tel. : 011-27185653, 9810064311

To my loving
Children
Rishit & Twisha

Preface to First Edition

The practice of supply chain management is guided by some basic underlying concepts that have not changed much over the centuries.

While developing my hypotheses, along with different ideas in supply chain management, I experimented in my classes at different management institutes over a number of years. I offer my grateful thanks to all my past and present students for raising several intelligent queries and doubts for help in my analysis later. I also owe my immense thanks to the work of all the authorson the subject, whom I have referred to during the course.

The objective of the text book is to explain these concepts of Supply Chain Management in simple and understandable language. Wherever required, the same have been explained with the help of illustrations and working examples to explain the numerical parts.

The idea behind this text book is to drive down the concepts of Supply Chain Management in the simplest form. Overall it shall be a good learning experience for the students of under-graduate and post-graduate programmes in management.

I am thankful to my beloved wife Vartika for typing the manuscript, doing the proof reading and being a source of continuous inspiration all through the work. I shall be grateful to the readers and academicians for their constructive suggestions in improving the contents of the book.

Author

Preface to the Second Edition

Welcome to the second edition of *Text Book of Supply Chain Management*. The practice of supply chain management has become widespread in all industries across the globe today and both small and large firms are realizing the benefits provided by effective supply chain management.

The objective of the book is to make readers think about how supply chain management impacts all of the areas and processes of the firm. Undergraduate business students, beginning MBA students as well as practicing managers can benefit from reading and using the text.

There are a number of additions to this second edition, which I hope will be interesting and useful. Each chapter contains new end-of-chapter discussion questions and exercises, wherever applicable. A new chapter on *Outsourcing* has been added and the chapters are supplemented by teaching cases covering most of the topics discussed. Some of the case companies and situations are real, while others are fictional and the cases are varied from easy to difficult and short to long.

I sincerely hope that the topics compiled in the text will keep the readers interested. I welcome the comments and suggestions of readers for the improvement of this text.

Author

Contents

1	**Introduction to Supply Chain Management**	**1**
	Role of SCM in Enterprise Management	3
	Evolution of the Concept of SCM	5
	Drivers of SCM	9
	Aligning the Supply Chain with Business Strategy	19
	Value Chains versus Supply Chains	27
	SCM and Related Disciplines: Logistics	34
	For Discussion	36
2.	**Inventory**	**37**
	Inventory Functionality	38
	Classification of Inventory	40
	Inventory Management	43
	Model I: The Retailer's EOQ Model of Inventory Management	45
	Model II: The Producer's EBQ Model	50
	Model III: The Discounting Model	54
	ABC Analysis or Value Distribution	56
	Numerical Problems	62
	For Discussion	71
	Numerical Exercises	72
3.	**Purchasing**	**75**
	Centralized Vs Decentralized Purchasing	81
	Purchasing Principles or Policies	82
	Ten Keys to Effective Purchasing	83
	For Discussion	87
4	**Source Selection & Management**	**89**
	Source Selection and Development	89
	Single Vendor Development	98
	Negotiations	100
	Storekeeping	100
	Stores Accounting	102
	For Discussion	103
5.	**Just-In-Time (JIT)**	**105**
	Development of the JIT Concept	107
	KANBAN and Pull System	112
	Lean Thinking for the Supply Chain	115
	Path Forward to a Lean Supply Chain	120
	For Discussion	120

6. **Logistics** 123
Logistics Costs 131
Models in Logistics Management 133
The Bullwhip Effect 145
For Discussion 148

7. **Outsourcing** 151
Outsourcing Operations 155
Outsourcing Functions 156
For Discussion 159

8. **Materials Handling** 161
Handling Requirements 162
Storage Requirements 163
Mechanized Systems 165
Semi-automated Handling 168
Automated Handling 170
Best Practices in Material Handling and Put-away 174
For Discussion 177

9. **Transportation** 179
Transport Functionality 179
Transport Infrastructure 184
Transport Economics 187
Cost Structures 189
Pricing Strategies 190
Rating 191
Where Are You on the Transportation Best-Practice Continuum? 194
For Discussion 196

10. **Packaging** 197
Packaging Design 198
Packaging Materials 198
Cost of Packing 207
Environmental Requirements 210
Best Practices in Fulfilment: On Picking and Packing 211
For Discussion 214

11. **Information Technology and Supply Chain Management** 215
Enterprise Information Technologies 215
Supply Chain Information Processing 216
Supply Chain Information Systems 220
For Discussion 227

12. **Benchmarking** 229
What is Best Practice? 230
Who uses best practices? 231
The Benchmarking Process 232
For Discussion 235

AN APPROACH TO CASE ANALYSIS **237**
Case 1: Mother Dairy: A Case for Supply Chain Management? 243
Case 2: To Buy or Not to Buy? 244
Case Study 3: Supply Chain Management at Bose Corporation 244
Case 4: HUL – Leveraging Growth through Information Tech. 246
Case 5: Transporting Samsung 248
Case 6: Routing And Backhauling 249
Case 7: Reducing Inventory 249
Case 8: Managing The Materials 251
Case 9: Managing Movement Of Medical Products 251
Case 10: Warehouse Management System 252

References 255
Subject Index 257

Introduction to Supply Chain Management

A *supply chain* is a network of facilities and distribution options that performs the functions of procurement of materials, transformation of these materials into intermediate and finished products, and the distribution of these finished products to customers. Supply chains exist in both service and manufacturing organizations, although the complexity of the chain may vary greatly from industry to industry and firm to firm.

An example of a simple supply chain for a single product is where raw material is procured from vendors, transformed into finished goods in a single step, and then transported to distribution centers, and ultimately, customers. Realistic supply chains have multiple end products with shared components, facilities and capacities. The flow of materials is not always along an arborescent network, various modes of transportation may be considered, and the bill of materials for the end items may be both deep and large.

Traditionally, marketing, distribution, planning, manufacturing, and the purchasing organizations along the supply chain operated independently. These organizations had their own objectives and these were often conflicting. Marketing's objective of high customer service and maximum sales, conflicts with manufacturing and distribution goals. Many manufacturing operations are designed to maximize throughput and lower costs with little consideration for the impact on inventory levels and distribution capabilities. Purchasing contracts are often negotiated with very little information beyond historical buying patterns. The result of these factors is that there is not a single, integrated plan for the organization—there were as many plans as businesses. Clearly, there is a need for a mechanism through which these different functions can be integrated together. Supply chain management is a strategy through which such integration can be achieved.

Supply chain management is typically viewed to lie between fully vertically integrated firms, where the entire material flow is owned by a single firm and those where each channel member operates independently. Therefore, co-ordination between the various players in the chain is critical in its effective management. Supply chain management can be compared to a well-balanced and well-practiced relay team. Such a team is more competitive when each player knows how to be positioned for the hand-off. The relationships are the strongest between players who directly pass the baton, but the entire team needs to make a co-ordinated effort to win the race.

It will not be less than correct to mention that marketing starts with customers and also ends with customers only. So to say, customer and marketing are inseparable from each other. Customer is considered king in the market who dictates the market and makes the enterprise run. Today, what customer wants are better products, lower prices and faster supplies of goods and services. These enhance the customer delight and enterprise plight. Meeting customer's wants has never been simple in a competitive market. Marketers have been engaged in evolving devices to gain competitive advantage that enables them to satisfy the customer's wants and stay and survive in market. In fact, innovate and invent have become, of late, the new mantras in modern marketing to possess competitive advantage, especially in a highly competitive market. Earlier logistics was used as one of the devices to gain competitive advantages in the market. Of late, there has been a paradigm shift from logistics to its modern day avatar, better known as Supply Chain Management (SCM) which has been discovered as a source of competitive advantage.

Let us first understand what these two terms, namely, logistics and SCM mean. Simply stating, logistics is a logical extension of transportation and its related areas to achieve an efficient and effective goods distribution system. Thus, logistics encompasses the activities of inventory management, order processing, warehouse and materials handling and physical distribution. SCM is the design and operation of the physical and managerial systems needed to transfer goods and services from vendor to customer in an effective and efficient manner.

The Council of Logistics Management defines SCM as:

> *The process of planning, implementing and controlling efficient flow of raw materials, in-process inventory, finished goods and related information from point of origin to point of consumption, for the purpose of conforming to customer requirements.*

Thus, SCM integrates various links involved in the customer order fulfilment, viz., supplier, transporters, manufacturer, wholesaler, retailer and consumer and transforms the business processes that bring products and services to the market place. In this way, SCM includes all those business processes involved in the value chain of an organisation that transform a concept into product and take it to the market.

Now, SCM can easily be differentiated from logistics. While logistics is a function, SCM is a process involving entire business activity.

Role of SCM in Enterprise Management

Only a few years have passed since enterprise management and organizational structure have been considered from the functional perspective: marketing, research and development, procurement, warehousing, manufacturing, sales and finance. The modern value creation logic challenges other schemes (as given in figure below).

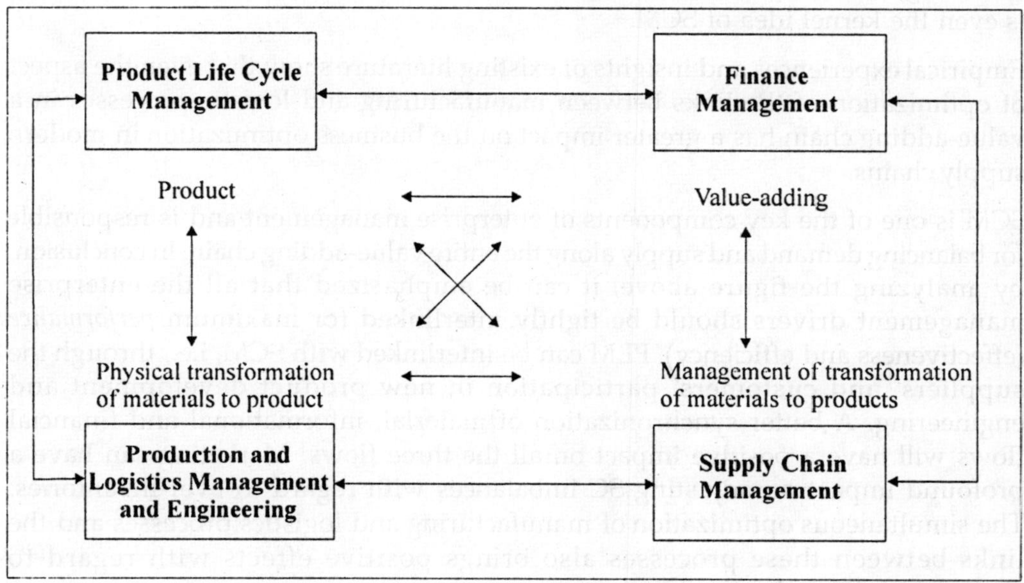

Main Elements of Enterprise Management

The basic element of entrepreneurship is the creation of *added value*. This is the basis for all further consideration. In normal business conditions, this value is connected with a product or a service. To be more precise, the added value creation is dispersed over the whole value chain, from raw materials to product distribution and consumption. The product life cycle management (PLM) is the first component of enterprise management. Its impact on enterprise growth is different in different branches and industrial environments.

The second enterprise management component is *finance*. The financial flows that accompany the material flows need to be handled efficiently. This concerns both the direct financial flows for product creation and indirect financial flows such as stock exchange activities, investments, etc. Study of financial management is out of scope of this book.

The physical production of a product is based on local product transformation (*manufacturing*) and transition (*logistics*) processes.

In the modern customer-driven economy, a product must not only be produced but also marketed. This means that a product is to be produced according to customers' requirements. Besides, minimum costs for product creation are usually desired. To achieve this, on the one hand, manufacturing and logistics process optimization is required. On the other, a continuous balance of demands and supplies is needed. This balance can be ensured by means of integrating and balancing the local processes along the entire value-adding chain. The last aspect is even the kernel idea of SCM.

Empirical experiences and insights of existing literature show that even the aspect of optimization of the links between manufacturing and logistic processes in a value-adding chain has a greater impact on the business optimization in modern supply chains.

SCM is one of the key components of enterprise management and is responsible for balancing demand and supply along the entire value-adding chain. In conclusion, by analyzing the figure above, it can be emphasized that all the enterprise management drivers should be tightly interlinked for maximum *performance* (effectiveness and efficiency). PLM can be interlinked with SCM, i.e., through the suppliers' and customers' participation in new product development and engineering. A better synchronization of material, informational and financial flows will have a positive impact on all the three flows. Marketing can have a profound impact on adjusting SC imbalances with regard to over-inventories. The simultaneous optimization of manufacturing and logistics processes and the links between these processes also brings positive effects with regard to shareholders' satisfaction.

Supply Chain Decisions

We classify the decisions for supply chain management (SCM) into two broad categories — strategic and operational. As the term implies, strategic decisions are made typically over a longer time horizon. These are closely linked to the corporate strategy, and guide supply chain policies from a design perspective. On the other hand, operational decisions are short-term, and focus on activities over a day-to-day basis. The effort in these types of decisions is to effectively and efficiently manage the product flow in the "strategically" planned supply chain.

There is a basic pattern to the practice of supply chain management. Each supply chain has its own unique set of market demands and operating challenges and yet the issues remain essentially the same in every case. Companies in any supply chain must make decisions individually and collectively regarding their actions in five areas:

1. *Production*—what products does the market want? How much of which products should be produced and by when? This activity includes the creation of master

production schedules that take into account plant capacities, workload balancing, quality control and equipment maintenance.

2. *Inventory*—what inventory should be stocked at each stage in a supply chain? How much inventory should be held as raw materials, semi-finished or finished goods? The primary purpose of inventory is to act as a buffer against uncertainty in the supply chain. However, holding inventory can be expensive, so what are the optimal inventory levels and reorder points?

3. *Location*—where should facilities for production and inventory storage be located? Where are the most cost efficient locations for production and for storage of inventory? Should existing facilities be used or new ones built? Once these decisions are made they determine the possible paths available for product to flow through for delivery to the final consumer.

4. *Transportation*—how should inventory be moved from one supply chain location to another? Air freight and truck delivery are generally fast and reliable but they are expensive. Shipping by sea or rail is much less expensive but usually involves longer transit times and higher uncertainty. This uncertainty must be compensated for by stocking higher levels of inventory. When is it better to use which mode of transportation?

5. *Information*—how much data should be collected and how much information should be shared? Timely and accurate information holds the promise of better co-ordination and better decision making. With good information, people can make effective decisions about what to produce and how much, about where to locate inventory and how best to transport it.

The sum of these decisions will define the capabilities and effectiveness of a company's supply chain. The things a company can do and the ways that it can compete in its markets are all dependent on the effectiveness of its supply chain. If a company's strategy is to serve a mass market and compete on the basis of price, it had better have a supply chain that is optimized for low cost. If a company's strategy is to serve a market segment and compete on the basis of customer service and convenience, it had better have a supply chain optimized for responsiveness. Who a company is and what it can do is shaped by its supply chain and by the markets it serves.

Evolution of the Concept of SCM

Over the last 50 years, a transition from the producers' market to the customers' markets has occurred. This transition began in the 1960s with an increasing role of marketing in the conditions of *mass production* of similar products to an anonymous market. This period is known as the economy of scale. After filling the markets with products, the quality problems came to the forefront of enterprise management. In the 1970s, Total Quality Management (TQM) was established.

The increased quality caused the *individualization* of customers' requirements in the 1980s. This was the launching point for the establishment of the economy of the customer. This period is characterized by efforts for optimal inventory management and a reduction in production cycles.

In the 1980-1990s, handling a high product variety challenged enterprise management. Another trend was the so-called *speed effect*. The speed of reaction to market changes and cutting time-to-market became even more important. Consequently, the optimization of internal processes simultaneously with external links to suppliers was rooted in the concepts of lean production and just-in-time.

Throughout the 1990s, companies concentrated in development approaches to core competencies, outsourcing, innovations and collaboration. These trends were caused by globalization, advancements in IT and integration processes into the world economy. The paradigm of SCM was established, particularly in the 1990s.

The development of SCM was driven in the 1990s by three *main trends*: customer orientation, market globalization and establishment of an information society. These trends caused changes in enterprise competitive strategies and required new adequate value chain management concepts (See figure below).

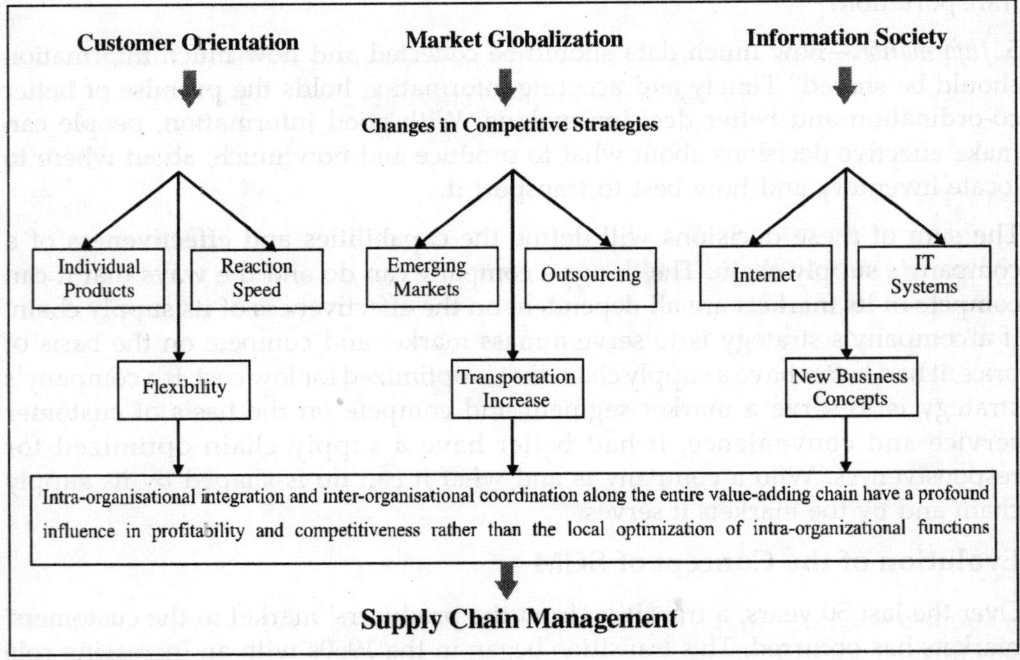

Development of SCM

First, to remain competitive, enterprises concentrated on *product individualization* and maximum satisfaction of customers' requirements. *Flexibility* and *responsiveness* came to be the key factors in supply management. Second, in the 1990s new markets in Asia, Eastern Europe and South America were extensively acquired and the production facilities actively shifted to these regions. Thirdly, remarkable advances in IT and establishing the World Wide Web (WWW) provided the basis for innovative business concepts. On the whole, the focus turned to the consideration of entire value-adding chains, all the elements and links within them and outside the own enterprise to ensure business profitability and competitiveness. This launched the mass establishment of SCM.

The practice of SCM has provided enough evidence that intra-organizational integration and inter-organizational co-ordination along the *entire value-adding chain* have a profound influence on profitability and competitiveness, rather than the local optimization of intra-organizational functions.

In the recent years, SCM has been increasingly established in different branches, such as aerospace, automotive, pharmaceutical, telecommunications, textiles and clothing, retail, 3PL, FMCG (fast moving consumer goods), construction and material, health care, food and beverages and high-tech manufacturing. The research on SCM has a different emphasis, i.e., in the automotive industry, the issues of alignment of market demands and supply and costing are at the forefront of discussions. For the FMCG sector, stockless processes, agility and mobile (IT) are the most important issues. For retail and clothing, the issues of outsourcing, uncertainty, collaboration and reverse logistics have a greater impact. In aerospace, the stage of product utilization and service is of a crucial nature.

Need for SCM

Before we appreciate the need for SCM, let us first trace out the evolution of the concept of SCM. The concept of SCM has only recently stepped into the marketing world. It rooted three decades back and has passed through three phases:

Phase I: Physical Distribution Management: This phase is better characterised as 'inventory push phase' when manufacturing was handled in isolation and output was pushed down to the finished goods warehouses.

Phase II: Integrated Logistics Management: This phase recognised the importance of integrating operations within the organisation like sales, procurement, manufacturing, warehousing, distribution and transportation to achieve an efficient and effective goods distribution system.

Phase III: SCM: The graduation of logistics management to its modern day avatar is better known as 'SCM'. SCM extends the scope to link external partners like suppliers, vendors, distributors and customers with a view to deliver enhanced customer and economic value through synchronized management of the flow of physical goods and associated information from source to consumption.

In fact, the need for supply chain management is felt to benefit both customer and enterprise. While it enhances customer delight by satisfying the customer need for better products, lower costs and fastest supply, it improves enterprise plight by improving its productivity. In a nutshell, the benefits derived by applying SCM are:

(i) Reduced operational costs.
(ii) Improved flow of supplies.
(iii) Compelling bottom-line benefits to enterprise.
(iv) Reduction of delays in distribution.
(v) Increased customer satisfaction.

The corporate profitability can be linked to the deliverables of a supply chain with the help of following equation:

Profit = Revenue + Customer Service/Cost + Capital Employed

Use of Internet has also enabled companies to realize several supply chain related benefits. These are:

1. More collaborative, timely product development through enhanced communication among functional departments, suppliers, customers and even regulatory agencies.
2. Reduction of channel inventory and product obsolescence owing to closer linkage across the supply chain and better insights into demand signals to drive products schedule and ultimately achieve build-to-order capability.
3. Reduction in communication costs and customer support costs with more interactive, tailored support capability inherent with Internet technologies.
4. New channel capability to reach different customer segments and further exploit current market.
5. Ability to enhance traditional products and customer relationships through customization driven by Internet connectivity and interactivity.

Features of SCM

The key features of Supply Chain Management can be summarized as follows:

1. Supply chain basically involves integration of business processes.
2. Supply chain establishes linkages with suppliers, customers and within the value chain of a business unit.
3. Supply chain encompasses all activities involved in the flow and transformation of goods from the raw material stage to the finished product as well as associated with information flows, cash flows and product flows in an organization.
4. Supply chain is to be managed from upstream to downstream by relationships with suppliers and customers to deliver superior customer value at the least possible cost.

Objectives of Supply Chain Management

The major objectives of SCM are:

1. To provide an uninterrupted flow of material and services required operating the organization.
2. To keep the inventory investment at a minimum level.
3. To improve and maintain quality.
4. To find and develop competent suppliers.
5. To purchase the required items and services at the lowest possible cost.
6. To improve the organization's competitive position.
7. To accomplish the purchasing and marketing objectives at the lowest possible level of cost.

Advantages of SCM

1. Reduced inventory at all sites of supply chain.
2. Reduced costs.
3. Faster order processing speed.
4. Reduced lead times.
5. Reduced warehouse costs.
6. Reduced obsolescence.
7. Greater responsiveness to customer changes.
8. Electronic links to suppliers and customers.
9. Speeding up the development cycle.

Types of Supply Chain

A supply chain comprises of 3 or more companies directly linked. Based on the span, supply chain can be:

1. A basic supply chain - a company, an immediate supplier and an immediate buyer.
2. An extended supply chain – it includes suppliers of the immediate supplier and buyer of the immediate buyer.
3. An ultimate supply chain – it includes all the companies involved in all the upstream and downstream flows, from initial supplier to the ultimate buyer.

Drivers of SCM

What drove logistics to SCM? One can identify a number of drivers for a paradigm shift from logistics to SCM. The major ones are:

First, the expectations of customer for increased value addition, response time sensitivity, need for reliability, cost consciousness and information sensitivity.

Second, the nature of competition favouring firms that have been in a position to decrease lead times as well as operational costs.

Third, the recent revolution taken place in the field of information technology has enabled and encouraged the firms to initiate newer means in the field of distribution management.

Fourth, managers have realized and recognised the need for continuous improvement of process involved in marketing activity. The attitude of managers has changed in favour of integrating all activities in the chain from sourcing to consumption.

Fifth, perception of firms to have inventories has changed to JIT philosophy. While money locked up in inventories leadsto poor use of working capital, higher inventories lead to higher lead times for procurement, manufacture and distribution.

As we saw in the previous section, there are five areas where companies can make decisions that will define their supply chain capabilities: Production; Inventory; Location; Transportation and Information. Chopra and Meindl define these areas as performance drivers that can be managed to produce the capabilities needed for a given supply chain.

Effective supply chain management first calls for an understanding of each driver and how it operates. Each driver has the ability to directly affect the supply chain and enable certain capabilities. The next step is to develop an appreciation for the results that can be obtained by mixing different combinations of these drivers. Let's start by looking at these performance drivers individually.

Production

Production refers to the capacity of a supply chain to make and store products. The facilities of production are factories and warehouses. The fundamental decision that managers face when making production decisions is how to resolve the trade-off between responsiveness and efficiency. If factories and warehouses are built with a lot of excess capacity, they can be very flexible and respond quickly to wide swings in product demand. Facilities where all or almost all capacity is being used are not capable of responding easily to fluctuations in demand. On the other hand, capacity costs money and excess capacity is idle capacity not in use and not generating revenue. So the more excess capacity that exists, the less efficient the operation becomes.

Factories can be built to accommodate one of two approaches to manufacturing:

1. *Product focus*—a factory that takes a product focus performs the range of different operations required to make a given product line from fabrication of different

product parts to assembly of these parts.

2. *Functional focus*—a functional approach concentrates on performing just a few operations such as only making a select group of parts or only doing assembly. These functions can be applied to making many different kinds of products.

A product approach tends to result in developing expertise about a given set of products at the expense of expertise about any particular function. A functional approach results in expertise about particular functions instead of expertise in a given product. Companies need to decide which approach or what mix of these two approaches will give them the capability and expertise they need to best respond to customer demands.

As with factories, warehouses too can be built to accommodate different approaches. There are three main approaches to use in warehousing:

1. *Stock keeping unit (SKU) storage*—in this traditional approach, all of a given type of product is stored together. This is an efficient and easy to understand way to store products.

2. *Job lot storage*—in this approach, all the different products related to the needs of a certain type of customer or related to the needs of a particular job are stored together. This allows for an efficient picking and packing operation but usually requires more storage space than the traditional SKU storage approach.

3. *Cross-docking*—an approach that was pioneered by Wal-Mart in its drive to increase efficiencies in its supply chain. In this approach, product is not actually warehoused in the facility. Instead, the facility is used to house a process where trucks from suppliers arrive and unload large quantities of different products. These larger lots are broken down into smaller lots. Smaller lots of different products are then recombined according to the needs of the day and quickly loaded onto outbound trucks that deliver the products to their final destination.

Inventory

Inventory is spread throughout the supply chain and includes everything from raw material to work-in-process to finished goods that are held by the manufacturers, distributors, and retailers in a supply chain. Again, managers must decide where they want to position themselves in the trade-off between responsiveness and efficiency. Holding large amounts of inventory allows a company or an entire supply chain to be very responsive to fluctuations in customer demand. However, the creation and storage of inventory is a cost and to achieve high levels of efficiency, the cost of inventory should be kept as low as possible.

There are three basic decisions to make regarding the creation and holding of inventory:

1. *Cycle Inventory*—this is the amount of inventory needed to satisfy demand for

the product in the period between purchases of the product. Companies tend to produce and to purchase in large lots in order to gain the advantages that economies of scale can bring. However, with large lots also come increased carrying costs. Carrying costs come from the cost to store, handle, and insure the inventory. Managers face the trade-off between the reduced cost of ordering and better prices offered by purchasing product in large lots and the increased carrying cost of the cycle inventory that comes with purchasing in large lots.

2. *Safety Inventory*—inventory that is held as a buffer against uncertainty. If demand forecasting could be done with perfect accuracy, then the only inventory that would be needed would be cycle inventory. But since every forecast has some degree of uncertainty in it, we cover that uncertainty to a greater or lesser degree by holding additional inventory in case demand is suddenly greater than anticipated. The trade-off here is to weigh the costs of carrying extra inventory against the costs of losing sales due to insufficient inventory.

3. *Seasonal Inventory*—this is inventory that is built up in anticipation of predictable increases in demand that occur at certain times of the year. For example, it is predictable that demand for anti-freeze will increase in the winter. If a company that makes anti-freeze has a fixed production rate that is expensive to change, then it will try to manufacture product at a steady rate all year long and build up inventory during periods of low demand to cover for periods of high demand that will exceed its production rate. The alternative to building up seasonal inventory is to invest in flexible manufacturing facilities that can quickly change their rate of production of different products to respond to increases in demand. In this case, the trade-off is between the cost of carrying seasonal inventory and the cost of having more flexible production capabilities.

Location

Location refers to the geographical setting of supply chain facilities. It also includes the decisions related to which activities should be performed in each facility. The responsiveness versus efficiency trade-off here, is the decision whether to centralize activities in fewer locations to gain economies of scale and efficiency, or to decentralize activities in many locations close to customers and suppliers in order for operations to be more responsive.

When making location decisions, managers need to consider a range of factors that relate to a given location including the cost of facilities, the cost of labour, skills available in the workforce, infrastructure conditions, taxes and tariffs, and proximity to suppliers and customers. Location decisions tend to be very strategic decisions because they commit large amounts of money to long-term plans.

Location decisions have strong impacts on the cost and performance characteristics of a supply chain. Once the size, number, and location of facilities is determined, that also defines the number of possible paths through which products can flow on the way to the final customer. Location decisions reflect a company's basic strategy for building and delivering its products to market.

Transportation

This refers to the movement of everything from raw material to finished goods between different facilities in a supply chain. In transportation, the trade-off between responsiveness and efficiency is manifested in the choice of transport mode. Fast modes of transport such as airplanes are highly responsive but also more costly. Slower modes such as ship and rail are cost-efficient but not as responsive. Since transportation costs can be as much as a third of the operating cost of a supply chain, decisions made here are important.

There are six basic modes of transport that a company can choose from:

1. *Ship* is highly cost-efficient but also the slowest mode of transport. It is limited to use between locations that are situated next to navigable waterways and facilities such as harbors and canals.

2. *Rail* is also cost-efficient but can be slow. This mode is also restricted to use between locations that are served by rail lines.

3. *Pipelines* can be efficient but are restricted to commodities that are liquids or gases such as water, oil, and natural gas.

4. *Trucks* are relatively quicker and a flexible mode of transport. They can go almost anywhere. The cost of this mode is prone to fluctuations though, as the cost of fuel fluctuates and the condition of roads varies.

5. *Airplanes* are the fastest mode of transport and are highly responsive. This is also the most expensive mode and it is somewhat limited by the availability of appropriate airport facilities.

6. *Electronic Transport* is amongst the fastest mode of transport, it is flexible and highly cost-efficient. However, it can only be used for movement of certain types of products such as electric energy, data, and products composed of data such as music, pictures, and text. Someday, technology that allows us to convert matter to energy and back to matter again may completely rewrite the theory and practice of supply chain management.

Given these different modes of transportation and the location of the facilities in a supply chain, managers need to design routes and networks for moving products. A route is the path through which products move and networks are composed of the collection of the paths and facilities connected by those paths. As a general rule, the higher the value of a product (such as electronic components or pharmaceuticals), the more its transport network should emphasize responsiveness and the lower the value of a product (such as bulk commodities like grain or lumber), the more its network should emphasize efficiency.

Information

Information is the basis upon which decisions regarding the other four supply chain drivers are made. It is the connection between all of the activities and operations in a supply chain. To the extent that this connection is a strong one, (i.e., the data is accurate, timely, and complete), the companies in a supply chain will each be able to make good decisions for their own operations. This will also tend to maximize the profitability of the supply chain as a whole. That is the way the stock markets or other free markets work and supply chains have many of the same dynamics as markets. Information is used for two purposes in any supply chain:

1. *Coordinating daily activities* related to the functioning of the other four supply chain drivers: production; inventory; location; and transportation. The companies in a supply chain use available data on product supply and demand to decide on weekly production schedules, inventory levels, transportation routes, and stocking locations.

2. *Forecasting and planning* to anticipate and meet future demands. Available information is used to make tactical forecasts to guide the setting of monthly and quarterly production schedules and timetables. Information is also used for strategic forecasts to guide decisions about whether to build new facilities, enter a new market, or exit an existing market.

Within an individual company the trade-off between responsiveness and efficiency involves weighing the benefits that good information can provide against the cost of acquiring that information. Accurate information can enable efficient operating decisions and better forecasts but the cost of building and installing systems to deliver this information can be high.

Within the supply chain as a whole, the responsiveness versus efficiency trade-off that companies make is one of deciding how much information to share with the other companies and how much information to keep private. The more information about product supply, customer demand, market forecasts, and production schedules that companies share with each other, the more responsive everyone can be. Balancing this openness however, are the concerns that each company has about revealing information that could be used against it by a competitor. The potential costs associated with increased competition can hurt the profitability of a company.

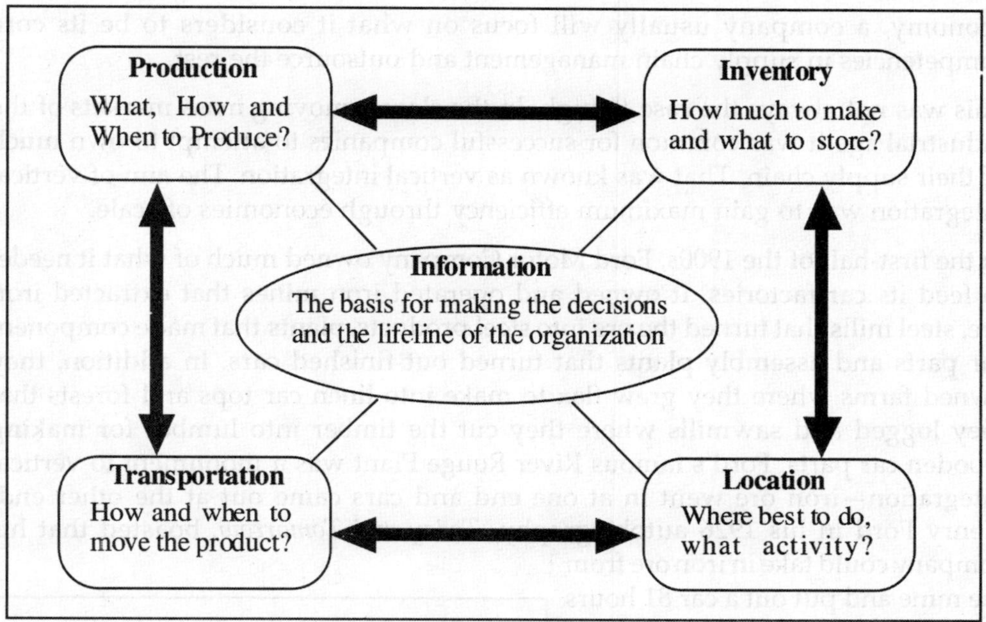

Major Drivers of Supply Chain

Basic Components for SCM

1. **Plan :** it is the strategic part of SCM to monitor the supply chain so that it is efficient, costs less and delivers high quality and value to customers in the most cost-effective manner.
2. **Source :** developing a set of pricing, delivery payment processes with the suppliers for monitoring and improving the relationships.
3. **Make :** involves making schedule for the activities necessary for production, testing, packaging and preparation for delivery.
4. **Deliver :** involves co-ordination of the receipt of orders from customers, developing a network of warehouses, picking carriers to get products to the customers and setting up an invoicing system to receive payments.
5. **Return/Reverse Flow :** refers to the reverse flow of goods from the customers back to the manufacturer and involves creating a network for receiving defective and excess products back from the customers and supporting customers who have problems with the delivered goods.

Supply Chain Management Today

The participants in a supply chain are continuously making decisions that affect how they manage the five supply chain drivers. Each organization tries to maximize its performance in dealing with these drivers through a combination of outsourcing, partnering, and in-house expertise. In the fast-moving markets of our present economy, a company usually will focus on what it considers to be its core competencies in supply chain management and outsource the rest.

This was not always the case though. In the slower-moving mass markets of the industrial age it was common for successful companies to attempt to own much of their supply chain. That was known as vertical integration. The aim of vertical integration was to gain maximum efficiency through economies of scale.

In the first-half of the 1900s, Ford Motor Company owned much of what it needed to feed its car factories. It owned and operated iron mines that extracted iron ore, steel mills that turned the ore into steel products, plants that made component car parts and assembly plants that turned out finished cars. In addition, they owned farms where they grew flax to make into linen car tops and forests that they logged and sawmills where they cut the timber into lumber for making wooden car parts. Ford's famous River Rouge Plant was a monument to vertical integration—iron ore went in at one end and cars came out at the other end. Henry Ford in his 1926 autobiography, *Today and Tomorrow*, boasted that his company could take in iron ore from the mine and put out a car 81 hours later.

This was a profitable way of doing business in the more predictable, one-size-fits-all industrial economy that existed in the early 1900s. Ford and other businesses churned out mass amounts of basic products. But as the markets grew and customers became more particular about the kind of products they wanted, this model began to break down. It could not be responsive enough or produce the variety of products that were being demanded. For instance, when Henry Ford was asked about the number of different colors a customer could request, he said, "they can have any color they want as long as it's black." In the 1920s, Ford's market share was over 50 percent but by the 1940s, it had fallen to below 20 percent. Focusing on efficiency at the expense of being responsive to customer desires was no longer a successful business model.

Old Supply Chains Vs New

Vertically integrated companies serving slow-moving mass markets once attempted to own much of their supply chains. Today's fast moving markets require more flexible and responsive supply chains.

Divisions of a Vertically Integrated Conglomerate

Raw Material

Transportation

Manufacturing

Distribution

Retail

Slow-Moving Industrial Mass Markets

Raw Material Company

Transportation Company

Manufacturing Company

Independent Distributor

Independent Retailer

Fragmented Fast-Moving Markets

Globalization, highly competitive markets, and the rapid pace of technological change are now driving the development of supply chains where multiple companies work together, each company focusing on the activities that it does best. Mining companies focus on mining, timber companies focus on logging and making lumber and manufacturing companies focus on different types of manufacturing from making component parts to doing final assembly. This way, people in each company can keep up with rapid rates of change and keep learning the new skills needed to compete in their particular business.

Where companies once routinely ran their own warehouses or operated their own fleet of trucks, they now have to consider whether those operations are really a core competency or whether it is more cost-effective to outsource those operations to other companies that make logistics the center of their business. To achieve high levels of operating efficiency and to keep up with continuing changes in technology, companies need to focus on their core competencies. It requires this kind of focus to stay competitive.

Instead of vertical integration, companies now practice "virtual integration". Companies find other companies who they can work with to perform the activities called for in their supply chains. How a company defines its core competencies and how it positions itself in the supply chain it serves is one of the most important decisions it can make.

Participants in the Supply Chain

In its simplest form, a supply chain is composed of a company, the suppliers and customers of that company. This is the basic group of participants that creates a simple supply chain. Extended supply chains contain three additional types of participants. First, there is the supplier's supplier or the ultimate supplier at the beginning of an extended supply chain. Then, there is the customer's customer or ultimate customer at the end of an extended supply chain. Finally, there is a whole category of companies who are service providers to other companies in the supply chain. These are companies who supply services in logistics, finance, marketing, and information technology.

In any given supply chain there is some combination of companies who perform different functions. There are companies that are producers, distributors or wholesalers, retailers, and companies or individuals who are the customers, the final consumers of a product. Supporting these companies there will be other companies that are service providers that provide a range of needed services.

Producers

Producers or manufacturers are organizations that make a product. This includes companies that are producers of raw materials and companies that are producers of finished goods. Producers of raw materials are organizations that mine for minerals, drill for oil and gas, and cut timber. It also includes organizations that farm the land, raise animals, or catch seafood. Producers of finished goods use these raw materials and subassemblies made by other producers to create their products.

Producers can create products that are intangible items such as music, entertainment, software, or designs. A product can also be a service such as mowing a lawn, cleaning an office, performing surgery, or teaching a skill. In many instances the producers of tangible, industrial products are moving to areas of the world where labour is cheap. Producers in the developed world of North America, Europe, and parts of Asia are increasingly producers of intangible items and services.

Distributors

Distributors are companies that take inventory in bulk from producers and deliver a bundle of related product lines to customers. Distributors are also known as wholesalers. They typically sell to other businesses in larger quantities than an individual consumer would usually buy. Distributors buffer the producers from fluctuations in product demand by stocking inventory and doing much of the sales work to find and service customers. For the customer, distributors fulfill the "Time and Place" function—they deliver products when and where the customer wants them.

A distributor is typically an organization that takes ownership of significant inventories of products that they buy from producers and sell to consumers. In addition to product promotion and sales, other functions the distributor performs are inventory management, warehouse operations, and product transportation as well as customer support and post-sales service. A distributor can also be an organization that only brokers a product between the producer and the customer and never takes ownership of that product. This kind of distributor performs mainly the functions of product promotion and sales. In both these cases, as the needs of customers evolve and the range of available products changes, the distributor is the agent that continually tracks customer needs and matches them with products available.

Retailers

Retailers stock inventory and sell in smaller quantities to the general public. This organization also closely tracks the preferences and demands of the customers that it sells to. It advertises to its customers and often uses some combination of price, product selection, service, and convenience as the primary draw to attract customers for the products it sells. Discount department stores attract customers using price and wide product selection. Upscale specialty stores offer a unique line of products and high levels of service. Fast food restaurants use convenience and low prices as their draw.

Customers

Customers or consumers are any organization that purchases and uses a product. A customer organization may purchase a product in order to incorporate it into another product that they in turn sell to other customers. Or a customer may be the final end user of a product who buys the product in order to consume it.

Service Providers

These are organizations that provide services to producers, distributors, retailers, and customers. Service providers have developed special expertise and skills that focus on a particular activity needed by a supply chain. Because of this, they are able to perform these services effectively and at a better price than producers, distributors, retailers, or consumers could do on their own.

Some common service providers in any supply chain are providers of transportation and warehousing services. These are truck companies and public warehouse companies and are known as logistics providers. Financial service providers deliver services such as making available loans, doing credit analysis, and collecting on past due invoices. These are banks, credit rating companies, and collection agencies. Some service providers deliver market research and advertising, while others provide product design, engineering services, legal services, and management advice. Still other service providers offer information technology and data collection services. All these service providers are integrated to a greater or lesser degree into the ongoing operations of the producers, distributors, retailers, and consumers in the supply chain.

Supply chains are composed of repeating sets of participants that fall into one or more of these categories. Over time the needs of the supply chain as a whole remain fairly stable. What changes is the mix of participants in the supply chain and the roles that each participant plays. In some supply chains, there are few service providers because the other participants perform these services on their own. In other supply chains, very efficient providers of specialized services have evolved and the other participants outsource work to these service providers instead of doing it themselves. Examples of supply chain structure are shown in Fig. on following page.

Aligning the Supply Chain with Business Strategy

A company's supply chain is an integral part of its approach to the markets it serves. The supply chain needs to respond to market requirements and do so in a way that supports the company's business strategy. The business strategy a company employs starts with the needs of the customers that the company serves or will serve. Depending on the needs of its customers, a company's supply chain

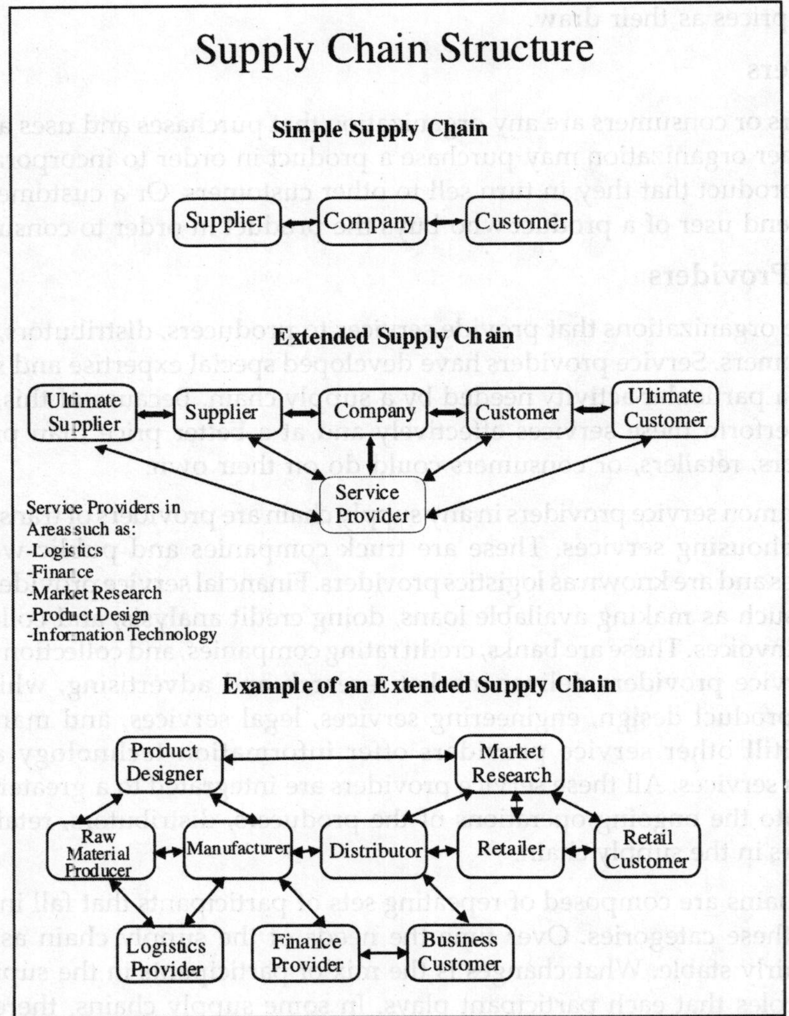

must deliver the appropriate mix of responsiveness and efficiency. A company whose supply chain allows it to efficiently meet the needs of its customers will gain market share at the expense of other companies in that market and also will be profitable.

There are three steps to use in aligning the supply chain with the business strategy. The first step is to understand the markets that the company serves. The second step is to define the strengths or core competencies of the company and the role the company can or could play in serving its markets. The last step is to develop the needed supply chain capabilities to support the roles the company has chosen.

1. Understand the Markets Your Company Serves

Begin by asking questions about your customers. What kind of customer does your company serve? What kind of customer does your customer sell to? What kind of supply chain is your company a part of? The answers to these questions will tell you what supply chains your company serves and whether your supply chain needs to emphasize responsiveness or efficiency. Chopra and Meindl have defined the following attributes that help to clarify requirements for the customers you serve. These attributes are:

(i) *The quantity of the product needed in each lot*—do your customers buy small amounts of products or do they buy large quantities? A customer at a convenience store or a drug store buys in small quantities. A customer of a discount warehouse club buys in large quantities.

(ii) *The response time that customers are willing to tolerate*—do your customers buy on short notice and expect quick service or is a longer lead time acceptable? Customers of a fast food restaurant certainly buy on short notice and expect quick service. Customers buying custom machinery would plan the purchase in advance and expect some lead time before the product could be delivered.

(iii) *The variety of products needed*—are customers looking for a narrow and well-defined bundle of products or are they looking for a wide selection of different kinds of products? Customers of a fashion boutique expect a narrowly defined group of products. Customers of a "big box" discount store like Wal-Mart expect a wide variety of products to be available.

(iv) *The service level required*—do customers expect all products to be available for immediate delivery or will they accept partial deliveries of products and longer lead times? Customers of a music store expect to get the CD they are looking for immediately or they will go elsewhere. Customers who order a custom-built new machine tool expect to wait a while before delivery.

(v) *The price of the product*—how much are customers willing to pay? Some customers will pay more for convenience or high levels of service and other customers look to buy based on the lowest price they can get.

(vi) *The desired rate of innovation in the product*—how fast are new products introduced and how long before existing products become obsolete? In products such as electronics and computers, customers expect a high rate of innovation. In other products, such as house paint, customers do not desire such a high rate of innovation.

2. Define Core Competencies of Your Company

The next step is to define the role that your company plays or wants to play in these supply chains. What kind of supply chain participant is your company? Is your company a producer, a distributor, a retailer, or a service provider? What does your company do to enable the supply chains that it is part of ? What are the core competencies of your company? How does your company make money? The answers to these questions tell you what roles in a supply chain will be the best fit for your company.

Be aware that your company can serve multiple markets and participate in multiple supply chains. A company like W.W. Grainger serves several different markets. It sells maintenance, repair, and operating (MRO) supplies to large national account customers such as Ford and Boeing and it also sells these supplies to small businesses and building contractors. These two different markets have different requirements as measured by the above customer attributes.

When you are serving multiple market segments, your company will need to look for ways to leverage its core competencies. Parts of these supply chains may be unique to the market segment they serve while other parts can be combined to achieve economies of scale. For example, if manufacturing is a core competency for a company, it can build a range of different products in common production facilities. Then different inventory and transportation options can be used to deliver the products to customers in different market segments.

3. Develop Needed Supply Chain Capabilities

Once you know what kind of markets your company serves and the role your company does or will play in the supply chains of these markets, then you can take this last step, which is to develop the supply chain capabilities needed to support the roles your company plays. This development is guided by the decisions made about the five supply chain drivers discussed earlier. Each of these drivers can be developed and managed to emphasize responsiveness or efficiency depending on the business requirements.

(i) Production—this driver can be made very responsive by building factories that have a lot of excess capacity and that use flexible manufacturing techniques to produce a wide range of items. To be even more responsive, a company could do their production in many smaller plants that are close to major groups of customers so that delivery times would be shorter. If efficiency is desirable, then a company can build factories with very little excess capacity and have the factories optimized for producing a limited range of items. Further efficiency could be gained by centralizing production in large central plants to get better economies of scale.

(ii) Inventory—responsiveness here can be had by stocking high levels of inventory for a wide range of products. Additional responsiveness can be gained by stocking products at many locations so as to have the inventory close to customers and available to them immediately. Efficiency in inventory management would call

for reducing inventory levels of all items and especially of items that do not sell as frequently. Also, economies of scale and cost savings could be achieved by stocking inventory in only a few central locations.

(iii) Location—a location approach that emphasizes responsiveness would be one where a company opens up many locations to be physically close to its customer base. For example, McDonald's has used location to be very responsive to its customers by opening up lots of stores in its high volume markets. Efficiency can be achieved by operating from only a few locations and centralizing activities in common locations. An example of this is the way Dell serves large geographical markets from only a few central locations that perform a wide range of activities.

(iv) Transportation—responsiveness can be achieved by a transportation mode that is fast and flexible. Many companies that sell products through catalogues or over the Internet are able to provide high levels of responsiveness by using transportation to deliver their products, often within 24 hours. FedEx and UPS are two companies who can provide highly responsive transportation services. Efficiency can be emphasized by transporting products in larger batches and doing it less often. The use of transportation modes such as ship, rail, and pipelines can be efficient. Transportation can be made more efficient if it is originated out of a central hub facility instead of from many branch locations.

(v) Information—the power of this driver grows stronger each year as the technology for collecting and sharing information becomes more widespread, easier to use, and less expensive. Information, much like money, is a very useful commodity as it can be applied directly to enhance the performance of the other four supply chain drivers. High levels of responsiveness can be achieved when companies collect and share accurate and timely data generated by the operations of the other four drivers. The supply chains that serve the electronics markets are some of the most responsive in the world. Companies in these supply chains from manufacturers, to distributors, to the big retail stores collect and share data about customer demand, production schedules, and inventory levels.

Where efficiency is more the focus, less information about fewer activities can be collected. Companies may also elect to share less information among them so as not to risk having that information used against them. Please note, however, that these information efficiencies are only efficiencies in the short-term and they become less efficient over time because the cost of information continues to drop and the cost of the other four drivers usually continues to rise. Over the longer term, those companies and supply chains that learn how to maximize the use of information to get optimal performance from the other drivers will gain the most market share and be the most profitable.

Three Steps to Align Supply Chain & Business Strategy

1. Understand the requirements of the customers
2. Define core competencies and the roles your company will play to serve your customers
3. Develop supply chain capabilities to support the roles your company has chosen

	Responsiveness	Efficiency
1. Production	- Excess capacity - Flexible manufacturing - Many smaller factories	- Little excess capacity - Narrow focus - Few central plants
2. Inventory	- High inventory levels - Wide range of items	- Low inventory levels - Fewer items
3. Location	- Many locations close to customers	- Few central locations serve wide areas
4. Transportation	- Frequent shipments - Fast and flexible modes	- Shipments few, large - Slow, cheaper modes
5. Information	- Collect and share timely accurate data	- Cost of information drops while other costs rise

Supply chain capabilities of responsiveness and efficiency come from decisions made about five supply chain drivers

A supply chain is composed of all the companies involved in the design, production, and delivery of a product to market. Supply chain management is the co-ordination of production, inventory, location, and transportation among the participants in a supply chain to achieve the best mix of responsiveness and efficiency for the market being served. The goal of supply chain management is to increase sales of goods and services to the final, end use customer while at the same time reducing both inventory and operating expenses.

The business model of vertical integration that came out of the industrial economy has given way to "virtual integration" of companies in a supply chain. Each company now focuses on its core competencies and partners with other companies that have complementary capabilities for the design and delivery of products to market. Companies must focus on improvements in their core competencies in order to keep up with the fast pace of market and technological change in today's economy.

To succeed in the competitive markets that make up today's economy; companies must learn to align their supply chains with the demands of the markets they serve. Supply chain performance is now a distinct competitive advantage for companies who excel in this area. One of the largest companies in North America is a testament to the power of effective supply chain management. Wal-Mart has grown steadily over the last 20 years and much, if not most, of its success is directly related to its evolving capabilities to continually improve its supply chain.

Adding Value to the Supply Chain

As technology products mature and become commoditized and competition intensifies, manufacturers are increasingly looking to electronic channels to bypass elements of the supply chain and thereby retain a higher proportion of their margins. More than often, it is the distributor's role within the channel that is most open to challenge from these new electronic channels. After all, products need to be made by the manufacturer and resellers have the relationships with the end user. Yet, replacing existing distributor partners with an Internet-based system may seem attractive from a short-term financial perspective but in the long-run, this underestimates the role of distributors and the value they bring to the supply chain.

Firstly, distributors play a vital role as intermediaries between globalized manufacturers and localized resellers and end users. The fact is that distributors typically serve regions that are more widespread than any reseller and yet have a strong understanding of local circumstances. The sheer scale of logistical support required for effective management of a global distribution process is beyond the scope of most manufacturers. Distributors are therefore able to provide a 'buffering' function enabling global manufacturers to more effectively meet demand on a regional basis.

Combined with this is the ability of distributors to provide manufacturers with valuable market sizing information. The fact that resellers operate on a local level with small product volumes means that they cannot serve as statistically valid indicators of future demand. Furthermore, manufacturers deal with products across large geographies and thus don't have the detailed insight into local market conditions that can yield accurate forecasts.

Distributors can aggregate resellers' sales into meaningful volumes and are therefore ideally placed to provide market-sizing information which enables manufacturers to effectively balance their product portfolios.

After all, manufacturers are geared to producing goods on a large-scale consistently over the year while customers only buy sporadically. To avoid large stock piles of products taking up valuable warehouse space, distributors provide not only essential sales forecasting information but also the logistical support necessary to keep goods flowing to where they are needed.

In addition to manufacturers, distributors are also well placed to provide this sales analysis to resellers. Through examining sales patterns and product life cycles, distributors can deliver a crucial component of the reseller's information needs, which is essential if they are to eliminate the prospect of 'fire sales' of obsolete equipment at the end of the working life of the products they stock.

Distributors also play a valuable role in facilitating such tasks as returns management. Inevitably products purchased by end users will be returned, which can often lead to a variety of complex processes including testing, refurbishment, disposal or returning to the manufacturer. Traditionally, the distributor will act as an intermediary between the manufacturer and reseller or customers to ensure that the goods are received by the manufacturer and any rebates due are passed on to the end user. Electronic channels simply cannot provide a replacement for the complex processes distributors have set in place to handle returns.

Take for instance, the recent European Union legislation compelling manufacturers to adopt responsibility for recycling electronic goods. This means manufacturers are going to have to implement processes for collecting these goods and then recycling them or alternatively paying a reseller or distributor to undertake this. While electronic channels may be used by resellers to procure goods from the manufacturers, they cannot effectively replace the role of the distributor in the reverse supply channel.

Finally, distributors are increasingly providing a great deal of pre- and post-sales support, particularly as a first line response to technical enquiries. Resellers typically don't sell products in the kind of volume that would justify having product specialists on staff and they therefore look further up the supply chain for that service. Manufacturers that argue in favor of the removal of distributors from the supply chain have clearly given little thought to the costs and resources that this level of technical support - on a 24 x 7 day basis - would entail.

There can be little doubt that distributors have a great deal of value to offer the supply chain. It is essential therefore those distributors threatened with removal from the supply chain stress these and other benefits they can bring to both manufacturers and resellers. The ability to provide sophisticated sales analysis and forecasting information, returns processes and technical support should be at the heart of any dialogue a distributor has with a manufacturer. However, to be in a position to provide these higher value services, distributors must invest in the necessary technology solutions.

Unfortunately, it is too often the case that distributors are reluctant to make the necessary investment. Sales forecasting, for instance, requires business information systems to provide hard, statistical evidence while schemes such as returns management require sophisticated back-end systems to automate processes within the supply chain. If distributors do not take the necessary steps and invest in the required technology then they run the risk of becoming irrelevant to the supply chain.

The temptation for manufacturers to replace elements of the supply chain with electronic channels is perfectly understandable, especially in current economic conditions. Yet, while cost savings may be forthcoming in the short-term, the effect of so-called disintermediation (the removal of links from the supply chain) will certainly be more harmful in the long-term. To remove the role of the distributor from the supply chain is to ignore the inherent value their role adds to both manufacturers and resellers.

Value Chains versus Supply Chains

The Value Chain concept was developed and popularized in 1985 by Michael Porter, in "Competitive Advantage", a seminal work on the implementation of competitive strategy to achieve superior business performance. Porter defined value as the amount buyers are willing to pay for what a firm provides, and he conceived the "value chain" as the combination of nine generic value-added activities operating within a firm – activities that work together to provide value to customers. Porter linked up the value chains between firms to form what he called a Value System; however, in the present era of greater outsourcing and collaboration the linkage between multiple firms' value creating processes has more commonly been called the "value chain". As this name implies, the primary focus in value chains is on the benefits that accrue to customers, the interdependent processes that generate value, and the resulting demand and funds flows that are created. Effective value chains generate profits.

To bring the concept of value into focus, consider for a moment a person walking in the desert, a person who is dying of thirst. As that person walks he has only one thing in his mind, and that is water. At that moment there is little consideration for the form of the water, the container, or who will be providing it. Water has a unique value to that person. When he finds water, or is offered some, money would be of little concern. What is the point of this example? First is that value is a subjective experience that is dependent on context. In the context of a busboy clearing a table, a glass of water kept there has no value, or even negative value – it's just more work for him. But for the man dying of thirst, that same glass of water is extremely valuable. Second, value occurs when needs are met through the provision of products, resources, or services – usually during some form of transaction or exchange. Finally, value is an experience, and it flows from the person (or institution) that is the recipient of resources – it flows from the customer.

This is a key difference between a value chain and a supply chain – they flow in opposite directions. Many views of Value Chains can be created. Examples of Value Chains are:

- One that takes an order from a customer;
- One that fulfills a customer requirement;
- One that defines a product or service etc.

We depict the Order Fulfillment Value Chain in Figure as a pictorial of the comparison.

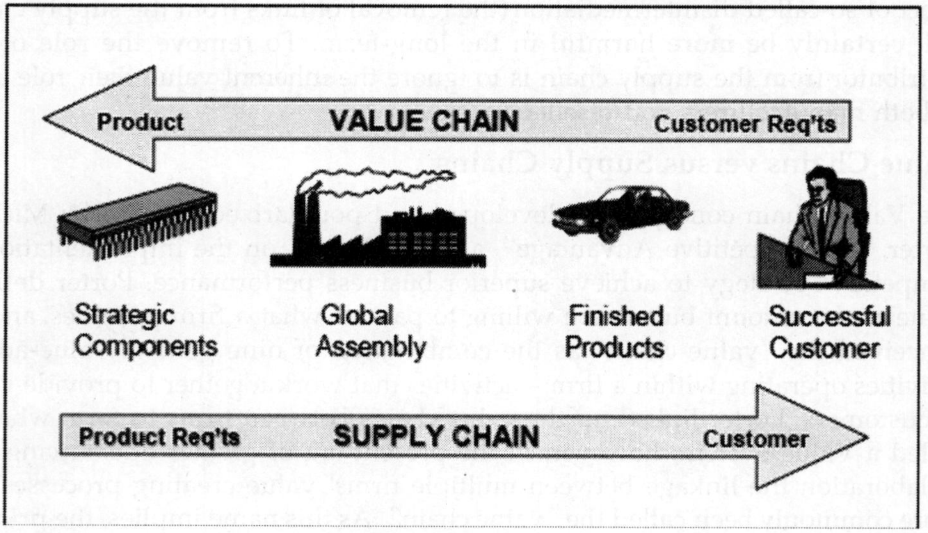

Figure: A Comparison of a Value Chain with a Supply Chain

From this simple example, we see that value, like beauty, is in the eye of the beholder. Value has meaning in a number of contexts, including trading relationships, consumer purchases, and the interests of company shareholders. In "Lean Thinking" by Womack and Jones, the first Lean Principle was "defining value from the customer's perspective". From this come two critical factors that need to be clarified when strategizing the creation of value:

1) Who is the customer?
2) What do they value?

Most corporate initiatives are really about developing appreciation and awareness of customer needs and values, and then organizing the firm's activities around efficiently providing for those needs – quickly, accurately, and at minimum cost. This is because value occurs when customer needs are satisfied through an exchange of products and/or services for some form of payment. The degree to which the needs that are met exceed the price paid in the exchange is one objective way that value can be measured. That is why paying Rs. 1,000 for a bottle of water in the desert when dying of thirst might seem reasonable if there were no other alternative.

A key distinction in defining value is whether the exchange that generates value is between firms - i.e., Business to Business (B2B) - or between a firm and a consumer - i.e., Business to Consumer (B2C).

There are three forms of value that occur in B2B commercial transactions.

- Technical (Resource Value);
- Organizational (Business Context); and
- Personal (Career and Idiosyncratic).

(i) *Technical value* is intrinsic to the resource being provided and occurs in virtually all exchanges. For the thirsty man, the water has a technical value regardless of the source or any other consideration. The cup can be used or even dirty, the man providing it a criminal and the water will still retain the same technical value.

(ii) *Organizational value* is built upon the context of the exchange, and may derive from a range of factors such as ethical standards, prestige, reliability, and association. Brand image may build organizational value, as well as company reputation. When at a fine dining establishment, the label on the water bottle generates value far in excess of the bottle's content.

(iii) *Personal value* is derived from the personal experiences and relationships involved in the exchange of resources and the benefits provided. While technical and organizational value accrues to the firms involved in a commercial exchange, personal value accrues to the individual. Manager motivation, preferences, feelings of comfort and trust create value for individuals that engage in trading relationships on behalf of firms, and can be extremely influential in the determination of successful exchange. For example, it is a cliché that many corporate IT managers responsible for purchasing computer systems have selected IBM equipment because "no one was ever fired for buying IBM", whether the system was the best choice or not.

Finally, there are competitive forces affecting the *market value* of any exchange of resources when comparisons can be made between competing offers. Competing offers can erode value (and margins) by making the lowest price a deciding factor in evaluating an exchange.

At the consumer level of exchange, value is layered, and has been described by three concentric rings. In the center ring is *product value*, the technical value derived from providing a source of supply. A second ring of *service value* is provided by the services that surround the product such as personal care and warranty service. The third ring has been called the new service/quality battleground, and was made popular by business thinkers such as Peters and Waterman ("In Search of

Excellence"). This third level of value is achieved by providing enhanced service, to "make your customer successful" rather than just satisfied. At this level, the experience surrounding the exchange of resources provides its own unique *"wow" value*, and the product itself is secondary. Ronald McDonald, happy-meal toys, and playgrounds have added value to McDonald's burgers for years without any nutritional or flavour change in the basic product.

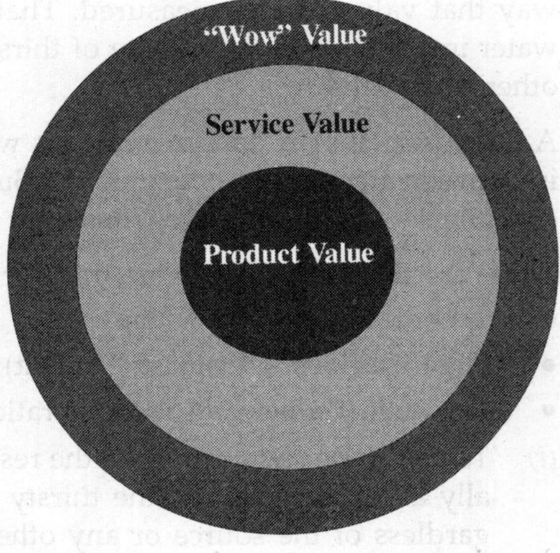

For corporations, the capability of providing value to customers generates revenues in excess of costs - creates profit, which in turn generates *shareholder value*. Thus, the exchange of value (or the value created in exchange) is the basic engine that drives our industrial economy. The upstream (value stream) impact of value creation is shareholder value. This is the value generated for the provider of those financial resources that enable value generation, based on a firm's stock price and dividends or a private company's return on investment.

Because value is derived from customer needs, activities that do not contribute to meeting these needs are "non-value-added" waste, or "muda" in the parlance of lean thinking. Careful consideration of the tasks and functions that occur in many of the industries we serve shows considerable waste still available for process improvement activities to uncover and reduce or eliminate. By streamlining the processes that generate the goods and services that customers value, fewer resources need to be expended, and the margin between customer value and the cost of delivery increases, improving a firm's profit margin. This is the essence of corporate strategies that focus on operational excellence. In contrast, innovation and marketing strategies focus on improving customer perceptions of the value of goods and services by innovatively improving the perception of what gets delivered. In either strategy, increasing the margin between delivery cost and perceived value is the foundation for improved business performance.

Similarities and Differences between a Supply Chain and a Value Chain

Supply Chain Management (SCM) emerged in the 1980s as a new, integrative philosophy to manage the total flow of goods from suppliers to the ultimate user, and evolved to consider a broad integration of business processes along the chain of supply. Keith Oliver coined the term "supply chain management" in 1982. Oliver, a vice president in Booz Allen Hamilton's London office, developed an integrated inventory management process to balance trade-offs between his clients' desired inventory and customer service goals. The original focus was the "management of a chain of supply as though it were a single entity, not a group of disparate functions", with the primary objective of fixing the suboptimal deployment of inventory and capacity caused by conflicts between functional groups within the company. SCM evolved quickly in the 1990s with the advent of rapid response initiatives in textile and grocery industries, and was refined by large retailer Wal-Mart who used point-of-sale data to enable continuous replenishment. Supply chain is a term "now commonly used internationally – to encompass every effort involved in producing and delivering a final product or service, from the supplier's supplier to the customer's customer". As the name implies, the primary focus in supply chains is on the costs and efficiencies of supply, and the flow of materials from their various sources to their final destinations. Efficient supply chains reduce costs.

In common parlance, a supply chain and a value chain are complementary views of an extended enterprise with integrated business processes enabling the flows of products and services in one direction, and of value as represented by demand and cash flow in the other. Both chains overlay the same network of companies. Both are made up of companies that interact to provide goods and services. When we talk about supply chains, however, we usually talk about a downstream flow of goods and supplies from the source to the customer. Value flows the other way. The customer is the source of value, and value flows from the customer, in the form of demand, to the supplier. That flow of demand, sometimes referred to as a "demand chain", is manifested in the flows of orders and cash that parallel the flow of value, and flow in the opposite direction to the flow of supply. Thus, the primary difference between a supply chain and a value chain is a fundamental shift in focus from the supply base to the customer. Supply chains focus upstream on integrating supplier and producer processes, improving efficiency and reducing waste, while value chains focus downstream, on creating value in the eyes of the customer. This distinction is often lost in the language used in the business and research literature.

For example, in 1998, the Global Supply Chain Forum (GSCF) defined supply chain management as "the integration of key business processes from end user through original suppliers that provide products, services, and information that **add value** for customers and other stakeholders", thereby adding the notion that supply chain processes must "add value" and blurring the distinction between a supply chain and a value chain. A recent study described supply chain management that seeks to optimize costs as second generation supply chains, and further the third generation supply chain management as being focused on customer intimacy, and being a synchronized supply chain where consumers have the power to pull value. This description reflects the evolution of supply chains that synchronize the flows of value and supply.

A recent survey of the main usages of the term "value" in the economics, marketing, strategy, and operations fields indicates that the notion of a value chain may actually be a misnomer, although a widely used one. According to this analysis, only resources move along the chain of linkages between firms - supplies going one way and money going the other, while value is a metaphysical perceived quality associated with the benefits that occur at the various points of exchange along the resource chain. According to this analysis, value surrounds the movement of resources - is perceptual - and accrues to both parties in a transaction, suppliers and customers. Therefore, value chains can be thought to operate in *both* directions, with suppliers accruing value from the financial resources, payment terms, stability, and future order cover that their customers provide, while customers derive value from the delivered products and services.

Misnomer or not, the value chain concept has become a staple idea in management and research, and is the focus for evolving strategies, enterprise models, and numerous efforts at improving business performance. Creating a profitable value chain therefore requires alignment between what the customer wants, i.e., the demand chain, and what is produced via the supply chain. And while supply chains focus primarily on reducing costs and attaining operational excellence, value chains focus more on innovation in product development and marketing.

Why Value Chains Now?

The growing interest in value chains began with Porter's seminal work, "Competitive Advantage", and has increased ever since. Clearly, the interest in value chains is not new. In Industrial Engineering, however, the primary focus has been on achieving operational efficiency - leading to a focus on production operations and supply chains. There are a number of significant trends that are now driving the need for operations oriented analysis from a value chain perspective. These include:

- Increasing competition and an increasing focus on innovation as an element of strategy;
- Evolving governance models for the extended enterprise;
- The trend towards globalization of supply and production;
- Benefits already wrung out of manufacturing and the supply chain;
- Trends in Management Discourse.

Increasing Competition and the Primacy of Strategy - The value chain is first and foremost a strategic concept, arising from a strategic theory of firm competition. As companies struggle to compete in an environment of globalization and intense competition, the focus shifts to alternative means to remain competitive. This creates an increasing interest in Value Chains as a tool to model the extended enterprise and formulate strategies for how to remain competitive.

Evolving Governance Models for the Extended Enterprise - The information era spurred on by the recent focus of capital investment on internet technologies and "dot-com" business models has increased general business and research interest in alternative value chain and business models. This has been promoted by the focus on Core Competencies and the Resource Based View (RBV) of the firm. This growth in modular/virtual collaborative enterprise business models has increased interest in the Value Chain as a primary construction for analysis of new models for business governance.

Globalization of Supply and Production - The growth in global sourcing and supply has begun a long-term process of leveling the playing field for adding value world wide. This leads to the need to model global value chains as the predominant mode of business in many industries.

Many Benefits Already Wrung out of Manufacturing and the Supply Chain - The Industrial Engineering and Operations Management disciplines, combined with management and operations improvement initiatives such as lean manufacturing, TQM, and Six Sigma, have been improving the efficiency of manufacturing and supply chain operations for many years. While there is still considerable work to do in the field, academic theoreticians and practitioners at many of the more advanced firms are beginning to turn to a broader view of the enterprise to continue making a contribution to improving competitive stance. Improving the operational capability of other value-added activities in the enterprise, such as product development, requires shifting perspective from the supply chain to the value chain.

Trends in Management Discourse - A final reason for the growing interest in Value Chains may simply be the nature of management fashion trends in academic and management discourse. A lifecycle process revealing how management knowledge entrepreneurs participate in the creation of trends in discourse was described in a study of Quality Circles by Abrahamson and Fairchild. This study derived two propositions that are relevant:

1) Management fashions tend to have a lifecycle characterized by a long latency phase followed by a wave-like, often asymmetrical and ephemeral popularity curve.
2) Three conditions occurring in conjunction trigger a management fashion within a niche:
    (a) A fashion in that niche must collapse;
    (b) There must be a widespread performance gap that a latency-phase replacement fashion in that niche can believably address; and
    (c) Discourse must have brought this gap to the attention of many management-fashion consumers.

The collapsing wave of interest in supply chain management associated with the dot-com era bubble bursting may qualify for condition (a). While the growing global competition in business certainly creates a performance gap (b). Value chains have had a long latency period since the mid 1980s, are an accepted terminology in academic discourse, and are believably positioned to address many of the concerns that business practitioners have in industry (c). Value chain discourse has come on as a strong contender in the past several years to fill the operations and supply management niche in management fashion, and may be ready for a continuing rise in popularity. Strategically, it is being positioned as a dynamic differentiator.

Value is highly conditioned by the larger social and economic environment through which complex and numerous interactions affect the human perception of value-based transactions. Advertising, social trends, and economic conditions all influence consumer and business valuations of products, services, and resources flowing through the value systems in our economy. One of the most watched figures in the marketplace is the consumer confidence index based on a survey of households. This index is an aggregate measure of confidence in the economy and a leading indicator of how consumers will value, and therefore how they will spend money on goods and services. When perceptions of value in a marketplace become exaggerated, market bubbles occur such as the internet technology bubble several years ago. When significant trends take hold in this larger environment it is difficult, if not impossible, for individual companies or households to avoid being swept along in the sudden creation and destruction of value that may result.

For supply chains to generate maximum value in this dynamic environment, they must synchronize the flows of supply with the flows of value from customers in the form of rapidly shifting tastes, preferences, and demand. We need to stop thinking of supply chains and value chains as different entities, but, rather, should integrate the two. Third generation supply chains require that the material flow and product delivery be synchronized and lean, and that the information, knowledge, and financial flows be fully integrated and instantaneous. SCM requires that product design be fully integrated with production capability, delivery processes, and information about customer demand. This can be achieved by taking a holistic view of the end to end business process throughout the product life cycle and across geographical borders. To continue to debate the importance of supply chain management versus the value chain concept would be folly. Instead, the next level of business performance will be achieved by companies that learn to integrate fully the concurrent flows of value and supply.

SCM and Related Disciplines: Logistics

The interrelation of logistics and SCM is "hot spot" in many discussions. Actually, the elaboration of a unique viewpoint on this aspect should not be counted on. Sometimes, these discussions appear very similar to discussions on interrelations of theatre and cinema in the 1940-1950s. Nevertheless, both the theatre and the cinema exist now. So both the logistics and SCM will exist in future.

In modern literature, four main viewpoints of the interrelation of logistics and SCM can be classified. These are:

- Logistics as a part of SCM;
- SCM as a part of logistics;
- SCM instead of logistics; and
- Logistics and SCM are independent and have some intersection points.

It can be concluded that logistics deals mostly with local functions for implementing the physical transition of material flows and SCM deals with the value-adding chain as a whole and concentrates on the managerial links between the local functions for implementing the physical transition of inbound and outbound material flows. Logistics is attracted to optimizing the realization of physical transitions; SCM is attracted to the management level. In other words, logistics takes care of providing the right goods, in the right place, at the right time, in the right volume, in the right package, in the right quality, with the right costs and SCM takes care of balancing the supplies along the entire value-adding chain subject to the full customer satisfaction.

SCM is interlinked with logistics, operations management, strategic management, marketing, industrial organization, production management and informatics. Some examples follow. Co-operation is the basis of SCM. However, the issue of

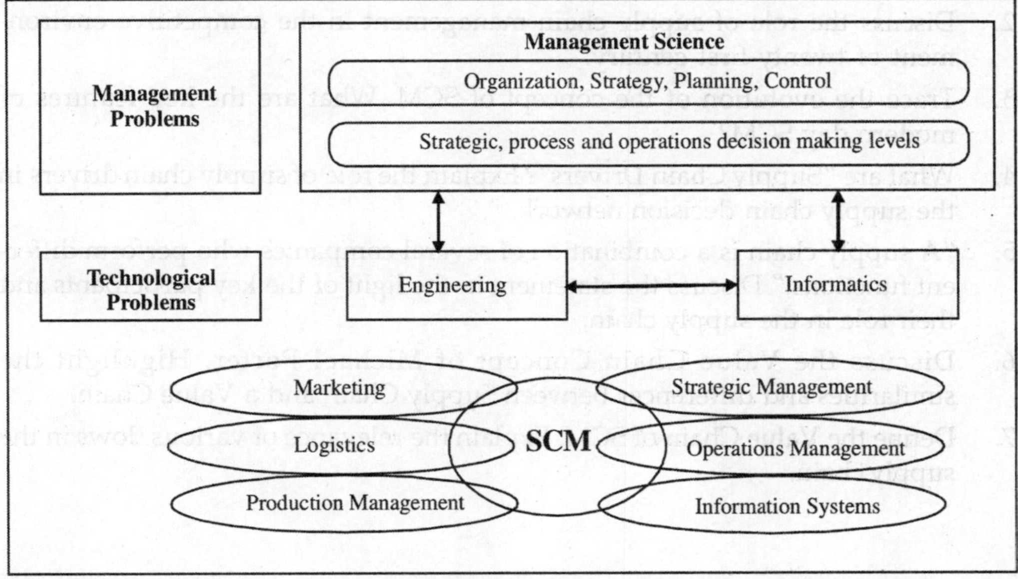

SCM as a Multi-disciplinary Framework

co-operation is within the scope of industrial studies. Co-operation process flows in turn belong to the logistics and SCM competences. SCM integrates the strategic goals of production (process flexibility, productivity and efficiency) and logistics (providing the production and customers with products, low logistic costs and a high logistic service level).

Besides co-operation, co-ordination belongs to the most important SCM components. The basis of the co-ordination is IT. The functionalities of IT can be different, i.e., SC planning, SC monitoring, data interchange, radio frequency identification (RFID), trace and tracking, etc. Hence, SCM is interlinked with informatics and engineering.

Only a few years have passed since SCM was considered as an extension of logistics and purchasing management. Modern SCM is a wider concept than just logistics. Moreover, SCM has been extensively developed into an independent research and management domain. For the last few years, the focus of SCM has shifted to the management level. Organization, strategies, planning and control at different decision-making levels are the subjects of management science. To implement the managerial functions, information and engineering technologies are needed. In its turn, the level of the existing technologies enables of disables management concepts. Hence, SCM should be considered as a multi-disciplinary framework of management science, engineering science and information science.

For Discussion

1. What is Supply Chain Management (SCM)? Discuss the critical decisions taken by the companies in the management of their supply chains.
2. Discuss the role of supply chain management in the competitive environment of twenty-first century.
3. Trace the evolution of the concept of SCM. What are the key features of modern day SCM?
4. What are "Supply Chain Drivers"? Explain the role of supply chain drivers in the supply chain decision network.
5. "A supply chain is a combination of several companies who perform different functions." Discuss the statement in the light of the key participants and their role in the supply chain.
6. Discuss the Value Chain Concept of Michael Porter. Highlight the similarities and differences between Supply Chain and a Value Chain.
7. Define the Value Chain of SCM. Explain the relevance of various flows in the supply chain.

Inventory

Inventory decisions are high-risk and high-impact from the perspective of logistics operations. Commitment to a particular inventory assortment and subsequent shipment to a market or region in anticipation of future sales determines a number of logistics activities. Without the proper inventory assortment, marketing may find that sales are lost and customer satisfaction will decline. Likewise, inventory planning is critical to manufacturing. Raw material shortages can shut down a manufacturing line or modify a production schedule, which, in turn, introduces added expense and potential for finished goods shortages. Just as shortages can disrupt planned marketing and manufacturing operations, overstocked inventories also create problems. Overstocks increase cost and reduce profitability through added warehousing, working capital requirements, deterioration, insurance, taxes, and obsolescence.

Inventory constitutes one of the most important elements of any system dealing with the supply, manufacturing and distribution of goods and services. In fact, inventories are common to farms, manufacturers, traders, hospitals, temples, prisons, zoos, universities and governments. The term inventory can be used to mean several different things such as:

(i) The stock on hand of materials at a given time (a tangible asset which can be seen, measured and controlled);

(ii) An itemized list of all the physical assets;

(iii) To determine the quality of items on hand; and

(iv) The value of the stock of goods owned by an organization at a particular time.

In logistics and supply chain perspective, inventory is any idle material resource of an enterprise awaiting future sales, use, or transformation. In other words, it refers to stocking of raw materials, in-process, finished, packaging, tools and equipments, spares and others in order to meet an expected demand or distribution in future.

Characteristics of Inventory

1. Manufacturing

For the manufacturer, inventory risk has a long-term dimension. The manufacturer's inventory commitment starts with raw material and component parts, includes work-in-process, and ends with finished goods. In addition, prior to sale, finished goods must often be transferred to warehouses in close proximity to wholesalers and retailers. Although a manufacturer may have a narrower product line than retailers or wholesalers, the manufacturer's inventory commitments are relatively deep and have long duration.

2. Wholesaler

Wholesalers' risk exposure is narrower but deeper and of longer duration than that of retailers. The merchant wholesaler purchases large quantities from manufacturers and sells small quantities to retailers. The economic justification of the merchant wholesaler is the capability to provide retail customers with assorted merchandise from different manufacturers in smaller quantities. When products are seasonal, the wholesaler is also forced to take an inventory position far in advance of selling, thus increasing depth and duration of risk.

One of the greatest hazards of wholesaling is product-line expansion to the point where the width of inventory risk approaches that of the retailer, while depth and duration of risk remain characteristic of traditional wholesaling.

3. Retail

For a retailer, inventory management is fundamentally a matter of buying and selling. The retailer purchases a wide variety of products and assumes a substantial risk in the marketing process. Retailer inventory risk can be viewed as wide but not deep. Because of high rents, retailers place prime emphasis on inventory turnover and direct product profitability. Turnover measures inventory velocity and is calculated as the ratio of annual sales divided by average inventory.

If an individual enterprise plans to operate at more than one level of the distribution channel, it must be prepared to assume additional inventory risk. For example, the food chain that operates a regional warehouse assumes risk related to the wholesaler operation over and above the normal retail operations. To the extent that an enterprise becomes vertically integrated, inventory must be managed at all levels of the marketing channel.

Inventory Functionality

The ideal inventory process consists of manufacturing a product to a customer's specifications once an order is placed. This is called a **make-to-order** operation and is characteristic of customized equipment. Such a system does not require stockpiles of materials or finished goods in anticipation of future sales.

Geographical Specialization

One function of inventory is to allow **geographical specialization** for individual operating units. Because of the requirements for factors of production such as power, materials, water, and labour, the economical location for manufacturing is often a considerable distance from major markets. For example, tires, batteries, transmissions, and springs are significant components in automobile assembly. The technology and expertise to produce each of these components are traditionally located in proximity to material sources in order to minimize transportation. This strategy leads to geographical separation of production so that each automobile component can be produced economically. However, geographical separation requires internal inventory transfer to completely integrate components into final assembly.

Geographical separation also requires inventories to create market assortments. Manufactured goods from various locations are collected at a single warehouse and then combined as a mixed-product shipment. For example, Procter & Gamble uses distribution centres to combine products from its laundry, food, and health care divisions to offer the customer a single integrated shipment. Such warehouses are examples of geographical separation and integrated distribution made possible by inventory.

Geographical separation permits economic specialization between the manufacturing and distribution units of an enterprise. When geographical specialization is utilized, inventory in the form of materials, semi-finished goods or components, and finished goods is introduced to the logistical system. Each location requires a basic inventory. In addition, in-transit inventories are necessary to link manufacturing and distribution. Although difficult to measure, the economies gained through geographical specialization are expected to more than offset the increased inventory and transportation cost.

Decoupling

A second inventory function, decoupling, provides maximumoperating efficiency within a single manufacturing facility by stockpiling work-in-process between production operations. Decoupling processes permit each product to be manufactured and distributed in economical lot sizes that are greater than market demands. Warehouse inventory produced in advance of need permits distribution to customers in large quantity shipments with minimum freight cost. In terms of marketing, decoupling permits products manufactured over time to be sold as an assortment. Thus, decoupling tends to "buffer", or cushion, the operations of the enterprise from uncertainty.

Decoupling differs from geographical specialization: the former enables increased operating efficiency at a single location, while the latter includes multiple locations.

Balancing Supply and Demand

A third inventory function, balancing, is concerned with elapsed time between consumption and manufacturing. Balancing inventory reconciles supply availability with demand. The most notable examples of balancing are seasonal production and year-round consumption. Orange juice is one such product. Another example of year-round production with seasonal consumption is antifreeze. Balancing inventories link the economies of manufacturing with variations of consumption.

Buffer Uncertainties

The safety stock or buffer stock function concerns short-range variation in either demand or replenishment. Considerable inventory planning is devoted to determining the size of safety stocks. In fact, most overstocks are the result of improper planning.

The safety stock requirement results from uncertainty concerning future sales and inventory replenishment. If uncertainty exists, it is necessary to protect inventory position. In a sense, safety stock planning is similar to purchasing insurance.

Safety stock protects against two types of uncertainty. The first type concerns demand in excess of forecast during the performance cycle. The second type of uncertainty involves delays in the performance cycle length itself. An example of demand uncertainty is a customer request of more or less units than planned. Performance cycle length uncertainty results from a delay in order receipt, order processing or transportation.

Classification of Inventory

In order to help the managers take effective inventory-related decisions, the inventory items are classified as :

(a) Production Inventories: Raw materials, parts and components, which are consumed in the production process of goods, come under the category of production material inventories.

(b) MRO Inventories: Maintenance, repair and operating supplies which are used in the production process but do not become a part of the products, called MRO items and their stocking is called MRO inventories. Items like lubricating oils, old cloth, machine spare parts etc. are not a part of the product produced but they are required for the smooth functioning of the production process and so their stock is maintained.

(c) In-process Inventories: These goods are partially completed/finished goods that are still in the production operation, i.e., semi-finished products found at various stages in the production process are called in-process inventories.

(d) Finished-goods Inventories: These inventory items are final products, available for sale and distribution, i.e., completed products ready for shipping.

Independent vs Dependent Demand Inventory

Some inventory items can be classified as independent demand items, and some can be classified as dependent demand items. While we need to make the timing and sizing decisions for all inventory items, we must be careful in the manner in which we make those decisions for these two types of items.

Independent demand inventory item: Inventory item whose demand is not related to (or dependent upon) some higher level item. Demand for such items is usually thought of as forecasted demand. Independent demand inventory items are usually thought of as finished products.

Dependent demand inventory item: Inventory item whose demand is related to (or dependent upon) some higher level item. Demand for such items is usually thought of as derived demand. Dependent demand inventory items are usually thought of as the materials, parts, components, and assemblies that make up the finished product.

Elements of Inventory Cost

When assessing the cost effectiveness of an inventory policy, it is helpful to measure the total inventory costs that will be incurred during some reference period of time. Most frequently, that time interval used for comparing costs is one year. Over that span of time, there will be a certain need, or demand, or requirement for each inventory item. In that context, the following describes how the annual costs in each of the four categories will vary with changes in the inventory lot sizing decision.

Item costs: How the per unit item cost is measured depends upon whether the item is one that is obtained from an external source of supply, or is one that is manufactured internally. For items that are ordered from external sources, the per unit item cost is predominantly the purchase price paid for the item. On some occasions, this cost may also include some additional charges, like inbound transportation cost, duties, or insurance. For items that are obtained from internal sources, the per unit item cost is composed of the labor and material costs that went into its production, and any factory overhead that might be allocated to the item. In many instances the item cost is a constant, and is not affected by the lot sizing decision. In those cases, the total annual item cost will be unaffected by the order size. Regardless of the order size (which impacts how many times we choose to order that item over the course of the year), our total annual acquisitions will equal the total annual need. Acquiring that total number of units at the constant cost per unit will yield the same total annual cost. (This situation would be somewhat different if we introduced the possibility of quantity discounts. We will consider that later.)

Holding costs (also called carrying costs): Any items that are held in inventory will incur a cost for their storage. This cost will be comprised of a variety of components. One obvious cost would be the cost of the storage facility (warehouse space charges and utility charges, cost of material handlers and material handling equipment in the warehouse). In addition to that, there are some other, more subtle expenses that add to the holding cost. These include such things as insurance on the held inventory; taxes on the held inventory; damage to, theft of, deterioration of, or obsolescence of the held items. The order size decision impacts the average level of inventory that must be carried. If smaller quantities are ordered, on average, there will be fewer units being held in inventory, resulting in lower annual inventory holding costs. If larger quantities are ordered, on average, there will be more units being held in inventory, resulting in higher annual inventory holding costs.

Ordering costs: Any time inventory items are ordered, there is a fixed cost associated with placing that order. When items are ordered from an outside source of supply, that cost reflects the cost of the clerical work to prepare, release, monitor, and receive the order. This cost is considered to be constant regardless of the size of the order. When items are to be manufactured internally, the order cost reflects the setup costs necessary to prepare the equipment for the manufacture of that order. Once again, this cost is constant regardless of how many items are eventually manufactured in the batch. If one increases the size of the orders for a particular inventory item, fewer of those orders will have to be placed during the course of the year, hence the total annual cost of placing orders will decline.

Shortage costs: Companies incur shortage costs whenever demand for an item exceeds the available inventory. These shortage costs can manifest themselves in the form of lost sales, loss of goodwill, customer irritation, backorder and expediting charges, etc. Companies are less likely to experience shortages if they have high levels of inventory, and are more likely to experience shortages if they have low levels of inventory. The order size decision directly impacts the average level of inventory. Larger orders mean more inventory is being acquired than is immediately needed, so the excess will go into inventory. Hence, smaller order quantities lead to lower levels of inventory, and correspondingly, a higher likelihood of shortages and their associated shortage costs. Larger order quantities lead to higher levels of inventory, and correspondingly, a lower likelihood of shortages and their associated costs. The bottom line is this: larger order sizes will lead to lower annual shortage costs.

Reasons for Maintaining Inventory

Anticipation Inventory or Seasonal Inventory: Inventory are often built in anticipation of future demand, planned promotional programmes, seasonal demand fluctuations, plant shutdowns, vacations, etc.

Fluctuation Inventory or Safety Stock: Inventory is sometimes carried to protect against unpredictable or unexpected variations in demand.

Lot-Size Inventory or Cycle Stock: Inventory is frequently bought or produced in excess of what is immediately needed in order to take advantage of lower unit costs or quantity discounts.

Transportation or Pipeline Inventory: Inventory is used to fill the pipeline as products are in transit in the distribution network.

Speculative or Hedge Inventory: Inventory can be carried to protect against some future event, such as a scarcity in supply, price increase, disruption in supply, strike, etc.

Maintenance, Repair, and Operating (MRO) Inventory: Inventories of some items (such as maintenance supplies, spare parts, lubricants, cleaning compounds, and office supplies) are used to support general operations and maintenance.

Inventory Management

The investment in inventory is very high in most of the undertakings engaged in manufacturing, wholesale and retail trade. The amount of investment is sometimes more in inventory than in other assets. About 90% part of the working capital is invested in inventories. It is necessary for every management to give proper attention to inventory management. A proper planning of purchasing, handling, storing and accounting should form a part of inventory management. An efficient system on inventory management will determine (a) what to purchase? (b) how much to purchase? (c) from where to purchase? (d) where to store? etc.

The purpose of inventory management is to keep the stock in such a way that neither there is over-stocking nor under-stocking. Over-stocking will mean a reduction of liquidity and starving of other production processes; under-stocking, on the other hand, will result in stoppage of work. The investment in inventory should be kept within reasonable limits.

Traditionally, for the proper management of inventory level, two issues need attention and analysis, namely:

1. *Order Quantity:* How much to order of each material with either outside suppliers or production department within organization. It is also called Lot Sizes or Economic Order Quantity (EOQ).
2. *Order Points:* When to place the orders. It is also called Reorder Point (RoP)

Objectives of Inventory Management

The main objectives of inventory management are operational and financial. They can be listed as:

Provide the desired level of customer service. Customer service refers to a company's ability to satisfy the needs of its customers. There are several ways to measure the level of customer service, such as: (1) percentage of orders that are shipped on schedule, (2) the percentage of line items that are shipped on schedule, (3) the percentage of dollar volume that is shipped on schedule, and (4) idle time due to material and component shortage. The first three measures focus on service to external customers, while the fourth applies to internal customer service.

Achieve cost-efficient operations. Inventories can facility cost-efficient operations in several ways. Inventories can provide a buffer between operations so that each phase of the transformation process can continue to operate even when output rates differ. Inventories also allow a company to maintain a level workforce throughout the year even when there is seasonal demand for the company's output. By building large production lots of items, companies are able to spread some fixed costs over a larger number of units, thereby decreasing the unit cost of each item. Finally, large purchases of inventory might qualify for quantity discounts, which will also reduce the unit cost of each item.

Minimize inventory investment. As a company achieves lower amounts of money tied up in inventory, that company's overall cost structure will improve, as will its profitability. A common measure used to determine how well a company is managing its inventory investment (i.e., how quickly it is getting its inventories out of the system and into the hands of the customers) is inventory turnover ratio, which is a ratio of the annual cost of goods sold to the average inventory level in dollars.

Some of the other objectives of inventory management are :

1. To ensure continuous supply of materials spares and finished goods so that production should not suffer at any time and customer's demand should also be met.
2. To avoid both over-stocking and under-stocking of inventory.
3. To maintain investment in inventories at optimum level as required by operational and sales activities.
4. To keep materials cost under control so that they contribute in reducing the overall cost of production.
5. To eliminate duplication in ordering or replenishing stocks. This is possible with the help of centralizing purchases.
6. To minimize losses through deterioration, pilferage, wastages and damages.
7. To design proper organization for inventory management. A clear-cut accountability should be fixed at various levels of the organization.
8. To ensure perpetual inventory control so that materials shown in stock ledgers should be actually lying in stores.
9. To ensure right quality goods at reasonable prices, of suitable quality and

quantity standards. The price analysis, the cost analysis and value analysis will ensure payment of proper prices.

10. To facilitate furnishing of data for short-term as well as long-term planning and control of inventory.

Model I: The Retailer's EOQ Model of Inventory Management

The Retailer's Model is based on the following assumptions:

1. Demand is known and constant, uniformly distributed throughout the year.
2. **Lead-time,** is the time between the placement of the order and the receipt of the order, is either zero, i.e., receipt of inventory is instantaneous, or it is known and constant.
3. The inventory from an order arrives in one batch, at one time.
4. Quantity discounts are not possible.
5. The only variable costs are the cost of setting up or placing an order (set-up cost) and the cost of holding or storing inventory over time (holding or carrying cost).
6. Stockouts (shortages) can be completely avoided if orders are placed at the right time.

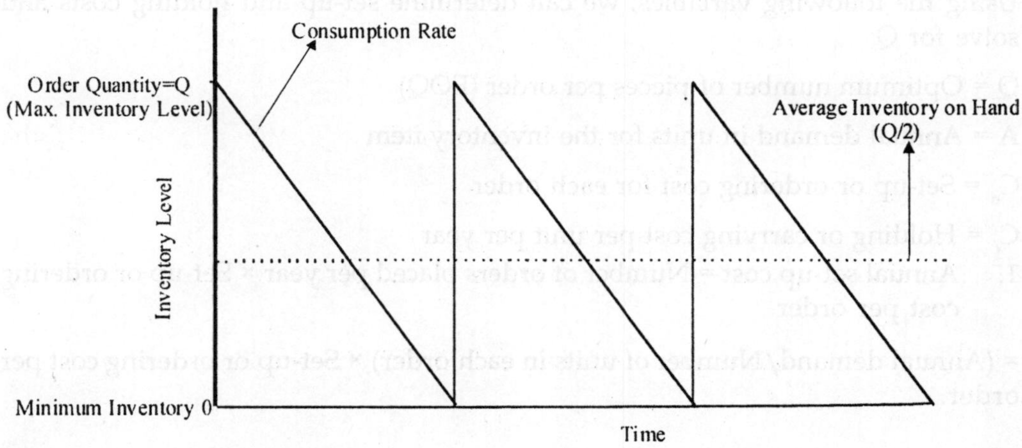

The figure shows the inventory usage over time under these assumptions. Q represents the amount that is ordered. If this amount is 500 units, all 500 units arrive at one time (when an order is received). Thus, the inventory level jumps from 0 to 500 units. In general, an inventory level increases from 0 to Q units when an order arrives. Because demand is constant, the inventory drops at a uniform rate over time. When the inventory level reaches zero the new order is placed and received, and the inventory level again jumps to Q units. This process continues indefinitely over time.

The objective of most inventory models is to minimize the total costs. Under the assumptions considered, the significant costs are the set-up (or ordering) cost and the holding (or carrying) cost. All other costs, such as thecost of the inventory itself, are constant. Thus, if we minimize the sum of the set-up and holding costs, we will also be minimizing the total costs. The optimal order size, Q, will be the quantity that minimizes the total costs. As the quantity ordered increases, the total number of orders placed per year will decrease. Thus, as the quantity ordered increases, the annual set-up or ordering cost will decrease. But as the order quantity increases, the holding cost or the carrying cost of the inventory will increase due to larger average inventories that are maintained.

With the EOQ model, the optimal order quantity will occur at a point where the total set-up cost is equal to the total holding cost.

The necessary steps in developing the model are:

1. Develop an expression for set-up or ordering cost;
2. Develop an expression for holding cost;
3. Set set-up cost equal to holding cost; and
4. Solve the equation for the best order quantity.

Using the following variables, we can determine set-up and holding costs and solve for Q:

Q = Optimum number of pieces per order (EOQ)

A = Annual demand in units for the inventory item

C_o = Set-up or ordering cost for each order

C_c = Holding or carrying cost per unit per year

1. Annual set-up cost = Number of orders placed per year × Set-up or ordering cost per order.

= (Annual demand/Number of units in each order) × Set-up or ordering cost per order.

Annual set-up cost = $\frac{A}{Q} \times C_o$

2. Annual carrying cost = Average inventory level × Carrying cost per unit per year.

Average inventory = (Max. Inv + Min. Inv)/2

i.e., Average inventory = (Q+0)/2 = Q/2

Annual carrying cost = $\left(\frac{Q}{2}\right) \times C_c$

3. Optimal order quantity is found when annual set-up costs equals annual carrying cost, namely,

$$\left(\frac{A}{Q}\right) \times C_0 = \left(\frac{Q}{2}\right) \times C_c$$

4. To solve for Q, simply cross-multiply terms and isolate Q on the left of the equal sign.

$$2A \times C_o = Q^2 \times C_c$$

$$Q^2 = \left(2A \frac{C_o}{C_c}\right)$$

$$\boxed{Q = \sqrt{\frac{(2AC_o)}{C_c}}}$$

This is called as the Wilson's Square Root Formula

The total annual inventory cost is the sum of the set-up and carrying costs:

Total annual cost = Set-up cost + Holding cost

In terms of variables the total cost TC can be expressed as:

$$TC = \left(\frac{A}{Q}\right) \times C_o + \left(\frac{Q}{2}\right) \times C_c$$

The Economic Order Quantity and Total Costs

A company purchases a critical component from a supplier. The manager wants to calculate the economic order quantity to ensure that the annual inventory cost is minimized. The following information is obtained:

Annual Demand = 7200 units;

Ordering cost = Rs 100 per order;

Carrying cost = Rs 4.00 per unit per year

$$EOQ = \sqrt{\frac{2AC_0}{C_C}} = \sqrt{\frac{2 \times 7200 \times 100}{4}} = 600 \text{ units}$$

$$\text{Total carrying cost} = \frac{600}{2} \times 4.00 = \text{Rs. } 1200$$

$$\text{Total ordering cost} = \frac{7200}{600} \times 100 = \text{Rs. } 1200$$

Therefore, the Total Cost = Total carrying cost + Total ordering cost = Rs. 2400.00

Quantity (Q)	Annual Carrying Cost	Annual Ordering Cost	Annual Total Cost	Variation (%)
540	1080.00	1333.33	2413.33	0.56
550	1100.00	1309.09	2409.09	0.38
560	1120.00	1285.71	2405.71	0.24
570	1140.00	1263.16	2403.16	0.13
580	1160.00	1241.38	2401.38	0.06
590	1180.00	1220.34	2400.34	0.01
EOQ = 600	1200.00	1200.00	2400.00 *	0.00
610	1220.00	1180.33	2400.33	0.01
620	1240.00	1161.29	2401.29	0.05
630	1260.00	1142.86	2402.86	0.12
640	1280.00	1125.00	2405.00	0.21
660	1320.00	1090.91	2410.91	0.45

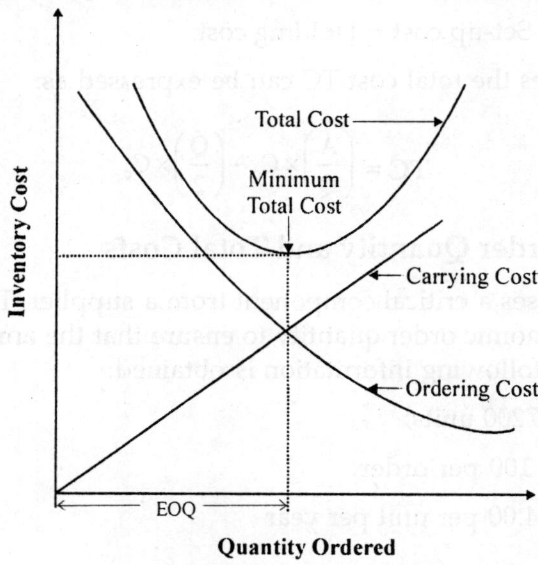

The figure shows the relationships between annual holding cost, annual ordering cost and the total annual holding plus order cost. At the EOQ, annual holding cost equals annual ordering cost. At or close to the EOQ, the total cost curve is rather flat, indicating that it is not very sensitive to small variations in the economic order quantity. Therefore, the Retailer's EOQ model is said to be very robust to minor errors in estimating cost parameters, such as holding rate, order cost or annual usage.

From the figure and the table above, it is also clear that if the order size is smaller than the EOQ, the annual holding cost is slightly lower, whereas the annual ordering cost is slightly higher. The net effect is a slightly higher annual total cost. Similarly, if the order quantity is slightly larger than the EOQ, the annual holding cost is slightly higher, whereas the annual ordering cost is slightly lower. The net effect is also a slightly higher annual total cost.

Example

Electronic Village stocks and sells a particular brand of personal computer. It costs the store Rs. 450 each time it places an order with the manufacturer for the personal computers. The annual cost of carrying the PCs in inventory is Rs. 170. The store manager estimates that annual demand for the PCs will be 1200 units. Determine the optimal order quantity and the total minimum inventory cost.

Solution:

A= 1200 personal computers, C_c = Rs. 170, C_o = Rs. 450

$Q= \sqrt{(2A\ C_o)/C_c}$

$= \sqrt{(2\ (450)(1200)\ /\ 170)}$

= 79.7 personal computers.

$TC = (A/Q)*C_o + (Q/2)*C_c$

= 450 (1200/79.7) + 170 (79.7/2)

= Rs. 13,549.91

Reorder Point

Once we have decided how much to order, now we will look at the second inventory question, when to order. The time between the placement and receipt of an order, called the **lead-time** or **delivery time**, can be as short as a few hours to as long as months. Thus, when-to-order decision is usually expressed in terms of a reorder point, the inventory level at which an order should be placed. The reorder point (RoP) is given as:

RoP = (Demand per day) × (Lead time for a new order in days)

RoP = d × L

This equation for RoP assumes that demand is uniform and constant. When this is not the case, extra stock, often called **safety stock**, should be added.

The demand per day, d, is found by dividing the annual demand, D, by the number of working days in a year:

d = D/(Number of working days in a year)

We will take an example to demonstrate how to calculate reorder point.

Example:

The I-75 Discount Carpet Store is open 311 days per year. If annual demand is 10,000 yards of Super Shag Carpet and the lead-time to receive an order is 10 days, determine the reorder point for carpets.

Solution:

r = d×L

= (10,000 yards/311 days) × 10 days

= 321.54 yards

Thus, when the inventory level falls to approximately 321 yards of carpet, a new order is placed. Notice that the reorder point is not related to the optimal order quantity or any of the inventory costs.

Model II: The Producer's EBQ Model

In the EOQ inventory model, we assumed that the entire inventory order was received at one time. There are times, however, when the firm may receive its inventory over a period of time. Such cases require a different model, one that does not require the instantaneous receipt assumption. This model is applicable when inventory continuously flows or builds up over a period of time after an order has been placed or when units are produced and sold simultaneously. Under these circumstances, we take into account the daily production(or inventory flow) rate and the daily demand rate. Figure shows inventory levels as a function of time.

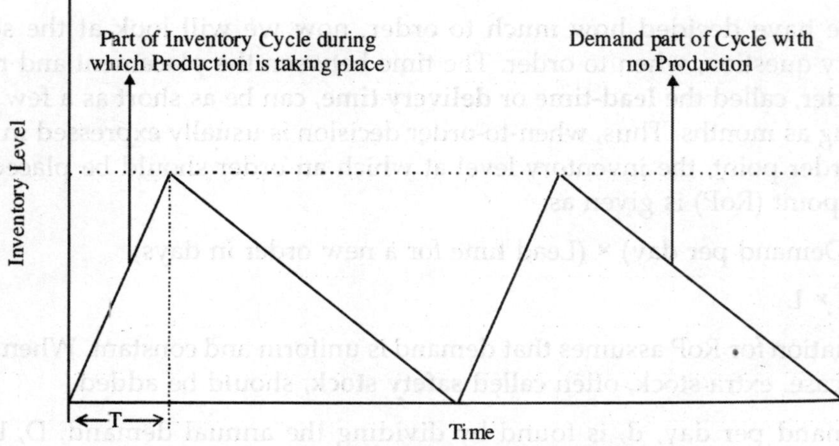

Figure: Inventory levels over time for the production model

Because this model is especially suitable for the production environment, it is commonly called the production order quantity model. It is useful when inventory continuously builds up over time and the traditional economic order quantity assumptions are valid. We derive this model by setting ordering or set-up costs equal to holding costs and solving for Q. Using the following symbols, we can determine the expression for annual inventory holding cost for the production run model:

A = Annual demand.

Q = Number of pieces produced per order or number of units produced in a lot.

C_c = Carrying cost per unit per year.

C_o = Ordering cost (per order) or Set- up cost per batch.

p = Daily production rate.

d = Daily demand rate, or usage rate.

t = Length of the production run in days.

1. Annual inventory carrying cost = (Average inventory level) × (Carrying cost per unit per year).

= (Average inventory level) × C_c.

2. Average inventory level = (Maximum inventory level)/2.

3. Maximum inventory level = (Total units produced during the production run)-(Total units used during the production run).

= pt - dt

But, Q=total units produced (defined earlier)

i.e., Q = pt, and thus $t = \frac{Q}{p}$

Therefore,

Maximum inventory level Q= pt - dt

Or, substituting $t = \frac{Q}{p}$, we get Q= $p \times \left(\frac{Q}{p}\right) - d \times \left(\frac{Q}{p}\right)$

$$= Q - \left(\frac{d}{p}\right)Q$$

$$= Q\left(1 - \frac{d}{p}\right)$$

4. Annual inventory carrying cost (or simply holding cost) =

(Maximum inventory level/2)$\times C_c = \left(\frac{Q}{2}\right)\left(1-\frac{d}{p}\right)\times C_c$

Since, in this case production takes place. Hence,

Ordering cost during the year= set-up cost of production = $\left(\frac{A}{Q}\right)\times C_o$

Using the expression for carrying cost above and the expression for set-up cost developed in the basic EOQ model, we solve for the optimal number of pieces per order by equating set-up cost and holding cost:

Set-up cost = $\left(\frac{A}{Q}\right)\times C_o$

Holding cost = $\left(\frac{Q}{2}\right)\left(1-\frac{d}{p}\right)\times C_c$

Set ordering cost equal to holding cost to obtain Q:

$$\left(\frac{A}{Q}\right)\times C_o = \left(\frac{Q}{2}\right)\left(1-\frac{d}{p}\right)\times C_c$$

$$\text{or}\quad \frac{A}{Q}\times\frac{2}{Q}\times C_o = \left(1-\frac{d}{p}\right)\times C_c$$

$$\text{or}\quad \frac{2A}{Q^2}\times C_o = \left(1-\frac{d}{p}\right)\times C_c$$

by cross-multiplication,

$$Q^2 = \frac{2AC_o}{C_c\left(1-\frac{d}{p}\right)}$$

$$\boxed{Q=\sqrt{\frac{2AC_o}{C_c\left(1-\frac{d}{p}\right)}}}$$

Total annual cost (TC)= Set-up cost + Holding cost

$$TC=\left(\frac{A}{Q}\right)\times C_o + \left(\frac{Q}{2}\right)\left(1-\frac{d}{p}\right)\times C_c$$

Here Q is also termed as EBQ or the **Economic Batch Quantity**. We can use the above equation, to solve for the optimum order or production quantity when inventory is consumed as it is produced.

We will take an example to see how to use it.

Example

We now assume that I-75 Outlet Store has its own manufacturing facility in which it produces Super Shag carpet. We further assume that the ordering cost or the cost of setting up the production process to make Super Shag carpet is Rs. 150. Estimated annual demand is 10000 meters of carpet, and annual carrying cost is Rs. 0.75 per meter. The manufacturing facility operates the same days the store is open (i.e., 311 days) and produces 150 meters of the carpet per day. Determine the optimal order size, total inventory cost, the length of time to receive an order, the number of orders per year, and the maximum inventory level.

Solution:

C_o = Rs. 150

C_c = Rs. 0.75

A = 10,000 metres

d = 10,000/311=32.2 metres per day

p = 150 metres per day

The optimal order size is determined as follows:

$$Q = \sqrt{\frac{2AC_o}{C_c\left(1-\frac{d}{p}\right)}}$$

$$= \sqrt{\frac{2\times150\times10000}{0.75\left(1-\frac{32.2}{150}\right)}}$$

=2256.8 metres

This value is substituted into the following formula to determine total minimum annual inventory cost:

$$TC = \left(\frac{A}{Q}\right)\times C_o + \left(\frac{Q}{2}\right)\left(1-\frac{d}{p}\right)\times C_c$$

$$= \left(\frac{10000}{2256.8}\right)\times150 + \frac{2256.8}{2}\left(1-\frac{32.2}{150}\right)\times0.75$$

=Rs. 1329

The length of time to receive an order for this type of manufacturing operation is commonly called the length of the production run. It is computed as follows:

Production run length = Q/p
= 2,256.8 / 150 = 15.05 days per order
The number of orders per year is actually the number of production runs that will be made:
Number of production runs (from orders) = A/Q
= 10,000 / 2256.8
= 4.43 runs per year
Finally, the maximum inventory level is
Maximum inventory level = Q (1 – d/p)
= 2256.8 (1 – 32.2/150)
= 1772 metres.

Model III: The Discounting Model

It is a common observation while purchasing items, that suppliers offer discounts on bulk purchases. They specify a particular percentage of discounts if items equal to or more than a particular quantity are purchased. Hence, such discounts are called *quantity discounts.*

The purchaser has to compare the EOQ model with the discount options, i.e., the total inventory costs are compared in both the options. The option having the lower total inventory cost is selected and adopted.

A supplier may offer different discounts for different quantities of an item. This is called *differential discounting*. In this situation, every discount option and the EOQ option are considered separately and the associated total cost is calculated. Then, a comparison of the total cost for the different options is made. The option with the least total cost is selected and adopted by the company.

Example

A hospital sources 20,000 disposable syringes every year from a supplier. The ordering cost per order is Rs. 100 and the carrying cost is Re. 1 per unit per year. The price of a syringe is Rs. 5. The supplier offers a 5% discount if purchases are made in lots of 10,000 syringes or more. Determine whether the discount model is better than the EOQ model in this situation.

Solution:

A=20000; C_o =Rs. 100 per order; C_c =Re. 1 per unit per year; price per unit= Rs. 5.

EOQ Model:

$Q = \sqrt{(2A\,C_o)/C_c}$

$Q = \sqrt{(2 \times 20000 \times 100)/1}$

Q=2000 units

Total Cost (by EOQ model) $T_{EOQ} = (A/Q)\times C_o + (Q/2)\times C_c$ +Cost of syringes

TC = (20,000/2,000)×100+(2,000/2)×1+20,000×5

TC= Rs. 1,02,000

Discount Model:

A=20,000 units. Therefore, two orders (of 10,000 units each) can be placed to get 20,000 units in a year.

Cost of 20,000 syringes =Rs. 1,00,000

Discount @ 5% = 5% of Rs. 1,00,000

$$= 1,00,000 \times \frac{5}{100}$$

= Rs. 5000

Therefore,

Net cost of 20,000 syringes after discount=Rs. 1,00,000 - Rs. 5,000 = Rs. 95,000

Total cost (after discount) $T_{discount} = (A/Q)\times C_o + (Q/2)\times C_c$ +Cost of syringes (after disc.)

= Rs. 95,000+(20,000/10,000)×Rs. 100+(10000/2)×Re. 1

= Rs. 95,000+Rs. 200+Rs. 5,000

= Rs. 1,00,200

$\therefore \quad T_{discount} < T_{EOQ}$

Hence, the discount model should be implemented.

Selective Inventory Management

As the size of the companies increases, the number of items to be purchased, and then to be taken care of, also increases. Purchase and control of all items at a time, in bulk, much before their use, irrespective of their usage value, price or procurement problems-blocks and involves a lot of money, man hours and is, therefore, uneconomical.

The inventory or an industrial firm generally comprises thousand of items with diverse prices, usages and lead time, as well as procurement and or technical problems. It is neither desirable nor possibleto exercise the same degree of control over all those items. The organization should pay more attention and care to those items whose usage value is high and less attention to those whose usage and consumption value is low. The organization has, therefore, to be selective in its approach to control its investment in various types of stocks and inventories. Such a system is known as '*selective inventory control*' system.

ABC Analysis or Value Distribution

In ordinary parlance, *ABC analysis* can be best compared with our class of society where the population is categorized into top, middle and lower classes. In the case of inventories also, it has been noticed that out of a large number of items that are generally held in stock, some of the items are quite significant, whereas the others are not that much important. Through *ABC* plan which is in fact an analytical approach based in common statistical techniques, the relative importance of the various items is established for the purpose of individual scrutiny and subsequent control.

ABC analysis contemplates to classify all the inventory items in number of categories, generally into three categories based on their economic values. Items of high value but small in number are classified as '*A*' items which would be under a strict control. '*C*' items represent relatively small value items and would be under simple control. Items of moderate value and consumption are classified as '*B*' items and would attract reasonable attention in the basis of the relative importance of the various items of the inventory, it is also known as '*control by importance and exception*'. As items are classified in order of their relative importance in terms of value, it is also known as '*proportional value analyses*'.

ABC analysis is a *Basic Technique* of materials management and can be applied over almost all the aspects of materials management. It is a system for inventory control where the inventory is analysed in terms of quality and quantity, thereby giving relative importance keeping in view the cost and usage factor of the inventory control. This method is the equivalent of creating a Pareto chart except that it is applied to inventory rather than quality. The Pareto principle states that there are a "critical few and trivial many". The idea is to focus resources on the few critical inventory parts and not the many trivial ones.

Control policies for A, B, C items are based upon two principles:

1. To keep capital tied-up in inventories as low as practicable.
2. To ensure that all the material would be available when required.

Figure below shows, class A items typically represent only about 20 percent of the items but account for 80 percent of the rupee usage. Class B items account for another 30 percent of the items but only 15 percent of the rupee usage. Finally, 50 percent of the items fall in class C, representing a mere 5 percent of the rupee usage.

The goal of ABC analysis is:- to identify the inventory levels of class A items and enable management to control them tightly by using the levels as discussed. To determine annual rupee volume for ABC analysis, we measure the annual demand of each inventory item times the cost per unit.

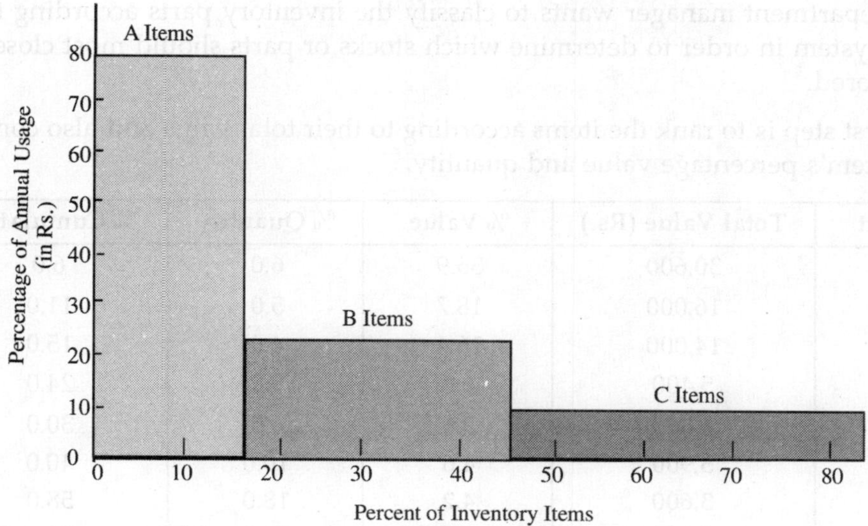

Figure: Graphic representation of ABC analysis

Procedural steps:

1. Identify all the items used in the industry.
2. List all the items as per their value.
3. Count the number of high value, medium value and low value items respectively.
4. Find the percentage of high value, medium value and low value items.
5. A graph can be plotted between percentage of items and percentage of total inventory cost.

Example

The maintenance department for a small manufacturing firm has responsibility for maintaining an inventory of spare parts for the machinery it services. The parts inventory, unit cost, and annual usage are as follows:

Part	Unit Cost (Rs.)	Annual Usage
1	60	90
2	350	40
3	30	130
4	80	60
5	30	100
6	20	180
7	10	170
8	320	50
9	510	60
10	20	120

The department manager wants to classify the inventory parts according to the ABC system in order to determine which stocks or parts should most closely be monitored.

The first step is to rank the items according to their total value and also compute each item's percentage value and quantity.

Part	Total Value (Rs.)	% Value	% Quantity	% Cumulative
9	30,600	35.9	6.0	6.0
8	16,000	18.7	5.0	11.0
2	14,000	16.4	4.0	15.0
1	5,400	6.3	9.0	24.0
4	4,800	5.6	6.0	30.0
3	3,900	4.6	10.0	40.0
6	3,600	4.2	18.0	58.0
5	3,000	3.5	13.0	71.0
10	2,400	2.8	12.0	83.0
7	1,700	2.0	17.0	100.0
	85,400			

Making an intuitive judgment, it appeared that the first three items form a group with the highest value, the next three items form a second group, and the last four items constitute a group. Thus, the ABC classification for these items is as follows:

Class	Items	% Value	% Quantity
A	9, 8, 2	71.0	15.0
B	1, 4, 3	16.5	25.0
C	6, 5, 10, 7	12.5	60.0

Criteria other than annual Rupee volume can determine item classification. For instance, anticipated engineering changes, delivery problems, quality problems, or high unit cost may dictate upgrading items to a higher classification. The advantage of dividing inventory items into classes allows policies and controls to be established for each class.

A Category

These are those items, which normally account for 70 to 80% of the total inventory cost. But in terms of volume and storage capacity, they are normally less than 20%. These categories of items need most close and careful inventory management because they are most important items from the control point of view. Such items being costly are purchased in small quantities often and just before their use.

This, of course, increases the procurement cost and involves risk of non-availability. However, lock-up inventory cost decreases and problem of storage and care taking are minimized. Any stock out on these items costs the company either in production halt or loss of a customer. Hence, frequent reviewing of stock position and consumption pattern along with maintenance of record to get the up-to-date position of stocks at any point of time are required.

B Category

These items account for 20 to 30% for inventory cost and 30 to 40% of the total storage space. They need simple control and medium level of the handling. Such items need moderate control. They are purchased on the basis of requirement. A record of receipts and issues is kept and a procurement order is placed as soon as the quantity touches the reorder point. These items are comparatively less costly. A safety stock of up to three months may be kept. These items cannot be overlooked but need a lesser degree of attention and control than those in class A but more than C category items.

C Category

They account for less than 10% inventory cost and 70% storage space is required. This category of items needs the least attention for inventory management. Casual supervision and simple records may be maintained and extra care is not required.

There is no hard and fast rule that all inventory items should be classified only in these three categories. There can be a larger number of classifications based on the requirements of the company and the nature of the items. For example *'A'* items may be further sub-classified as A_1, A_2, A_3 etc. The same principle may be extended to *'B'* items also or alternatively all the inventory items may be classified into *A, B, C, D, E, F* etc.

All items that the company consumes must be considered together while classifying into *ABC* classes. Separate classification of raw materials, spares and consumables is not really meaningful. While classifying as *ABC* items, what counts is the consumption Rupees and not the unit price of an item or its consumption in terms of the number of units. Even though, so far we have referred to annual consumption, it is not at all necessary that the consumption figures should be taken only for one year. It can be for 6 months or even 3 months. But the period should be so selected that the consumption figures would be representative. However, annual figures are far more convenient and are universally followed.

The objective of classifying inventory items into *'A'*, *'B'*, *'C'* categories is to develop policy guidelines for selective control. Such a policy can be designed in a variety of ways. In general, *'A'* items merit a tightly controlled inventory system with *constant attention*, *'B'* items moderately through routine inventory system with *periodic attention*, and *'C'* items to subject to loose control with *casual attention*.

Table showing features of *ABC* Analysis

S. No.	Nature	A Items *(High value)*	B Items *(Moderate value)*	C Items *(Low value)*
1	Extent of control	Rigid control	Moderate control	Loose control
2	Safety stock cover	Low safety stocks	Medium safety stock	Large safety stock
3	Frequency of order	Frequently	Less frequently	Bulk ordering
4	Degree of posting	Individual posting	In small groups	Group postings
5	Period of review	Every fortnight	Quarterly	Yearly
6	Sources of supplies	Large no. of sources	Few & reliable	One or two sources
7	Follow-up	Vigorous	Periodic	Occasional
8	Control statements	Weekly	Monthly	Quarterly
9	Forecasting	Accurate forecasts	Focus on past trends	Rough estimates
10	Management level	Senior management	Middle management	Stores supervisor
11	Lead time	Effort to reduce	Moderate efforts	Minimum efforts
12	Annual usage value	Rs 50000 or more	Rs 10000 and above	Below Rs 10000
13	% of stock	5%	10%	85%
14	% of value of item	50%	35%	15%

Advantages of *ABC* Analysis

The benefits derived from this analysis and its subsequent follow-up are summarized as follows:

(a) It facilitates selective control and thereby saves valuable time of busy executives.

(b) It helps in eliminating a lot of unnecessary paper work involved in various other control procedures.

(c) It facilitates inventory control and control over usage of stores materials which ultimately results in cost control.

Limitations of *ABC* Analysis

Although *ABC* analysis is a fundamental tool for exercising selective control over numerous inventory items, it does not, in its present form, permit precise consideration of all relevant problems of inventory management. For instance, a never-ending problem in inventory management is that of adequately handling thousands of low-value 'C' items. Low-value purchases frequently require more items and thereby reduce the time allowance available to purchasing personnel for value analysis, vendor investigation and other 'B' items.

Besides, if *ABC analysis* is not periodically reviewed and updated, the very approach of control may be defeated. For example, 'C' items like diesel oil in a firm, will become most high-value item during power crisis and should, therefore, deserve more attention, but this point may be overlooked if classification of items is not reviewed and updated.

ABC-VED Matrix

The emphasis of ABC analysis is to control the various inventory items on the basis of priority based on monthly/annual consumption value. To overcome this problem, logistics managers can have a matrix approach, which will be an integration of both ABC and VED analysis.

VED analysis emphasizes on classification of items on the basis of their criticality of use as shown in Fig.

Category of Items On the Basis of Criticality of use	Consequences in the case of stock out	Degree of Inventory Management
V (Vital)	Bring production to a halt/loss of corporate image	Significant
E (Essential)	Dislocation of production schedule/loss of sales	Special
D (Desirable)	Temporary additional cost due to arrangement of a substitute	Considerable

The ABC-VED matrix is a hybrid model wherein every category (A, B and C) of items is further classified into three sub-categories (V, E, D) so that an in-depth consideration and due recognition can be given to various items for their inventory management.

Consumption value of Item	Criticality of Items		
	Vital *(Significant)*	Essential *(Specific)*	Desirable *(Considerable)*
A (Best)	(A, V) Best-Significant	(A, E) Best-Specific	(A, D) Best-Considerable
B (Better)	(B, V) Better-Significant	(B, E) Better-Specific	(B, D) Better- Considerable
C (Good)	(C, V) Good-Significant	(C, E) Good-Specific	(C, D) Good-Considerable

Best Practices for Inventory Control

Every item used to produce goods or services is classified as inventory or stock. That includes raw material, goods used in the production process, and finished goods. The goal of inventory management is to have goods in stock when you need them. Not having enough stock at any stage of the production process may jeopardize sales, but tying up too much cash in inventory can hurt your cash flow as well.

It's important for all businesses to properly manage inventory. Here are some things for you to consider.

How much stock to keep?

What's right for a business will depend on the nature and size of the business, as well as the type of inventory. If the company delivers fresh food, for example, its inventory needs will be different (order in smaller quantities but more often) than a custom t-shirt maker who sells over the Internet.

Generally, keeping little stock can boost the cash flow and lower the storage costs, but may be vulnerable to the efficiency of its suppliers and it may cost more than if bought in bulk.

Best practice. Analyze each step of the inventory chain (raw goods, goods-in-progress, finished goods) based on past turnover, sales patterns, and seasonality to determine an optimum amount to keep on hand. Take into account minimum stock levels and re-order lead times.

Best practice. Conduct regular inventory reviews to help assess trends and manage the risks of holding too little or too much stock. If the business is more complex, consider investing in stock control software. Point-of-sale technology may also be used for inventory reviews.

Quality control

The goods should always be checked against the delivery receipts when they come in to look for damage to the goods and packaging.

Best practice. The inventory-receiving practices should be documented in the form of a checklist and it should be ensured that all employees who receive goods follow the proper procedures.

The stock should be stored properly; taking into account all possible factors which may damage it. This includes light, humidity, and improper hygiene. For perishables, a "first-in, first-out" policy should be followed.

Best practice. Expensive and potentially hazardous products should be stored securely. If necessary, expensive inventory that is portable should be identified and "tagged".

Best practice. All stocks should be securely stored after it is delivered and any packaging should be disposed off.

Numerical Problems

Problem 1: A purchase manager places order a lot of 800 units of a particular item. Following additional information is also available:

a) Inventory carrying cost 50%

b) Ordering cost per order Rs. 375

c) Cost per units is Rs. 60

d) Annual demand 1600 units

Comment on the decision of the purchase manager. Also calculate the effect of his decision.

Solution:

$$EOQ = \sqrt{\frac{2AC_0}{C_c}}$$

$$= \sqrt{\frac{2 \times 1600 \times 375}{50\% \times 60}}$$

$$= 200 \text{ units}$$

Evaluation of the ordering policies:

	Existing	EOQ
Total requirements (units)	1600	1600
Units per order	800	200
Number of orders	2	8
Average Inventory (units)	400	100
Carrying cost @ 50%	12000	3000
Ordering cost @ Rs 375	750	3000
Total Cost	12750	6000

It is evident that the firm is incurring a loss of (12750 – 6000 = Rs. 6750) by not following the EOQ model.

Problem 2: Assuming that the following quantity discount schedule for a particular product is available to a retail store:

Order size (units)	Discount
0 – 49	Nil
50 – 99	5%
100 – 199	10%
200 and above	12%

The cost of a single unit of the product without discount is Rs. 25. The annual demand for the product is 250 units. Ordering cost is Rs. 15 per order and annual inventory carrying cost is Rs. 3 per unit. Determine the optimal order quantity, the associated minimum total cost and total purchase cost of inventory if shortages are not allowed.

Solution:

$$\text{EOQ without discount} = \sqrt{\frac{2AC_0}{C_c}} = \sqrt{\frac{2 \times 250 \times 15}{3}} = 50 \text{ units}$$

Comparative Evaluation of EOQ and Discount Offer

	EOQ	100 units	200 units	250 units
No. of orders	5	3	2	1
Total order cost @ Rs. 15 (A)	75.00	45.00	30.00	15.00
Average Inventory	25 units	50 units	100 units	125 units
Carrying cost @ Rs. 3 (B)	75.00	150.00	300.00	375.00
Purchase price per unit	23.75	22.50	22.00	22.00
Total purchase cost (C)	5937.50	5625.00	5500.00	5500.00
Total cost (A + B + C)	6087.50	5820.00	5830.00	5890.00

The firm has minimum cost when it orders 100 units and avails a discount of 10%.

Problem 3: The following information is available from a retailer:

Cost per unit (Rs.)	25
Annual requirement (units)	5000
Carrying cost	20% of the cost per unit
Ordering cost (Rs.)	50 per order
Discount	2% on the order of 2500 or more

Evaluate and suggest whether to adopt the EOQ model or the discount model?

Solution: First of all, let us determine EOQ

$$EOQ = \sqrt{\frac{2AC_0}{C_c}} = \sqrt{\frac{2 \times 5000 \times 50}{5}} = 316 \text{ units}$$

Comparative Evaluation of EOQ and Discount Offer

	EOQ	Discount Offer
Annual requirement	5000	5000
Size of the order	316	2500
Number of orders	15.8 ? 16	2
Cost per order	50.00	50.00
Total ordering cost (A)	800.00	100.00
Carrying cost per unit	5.00	5.00
Average inventory	158	1250
Total carrying cost (B)	790.00	6250
Cost per unit	25	24.50*
Total cost of purchase (C) (Annual requirement × cost per unit)	125000	122500
Total Cost (A + B + C)	**126590**	**128850**

$$* \left(25 - \frac{2}{100} \times 25\right) = 24.50$$

Order shall be placed as per EOQ.

Problem 4: ABC Ltd. requires 4000 units of a certain item per year. The purchase price per unit Rs. 50. The carrying cost of inventory is 25% of unit cost and the cost per order is Rs. 1000. Calculate:

(i) The Economic Order Quantity.

(ii) What will be the total cost of ordering and cost of carrying inventories when 4 orders of equal sizes are placed?

Solution:

(i) Annual usage = 4000 units

Purchase price per unit = Rs. 50

Carrying cost of inventory = 25% of unit cost = Rs. 12.50

Cost per order = Rs. 1000

$$EOQ = \sqrt{\frac{2AC_O}{C_c}} = \sqrt{\frac{2 \times 4000 \times 1000}{12.50}} = 800 \text{ units.}$$

(ii) Ordering cost = 4 × 1000 = 4000

Carrying cost = Average inventory × carrying cost per unit

$$= \frac{1000}{2} \times 12.50 = 6250$$

Total cost = 4000 + 6250 = Rs. 10,250

Problem 5: ABC Motors purchases 9000 units of spare parts for its annual requirements, ordering one month usage at a time. Each spare part costs Rs. 25. The ordering cost per order is Rs. 20 and the carrying charges are 20% of the unit cost. Suggest whether the current purchasing policy of the company is acceptable or not. Give reasons.

Solution: The existing cost of maintaining inventory is as follows: since, the firm is buying 9000 units which are purchased in orders of 1 month usage, therefore, the number of units purchased in each order is9000/12 = 750 units and the firm is placing 12 orders in a year and the average inventory is 375 units (i.e. 750/2). Now,

Ordering cost = 12 × Rs. 20 = Rs. 240

Carrying cost = 375 × 20% of Rs. 25 = 375 × 5 = Rs. 1875

Total annual cost of the existing policy = 240 + 1875 = Rs. 2115

The Economic Order Quantity may be ascertained as follows:

$$EOQ = \sqrt{\frac{2\,AC_O}{C_c}} = \sqrt{\frac{2 \times 9000 \times 20}{5}} = 268 \text{ units}$$

So, when the EOQ is 268 units, the number of orders to be placed in a year would be (9000/268 = 33.5 = 34) and the average inventory would be 268/2 = 134 units. The cost of maintaining this economic order quantity is as follows:

Ordering cost (34 × Rs. 20) = Rs. 680
Carrying cost (134 × Rs. 5) = Rs. 670

Total annual cost according to EOQ policy = 680 + 670 = Rs. 1350

The current purchasing policy of the companyis not acceptable. The company can save (2115 - 1350 = Rs. 765) if it purchases according to the EOQ policy.

Problem 6: The following information is obtained from the purchase manager of an organization:

Interest on the locked up capital	20%
Ordering cost for each order	Rs. 100
Inspection cost per lot	Rs. 50
Follow-up cost for each order	Rs. 80
Pilferage while holding inventory	5%
Other holding cost	15%
Other procurement cost for each order	Rs. 170
Cost per item	Rs. 10

Discount for a minimum order quantity of 500 items is 10%. What should be the ordering policy of the purchase manager?

Solution:

The total inventory carrying cost (20% + 5% + 15%) = 40%
Ordering cost (100 + 50 + 80 + 170) = Rs. 400

$$\text{EOQ} = \sqrt{\frac{2\,AC_o}{C_c}} = \sqrt{\frac{2 \times 1000 \times 400}{4}} = 447 \text{ units}$$

$$\text{Number of orders to be placed in a year} = \frac{1000}{447} = 2.24 \cong 3$$

However, if the firm places 3 orders in a year, then instead of 447 units it should place order for 334 units (1000/3) only.

	Order of 500 Units	Order Based on EOQ	Order of 334 Units
Size of order (units)	500	447	334
No. of orders	2	3	3
Cost per order	Rs. 400	Rs. 400	Rs. 400
Total ordering cost (A)	Rs. 800	Rs. 1200	Rs. 1200
Carrying cost per unit	Rs. 3.60*	Rs. 4.00	Rs. 4.00
Average inventory	250	224	167
Total carrying cost (B)	Rs. 900	Rs. 896	Rs. 668
Total purchase cost (C)	Rs. 9000	Rs. 10000	Rs. 10000
Total Cost (A + B + C)	**Rs. 10700**	**Rs. 12096**	**Rs. 11868**

* (The carrying cost is 40% of the unit cost, the unit cost after 10% discount is Rs 9)

Since, the total cost is minimum when order is placed for 500 units, therefore, the benefit of 10% discount on purchase is fully justified.

Problem 7: A firm requires 1,20,000 units of a particular item annually. The cost per unit is Rs. 50, the cost per purchase order is Rs. 500 and the inventory carrying cost is Rs. 8 per unit per year. What is the EOQ and what should the firm do if the supplier offers discount as below:

Order Quantity	Discount
5000 – 6500	2%
6500 and above	3%

Solution:

$$\text{EOQ} = \sqrt{\frac{2\,AC_o}{C_c}} = \sqrt{\frac{2 \times 120000 \times 500}{8}} = 3873 \text{ units}$$

Evaluation of Ordering Policies

	3873 Units	5000 Units	6500 Units
No. of orders	31	24	19
Ordering cost @ Rs. 500 (A)	Rs. 15500	Rs. 12000	Rs. 9500
Carrying cost per unit	Rs 8	Rs 8	Rs. 8
Average inventory	1937	2500	3250
Total carrying cost (B)	Rs. 15496	Rs. 20000	Rs. 26000
Per Units cost	Rs. 50	Rs. 48	Rs. 48.50
Total purchase cost (C)	Rs. 6000000	Rs. 5880000	Rs. 5820000
Total Cost (A + B + C)	**Rs. 6030996**	**Rs 5912000**	**Rs. 5855500**

The total cost is minimum when order is placed for 6500 or more units.

Problem 8: A materials manager has the following information for procuring a particular item. Annual demand = 800 units. Ordering cost = Rs. 640. Inventory carrying cost = 35%. Cost per unit = Rs 50. If the order quantity is more than or equal to 250, the supplier offers a discount of 10%. Calculate the quantity for which order should be placed to reduce the total cost.

Solution:

$$EOQ = \sqrt{\frac{2\,AC_o}{C_c}} = \sqrt{\frac{2 \times 800 \times 640}{35\% \text{ of } 50}} = 241.89 \cong 242 \text{ units}$$

$$\text{Total carrying cost} = \frac{242}{2} \times 17.50 = \text{Rs. } 2117.50$$

$$\text{Total ordering cost} = \frac{800}{242} \times 640 = \text{Rs. } 2115.70$$

Total purchase cost = 50 × 800 = Rs 40000

Total inventory cost at 242 units = 40000 + 2117.50 + 2115.70 = Rs. 44233.20

For 250 units (with discount): cost per unit = Rs. 45

$$\text{Total carrying cost} = \frac{250}{2} \times 35\% \text{ of } 45 = \text{Rs. } 1968.75$$

$$\text{Total ordering cost} = \frac{800}{250} \times 640 = \text{Rs. } 2048.00$$

Total purchase cost = 45 × 800 = Rs. 36000

Total inventory cost at 250 units = 36000 + 1968.75 + 2048.00 = Rs. 40016.75

So, the firm should place order for 250 units in order to minimize the total cost.

Problem 9: From the following details, draw a plan of ABC selective control.

Item	Units	Unit Cost (Rs.)
1	7000	5.00
2	24000	3.00
3	1500	10.00
4	600	22.00
5	38000	1.50
6	40000	0.50
7	60000	0.20
8	3000	3.50
9	300	8.00
10	29000	0.40
11	11500	7.10
12	4100	6.20

Solution:

In order to arrange the items as per ABC analysis, they are to be arranged in order of total annual value.

Ranking of Items According to Total Annual Value

Item	Units	Unit cost	Total cost	% of total	Ranking
1	7000	5.00	35000	9.8	4
2	24000	3.00	72000	20.2	2
3	1500	10.00	15000	4.2	7
4	600	22.00	13200	3.7	8
5	38000	1.50	57000	16.0	3
6	40000	0.50	20000	5.6	6
7	60000	0.20	12000	3.4	9
8	3000	3.50	10500	3.0	11
9	300	8.00	2400	0.7	12
10	29000	0.40	11600	3.3	10
11	11500	7.10	81650	23.0	1
12	4100	6.20	25420	7.1	5
			355770	100.00	

The grouping for ABC analysis can now be done as follows:

Item	Total Value	% of Items	% of Value	Cum. Value	Group
11	81650		23.0		A
2	72000		20.2		A
5	57000	25%	16.0	59.2%	A
1	35000		9.8		B
12	25420		7.1		B
6	20000		5.6		B
3	15000	33.33%	4.2	26.7%	B
4	13200		3.7		C
7	12000		3.4		C
10	11600		3.3		C
8	10500		3.0		C
9	2400	41.7%	0.7	14.1%	C
		100.0%	100.0%		

Problem 10: Classify the inventory items according to ABC plan for the data given below:

Solution:

Item No.	Quantity Used	Cost per unit (Rs.)
1	2	40
2	200	5
3	30	1000
4	20	20
5	4	20
6	16	2000
7	24	50
8	5	40
9	100	8
10	250	4
11	120	8
12	140	7
13	10	10
14	20	10
15	200	5

Solution:

Item	Units	Unit cost (Rs.)	Total cost (Rs.)	Ranking
1	2	40	80	15
2	200	5	1000	5
3	30	1000	30000	2
4	20	20	400	10
5	4	20	80	14
6	16	2000	32000	1
7	24	50	1200	3
8	5	40	200	12
9	100	8	800	9
10	250	4	1000	6
11	120	8	960	8
12	140	7	980	7
13	10	10	100	13
14	20	10	200	11
15	200	5	1000	4
	1141		70000	

Classification into A, B, C

Item No.	Rank	Total Value (Rs.)	Cum. Value	% Total Value	Group
6	1	32000	32000		
3	2	30000	62000	88.57%	A (88.57%)
7	3	1200	63200		
2	4	1000	64200		
10	5	1000	65200		
15	6	1000	66200		
12	7	980	67180		
11	8	960	68140		
9	9	800	68940	98.48%	B (9.91%)
4	10	400	69340		
8	11	200	69540		
14	12	200	69740		
13	13	100	69840		
1	14	80	69920		
5	15	80	70000	100%	C (1.52%)
		70000			

For Discussion

1. What is Inventory? Discuss the distinguishing characteristics of inventory.
2. What is the basis for the classification of inventory?
3. What are the various elements of inventory cost? Discuss.
4. Why should we manage inventory? Enumerate the major objectives of inventory management.
5. Discuss the applicability of Retailer's Model and Producer's Model in inventory management.
6. What are the basic assumptions in the application of the Retailer's Model and the Producer's Model?
7. Describe the conditions in which a buyer gives preference to the Discounting Model over the Retailer's Model.
8. What is the basis for ABC method of inventory classification?
9. State whether the following statements are correct. Give reasons:
   a) Safety stock increases as the demand increases.
   b) In ABC analysis high cost items are most likely to fall in category A, and least cost items are likely to fall in category C.
   c) A large batch size is necessary to protect against stockouts.
   d) EOQ is based on balancing between inventory carrying costs and shortage costs.

e) Lead time is the time interval elapsing between the placement of a replenishment order and the receipt of last installment of goods against the order.

10. Write short-notes on:

a) VED Analysis

b) FSN Analysis

c) SOS Analysis

d) SDE Analysis

Numerical Exercises

1. A firm's annual requirement of inventory is 30,000 units. The purchasing costs amount to Rs. 150 per order. The carrying costs are likely to be Rs. 1.20 per unit per year. Assuming the following order sizes: (i) 30,000 units, (ii) 15,000 units, (iii) 6,000 units. Determine (a) ordering cost, (b) carrying cost, (c) average inventory, (d) economic order quantity.

2. A company required 10,000 units of an item every year. The cost of placing an order is Rs. 150. The inventory carrying cost is 20%. The unit price of the item is Rs. 10. Calculate the economic order quantity.

3. A company requires 2500 units of a product every month. Each order costs Rs. 50. The carrying cost is 15% per year while the unit cost of the product is Rs. 10. Determine the economic lot size and maximum total variable cost.

4. Anand Motors purchase 10,000 units of a spare part for its annual requirement. Each spare part costs Rs. 20. The ordering cost per order is Rs. 15 and the carrying charges are 15% of the average inventory per year. You are required to suggest a more economical purchasing policy for the company. What is your recommendation and how much would it save the company every year?

5. Determine the economic order quantity for a product whose average daily consumption rate is 80 units. The cost of each unit is Re. 0.50 and the inventory carrying charge is 205 per year. The cost of placing and receiving the order is Rs. 10. Assuming total working days in a year as 300, calculate the annual inventory cost also.

6. A purchase manager places order each time for a lot of 500 numbers of a spare part. The following results are obtained from the information available:

Inventory carrying cost = 40%

Ordering cost per order = Rs. 600

Cost per unit =Rs. 50

Annual Demand = 2500 units

Suggest whether the purchase manager has taken the right decision?

7. An automobile company uses metal at an approximate customer rate of 25,000 kg per year. The metal costs Rs. 30 per kg and the company personnel estimate that it costs Rs. 130 to place an order and the inventory carrying cost is 10% per year. How frequently should orders for the metal be placed and what quantity should be ordered?
8. The annual demand, buying cost per order and carrying cost per year as a percentage of the value of inventory in the case of two products A and B are the same. However, the price of A is 5 times as much as that of B. If EOQ for A is 100 units, what will be the EOQ for B?
9. Vishal manufactures 5000 bottles of a chemical in a year. The factory cost per bottle is Rs. 5; the set-up cost per production run is estimated to be Rs. 90, and the carrying costs on finished goods inventory amount to 20% of the cost per annum. The production rate is 600 bottles per day and sales amount to 150 bottles per day. What is the optimal production lot size and the number of production runs?
10. A production manager is reviewing the production lot size decision associated with a production operation where the production rate is 8000 units a year, annual demand is 2000 units, set-up cost is Rs. 300 per production run and carrying cost is Rs. 2 per unit per year. The current production run is 500 units every 3 months. Would your recommend a change in the production lot size? If so, why? How much could be saved by adopting the new production lot size?
11. A company requires 48,000 units of a raw material costing Rs 1.20 per unit. Placing each order costs Rs. 45 and the carrying cost is 15% per year of the average inventory. (i) Find the economic order quantity, and (ii) assuming that the company follows the EOQ purchasing policy, it operates for 300 days a year, the lead time is 12 days and the safety stock is 500 units, find the reorder point, the maximum, minimum and average inventories.
12. The estimated annual demand for a product is 5000 units, the ordering cost is Rs 49 per order and the inventory carrying cost is 20% of the value of inventory. The normal price charged by the supplier is Rs. 5 per unit. However, a discount @ 3% is allowed for an order for at least 1000 units. The discount is raised to 5% if the order is for 2500 units or more. What is the most economical order quantity?
13. A company buys 8,000 units of an item for its annual consumption. Each unit costs Rs. 10. The ordering cost per order is Rs. 30 and the carrying cost is 7½% of the average inventory per year.
    (i) Determine the EOQ and the total inventory cost.
    (ii) Should the company accept an offer of 2% discount in price on 4 bigger orders of quarterly requirements of the material?

14. From the following details, draw a plan of ABC inventory control.

Item	Units ('000)	Unit Cost (Rs.)
1	7	5
2	24	3
3	1.5	10
4	0.6	22
5	38	1.5
6	40	0.5
7	60	0.2
8	3	3.5
9	0.3	8
10	29	0.4
11	11.5	7.1
12	4.1	6.2

Chapter 3

Purchasing

Purchasing (procurement) is a strategic process for the development of a sound production set-up and an effective supply base so as to achieve logistics productivity. Purchasing refers to a functional activity carried out in every organization. In other words, purchasing can be defined as the procuring of materials, supplies, machines, tools and services, required for the equipment, maintenance and operation of a manufacturing plant. Purchasing has acquired the status of a dynamic management activity that includes:

a) Able administration.
b) Accurate forecasting.
c) Effective planning.
d) Developed capacity to organize.
e) Effective co-ordinating efforts.
f) Better control mechanisms.

Purchasing is of importance in the operation of a manufacturing concern because:

1. The efficient operations of an industrial concern depends upon the highest possible turnover of investment. The purchasing department must arrange its purchases so as to ensure receipt of proper materials in the quantities and at the same time required to maintain the continuity of production and the shipping promise to the customer, without increasing the investment beyond the required levels to meet the current needs.
2. It is a primary function. Proper sales cannot be made unless materials being used in manufacture or for resale are bought at an ultimate cost equal to or lower than that obtained by competitors.
3. By its close contacts with vendors and their representatives and the general market, the purchasing department is in a better position to advise its company on new materials, which may be used to advantage as substitutes for materials now in use, possible new lines of products to be added and policies and procedures that increase goodwill in the business concerns with which it deals.

Objectives of Purchasing

1. To maintain regular flow of materials.
2. To purchase at a competitive price the right quality, in right quantity and at a right time from a right source.
3. To ensure higher productivity.
4. To ensure the production of a better quality product at a competitive cost.
5. To act for standardization, variety reduction and value analysis.
6. To ensure a better margin of profit.

The Purchasing Process

Almost every one is familiar with the steps in a standard purchasing process. As consumers, we go through the procedural steps found in most purchasing systems every time a major purchase is made. For example, whether we are buying a new car or planning a dream vacation, we go through each of the following steps: 1) we identify or recognise a need; 2) we clearly describe what we need to buy; 3) we shop around to find the best place to buy the desired product; 4) we decide what we are willing to pay; 5) we make the purchase; 6) we make sure that the purchased item is delivered to us when we need it; 7) we receive the new purchase and carefully inspect it; 8) make payment for the purchase; and 9) maintain proper records of receipts and warranty cards etc.

The actual purchasing process varies depending on what we are buying. Typically more time is spent on buying products which are costly than low-priced products. The same is true for companies – different companies perform the above steps at varying levels of sophistication depending on the items being purchased, the skill of the purchasing managers and the resources dedicated to the purchasing process. The steps followed in a purchasing process shall now be discussed in detail.

1. Recognition of Need

The purchasing process begins in firm whenever a need to acquire some input is identified. This input may be materials, supplies or services required for use in production or in the general support of the day-to-day business activities of the firm. Recognising that a need exists is the responsibility of the user of the item to be purchased. With the advent of technology, standard production needs are communicated automatically through a computerised production control system that monitors inventory levels and reorder points. However, a clear and precise set of guidelines must be in place to facilitate communications regarding new, unique, or one-time purchases.

2. Description of Need

To ensure purchase of the right items as they are needed, the user must clearly specify what is needed. This specification process generally takes place as a purchase requisition is created. The purchase requisition contains all the information pertaining to the purchase of various items required. It includes the description of the item, requisitioning department, authorising signature, purchase quantity, and delivery date and location. The information should be stated clearly and precisely to ensure that the purchasing process is carried on smoothly. Item description is particularly critical since purchasing must have a clear understanding of what is needed to identify the appropriate supplier and then communicate the needs to that supplier. Each item can be described in several ways, depending on the item as well as the amount of experience in buying the item. Several items are easy to describe, description may be done in terms of a brand name or via an established part number; others require listing extensive physical and performance characteristics. The less experience purchasing has with an item, the more clear and specific the description must be. The items to be purchased can be described to the purchasing authorities and potential suppliers in terms of:

(a) a brand name;

(b) an established market grading system;

(c) a word picture that describes the item;

(d) a blue print;

(e) a sample or prototype; or

(f) a set of performance expectations.

3. Selection and Development of Suppliers

Once the needs of the user are understood, the next step is to find the best – capable and committed – supplier possible. The success of the purchase department depends on its skill in locating or developing suppliers, analysing vendor capabilities and then selecting the appropriate vendor.

One of the objectives of purchasing is to ensure that the highest quality product is made available at the lowest possible cost along with the best service. A supplier should be selected on the basis of his ability to meet these requirements. However, several other issues should also be considered in selecting a supplier. The definition of a good supplier is:

A good supplier is one who is at all times honest and fair in his dealings with the customers, his own employees, and himself; who has adequate plant facilities, and know-how so as to be able to provide materials which meet the purchaser's specifications, in the quantities required, and at the times promised; whose financial position is sound; whose prices are reasonable both to the buyer and to himself; whose management policies are progressive; who is alert to the need for continued improvement in both his products and his manufacturing processes; and who realizes that, in the last analysis, his own interests are best served when he best serves his customers. **(Dobler, 1996)**

The actual process used to identify good suppliers varies and is dependent on the importance of the item being purchased. Suppliers of maintenance and repair order (MRO) items do not receive a lot of attention while suppliers of major components are carefully analysed and developed by the purchasing department. In general, the higher the purchase value, or the greater the importance of the purchased item on the end product's performance, the more important the selection process of the supplier.

4 Acquisition and Analysis of Proposals

When qualified suppliers have been identified, requests for specific proposals will be made. Stage 3 and 4 may occur simultaneously in a straight re-buy. Buyers merely check a catalogue or contact suppliers to obtain up-to-date information about prices and deliveries. However, in more complex situations, the above stages are separate and distinct. A lot of time may be spent in exchanging proposals and counter-proposals. In such purchase situations, the need for information is extensive and a great deal of time is devoted to analysing proposals and comparing products, services and costs. Thus, this stage can be regarded as a distinct component of the purchasing process.

5 Evaluation of Proposals and Selection of Suppliers

Various proposals of competing suppliers are weighed and analysed. If a firm is facing a make-or-buy decision, proposals are compared to the cost of producing the needed item within the buying firm. If the buying firm decides it can produce the needed item more economically, the buying process terminates. If the firm is not facing a make-or-buy decision, one or more offers from competing suppliers are accepted. Further negotiations may continue with selected suppliers on terms, prices, delivery, or other aspects of the supplier's proposals.

6 Selection of an Order Routine

Order routines are established by forwarding purchase orders to the vendors and status reports to the using department and by determining the levels of inventory that will be needed over various time period. While this phase begins with the placement of an order, the purchase process is not actually completed until the ordered item is delivered and accepted for use. The user department, where the need originated, does not view its problems solved until the specified product has been received and is available for use. The effectiveness of suppliers in handling this phase is, therefore, critical.

7 Performance Feedback and Evaluation

The final phase in the purchasing process consists of a formal or informal review and feedback regarding product performance, as well as vendor performance. This phase involved a determination by the user department as to whether the purchased item solved the original problem. If it did not, the suppliers that were screened earlier may be given further consideration. Feedback that is critical, of the chosen vendor or product can cause the members of the decision-making unit to re-examine their positions. Research indicates that when this occurs, the views regarding previously rejected alternatives become more favourable.

Methods of Purchasing

The methods of purchasing vary according to the nature of the demand in the plant and the conditions in the market in which goods are to be bought. The major purchasing methods can be listed as follows:

1. **Market purchasing**: When purchases are made in accordance with the condition of the market, to take advantage of price fluctuations rather than to meet immediate needs or for a specified future period, the method is known as market purchasing. This method cannot be termed as speculative purchasing as long as it conforms to the production schedule and its possible changes, or to the demands of the plant or business. The advantages of this method are:

a) Greater margin of profit on finished products, the price of which does not fluctuate as widely as that of the raw material.

b) Lower purchase prices.

c) Consolidation of purchase of a given material into one transaction, with a resulting saving in purchase expense.

The disadvantages of this method are:

a) Liability of obsolescence in case of radical changes in specifications.

b) Possibility of error in judgment of market tendencies, which may mean larger losses.

c) Higher inventories with consequent higher carrying charges and tying up of storage space.

2. **Purchasing small items in groups:** The purchasing method in which small items are grouped and purchased from one dealer who agrees to sell them at a fixed percentage of profit above dealers cost, is proving worthwhile in may organizations. Agreements of these kinds often provide for an audit of dealer costs by the buyer. The problem is to handle such purchases as quickly and as inexpensively as possible.

3. **Speculative purchasing:** Speculative purchasing is buying in excess of needs. With the hope of selling the excess at a future date at a profit. The term is occasionally applied to an unusually large purchase made at a price, which is low enough to warrant taking the gamble that the savings in price will more than offset the cost of carrying the inventory. It does not base decisions on demands of the business itself, but on the possibility of market price savings. Speculative purchasing is not, properly, a function of the purchasing department. It should be authorized only by direct action of top management. For ordinary manufacturing, the method is discouraged. Its simple advantage is the possibility of huge

speculative profits. However, the disadvantages include:

- Endangering manufacturing schedules by waiting for profitable buying points.
- Using large storage spaces.
- Tying up large amounts of capital.
- Running the risk of obsolescence in case of radical change in specification.

4. **Purchasing for a specified future period:** Purchase for a specified future period is standard practice for buying goods regularly used but not in large quantity, and on which price variations are negligible. Most supplies are bought by this method. The period for which the purchase is made be fixed by a production schedule, by the stores record of past use, or by a combination of both. The savings to be gained by the purchase of a given quantity also affects the determination of the period, as does the cost of carrying the goods in inventory. It is important to note that no fixed periods should be set for all purchases. Rather, a separate and flexible period should be determined for each item.

5. **Schedule purchasing:** The schedule plan for purchasing materials, which are used regularly in large quantities, has been developed to reduce the investment in inventory. Essentially, the plan consists of giving suppliers approximate estimates of purchase requirements over a period of time, thus enabling them to anticipate the receipt of orders and be prepared to fill them when they arrive. Although, minimum inventory is probably the most important objective in this plan, other objectives sought are good quality, prompt delivery, and low price. Good quality can be obtained only by giving suppliers enough time to fulfil the order. Prompt delivery can be better assured if the supplier can include the purchaser's approximate materials requirements in his own production plans. Lower cost results from this opportunity to pre-plan production, because better methods and equipment can often be provided when the demand is known.

6. **Purchasing strictly by requirement:** Purchasing by requirement means that no purchase is made until a need arises, and then only that quantity is purchased which is necessary to meet the need. This method applies principally to emergency requirements, or to goods used so infrequently that they should not be carried in stock. It is essentially emergency buying and the task of the purchasing department is to have vendor relations, which can be depended upon to fulfil such orders promptly and without taking advantage of the situation.

7. **Contract purchasing:** All purchasing is by contract, and the term "contract purchasing" is applied to that special type of contract, which calls for deferred delivery over a period of time. Through this medium, advantage can be taken of low prices of materials, which are in effect at the time of placing the order, while providing for the delivery of the materials to meet estimated future requirements. Thus, the price advantage is obtained, without undue addition in inventory. Whenever such contracts are possible, they should be negotiated for those raw

materials that fluctuate widely in price. In some cases, the prices for spot purchases are more favourable, and market purchasing, even with the increase in inventory costs, may prove advantageous.

Functions of the Purchase Department

Purchasing is the most important function of materials management. The moment an order is placed for the purchase of materials, a substantial part of the companies finance is committed which affects the cash flow position of the company. Following are the functions of the purchase department :

1. To ensure continuous availability of materials so that there may be uninterrupted flow of materials for production.
2. To make purchases in reasonable quantities in order to keep investment in materials at a minimum.
3. To purchase proper quality of materials and to ensure minimum possible wastage and consequent loss in production.
4. To develop good supplier relationships that will ensure the best terms of supply of materials.
5. To make purchases competitively and wisely at the most economical prices.
6. To develop alternate sources of supply so that materials can be purchased from them in case a particular supplier fails to supply the materials.
7. To serve as an information centre on the materials knowledge relating to prices, sources of supply, specifications, mode of delivery etc.
8. To adopt the most advantageous method of purchase to ensure smooth delivery of materials form suppliers and to avoid the risks of any disputes or financial loss.
9. To see if the materials indented can be manufactured in the plant by utilizing spare capacity.
10. In many cases, purchase section also handles the disposal of surplus stock and scrap, because of its better knowledge of market conditions and of the dealers.

Centralized Vs Decentralized Purchasing

When it is centralized, it generally means that this department will procure all requirements of all the departments of the concern. If there is a decentralized system, a purchase section, vested with all the powers of a purchase department, is attached to all the departments and is responsible for purchasing all the requirements of the attached department.

Merits of Centralized Purchasing

1. The purchasing staff and its consequent overheads are reduced.
2. The procedure of purchasing is simplified. Also disposal is simplified and

facilitated.

3. The standardization of the quality of materials purchased is ensured. This also helps in reducing the variety.
4. The advantages of bulk purchases are achieved. Bargaining on better price, terms and conditions is possible.
5. The centralization of receiving, inspection and storage is rendered possible, resulting in reduction of handling and other miscellaneous storage costs.
6. The overall inventory is reduced and the inventory investment and carrying cost is reduced to a great extent.
7. The working of the accounts department is also simplified because of fewer payments and hence lesser clarifications.

Wherever, a centralized system of purchasing is followed and there are certain branches of the concern, the centralized purchasing of various branches is specified and central purchase department procures only the specified items and the rest is left to the purchasing section attached to various branches. Thus, the advantages of easy and timely purchasing action, greater efficiency, better utilization of budgetary provisions, economical purchasing due to better and local contact with suppliers, and timely replenishment accrue to the organization due to this arrangement of combining both the systems. However, a decentralized system is advisable only in those cases where different plants or associated companies are located at different places and are manufacturing or dealing in different products.

Purchasing Principles or Policies

1. Right Source: The various factors guiding the selection of the right source are reliability, cost, quality assurance, past performance, good public relations, after sales service, accessibility etc. Market research is conducted to locate potential sources (vendors) so that monopoly restrictions and proprietary conditions are avoided. It involves:

- Vendor selection.
- Vendor development.
- Vendor rating.

2. Right Quantity: In order to take a proper decision on the quantity, the purchase manager has to take many aspects into consideration. It is necessary for him to liaise with other departments, mainly, the production department. In case of recurring items, the right quantity is that which may be purchased at a particular time with the minimum total cost. If the quantity is large, the price is generally lower but the inventory carrying cost goes up.

3. Right Quality: Quality control and standardization refers to the following:

- Standardization and variety reduction.

- Quality assurance/inspection and grading.

4. **Right Price:** Price means the cost of ordering and cost of carrying. Price structure also influences the **'make or buy'** decision. The purchase manager is called upon to decide the most optimum quantity to reduce overall cost by inventory control. This quantity is obtained through several mathematical techniques.

When to Make ?

- When existing suppliers cannot meet the quality or performance.
- When the firm can produce the part at a lower cost.
- When the firm has excess capacity and the component value is sufficient to cover all the costs of producing it.
- When the firm's manufacturing experience and equipment are well-suited to manufacture the material.

When to Buy ?

- When the cost of the equipment needed to make the item is so large that the firm is not in a position to make the required material.
- When the desired quality is available from the existing suppliers.
- When the quantity of the components required is small.
- When other firms hold patents on the required materials.
- When the opportunity cost of producing is much greater than that of buying.

5. **Right Time:** Like correct quantity, right time of supply is also important. Delayed supply can cause shortages and upset production schedule and might mean tangible and intangible losses. In order to ensure the supply in time, the following steps are to be taken :

(i) Set-up effective method of expediting the supplies based on the following:
   - Routine reminders on C class items.
   - Detailed analysis on class A and B items.
   - Intensive follow-up on 'vital' and 'essential' items.

(ii) Provide logistics support in time for the following:
   - Assembly/Distribution.
   - Transportation.
   - Storage.

Ten Keys to Effective Purchasing

Price increases are impacting companies at unprecedented levels. Utility costs have increased 30% over the last year. Escalating paper prices are affecting the cost of copy paper, letterhead and other printing costs. Health insurance increases over the last four years upto 80%.

What are your plans to keep profits at the same level, or even increase your profitability despite this increase in costs?

- Reduce capital spending.
- Implement yet another round of layoffs; GM and Ford are currently pursuing this strategy.
- Increase employee share of health insurance.
- Raise prices.

However, if a company wants to maintain its stature as a "best in class organization" it cannot continue to rely on the above four methods to improve profits. The competitors are increasing capital spending, adding employees, offering competitive benefit packages and actually lowering prices to their customer's year after year. **Their Secret - Implementing best practices in purchasing.**

How long does it take to become a best in the world purchasing organization?

The short answer is, a very long time. That means inch-by-inch, day-by-day, and price increase by price increase.

A better answer: best practices evolve over time – if a company decides to become a master purchasing organization it has to recognize that change is inevitable, keep a positive attitude and passionately believe in the process improvement cycle.

The following ***"Ten Keys to Effective Purchasing"*** have been identified and developed. These keys have been developed by the best purchasing gurus in the world, continuously researching companies that are named Purchasing Magazines' best companies:

1. **Improve your vendor relationships - They don't stay the same from year to year**
   a) Avoid cosy or adversarial relationships with suppliers. Cinema tickets and free lunches are great as long as the supplier is bringing great cost improvement ideas along with them.
   b) Is your door open to suppliers or do you continue to shut them out? Sitting down with vendors once or twice a year to collaborate eliminates surprises from both you and them.
   c) Order in a manner that keeps the vendor's cost low.
   d) Work with the best vendors, taking into account local, regional, national and global players for the goods and services you are purchasing.

e) Competitive pricing is key, focus on the overall best total cost.

f) Companies are working with too many vendors, find a great vendor or two and utilize your leverage by giving them all of your business.

g) Develop an annual cost reduction plan; the best vendors will understand this concept.

h) Vendors should enjoy working with you (payment policies, return policies, returning phone calls).

2. Develop a scorecard for keeping track of vendors' service, quality, delivery and pricing

a) Track the quality, service and price performance of your vendors.

b) Communicate the results of your scorecard to the vendors.

c) Understand what is important to your vendors and make sure they understand what is important to your company.

d) Involve the vendor in the design of your product from the beginning.

3. Obtaining the right information = right sizing your vendor list and vendor costs

a) Leverage your volume with your vendors.

b) Purchasing and finance should form a team to identify current spending and where the greatest opportunities for improvement exist.

c) Engineering, manufacturing and sales should be included to brainstorm ideas for product improvements.

4. Create a purchasing staff with the following characteristics

a) **Analytical** - great purchasing is based on the ability to roll your sleeves up and get into the details of the items you are looking to buy.

b) **Great negotiation skills** - very few purchasing managers and buyers have had the benefit of negotiation training.

c) **Business knowledge** - Understanding your business goals and the focus of your suppliers business is critical to making sure you reach your companies goals while providing what is necessary to help your supplier reach their goals.

d) **Compliance to policies** - Creating purchase orders after the invoice has been generated is a waste of both your time and accounting's time. How many rogue buyers do you have in your organization that are buying from non-preferred vendors.

e) **Legal knowledge** - creating contracts that benefit the company, not solely the vendor, is not an easy process and requires training and understanding of the terms that must be met for a vendor to work with your company. You also have to monitor your vendors to make sure they comply with the agreements put in place.

f) Ability to work in other parts of the organization (Sales, operations, finance).

5. **Get the executive team behind purchasing 100%**
   a) Top purchasing executive should report to the CEO or COO, not to be stuck behind another executive in your company.
   b) Top officials must have a direct line to purchasing so that they can understand the impact, price increases will have on their business and make decisions as to whether increases should be passed on to your customers.
   c) Potential price increases need to be offset with decreases in other areas.
   d) Top executives may consider increasing the employee cost of group insurance.
   e) A team approach to purchasing helps to focus on the priority areas within a company.
6. **Enforce a preferred vendor list**
   a) Support the purchasing manager when a tough decision needs to be made.
   b) The purchasing manager has found a great new vendor, better quality, better service, better pricing and, will take responsibility for parts inventory. Don't nix this idea just because your neighbour is the current preferred supplier.
   c) Preferred vendor lists prevent your total vendor list from getting out of control.
   d) If every buyer continues to buy from those vendors they like to do business with, you will lose the leverage, the pricing and the efficiencies of consolidating your spend with one or two selected vendors for an expense area.
7. **Structure centrally led, but locally implemented teams**
   a) In order to obtain the best leverage available to your organization you will need to gather data in a central point so that you can evaluate your total spending by area.
   b) Once you have total spend by area you must put teams together that can help to identify the best suppliers for those areas.
   c) Once suppliers are selected, collaborate with them to see what ideas they have to help you achieve greater success.
   d) The local team will be critical to implementation of the suggested improvements.

e) It is extremely difficult to implement a process improvement without local support.

8. **Develop strong negotiation skills**

a) **Evergreen Clause** - Organizations are burned every day by agreements that force them to use a supplier for another year despite the desire to switch to a new vendor.

b) **Training** - On-going training and organizational development in the area of negotiation is the key to developing a win-win relationship with your supplier network.

c) **Planning** is the key to a great negotiation. Make sure that you always get your needs, mostly get your wants and frequently get the WOW!- that makes the CEO happy.

9. **Use technology to propel yourself ahead of your competition**

a) Utilize e-mail over fax and phone when possible.

b) The system you utilize everyday can handle incredible tasks and automate things that you are handling manually.

c) Capture the correct data in your system and then tap into that data when you need to begin a negotiation.

10. **Design an incentive program that actually profits the individual and the company**

a) Incentives paid to your employees are critical to the ability of your organization to accept and embrace implementing change.

b) **What gets rewarded is what gets done.**

In order to implement these best practices, an effective plan has to be developed, a team to be formed that will be compensated for their results, the plan to be implemented and performance monitored. Once the plan is implemented, there should be quarterly to share additional successes achieved along the way.

For Discussion

1. Define Purchasing. Discuss the importance of purchasing in the operation of a manufacturing concern.
2. "The methods of purchasing vary according to the nature of demand." Explain the various methods of purchasing in the light of this statement.
3. What are the major functions of the Purchase Department?
4. Discuss the applicability of Centralized and Decentralized purchasing along with their merits and demerits.
5. What are the key principles of purchasing?
6. Describe the steps to be followed in the Purchasing Process.

Chapter 4

Source Selection & Management

The ability to select reliable suppliers is a mark of successful purchasing. To paraphrase an old saying, "Tell me who your suppliers are, and I'll tell you what kind of a purchasing department you have". It's not always easy, however, to identify good suppliers. There is no substitute for an objective means of supplier appraisal.

What should buyers look for in a "world class" supplier? The term has come to mean those suppliers who can deliver their goods anywhere globally at competitive cost in all marketing arenas. Some other considerations affecting source decisions are the stage of economic development of the supplier, the buyer's expectations and preferences for geographical location, bulky items can be costly to transport long distances.

Source Selection and Development

Sourcing breaks down into two categories: source selection and source development. Source selection can be day-to-day buying for items now available on the marketplace, or looking for lower cost suppliers.

Source selection to get the "right" supplier runs the gamut from liking a salesman and believing you have a good supplier to the formalized and technical evaluation reserved for high tech or military procurement. Neither extreme suits most companies. The three steps of source selection are: search, screen and select.

Request for Quotation (RFQ)

A good approach when no established market prices are published is to decide whom to invite to quote. Much wasted time is avoided by picking the most logical sources for inquiry and this brings into play the experience of the buyer. Most companies use a simple request for a quote (RFQ). This is not to be confused with a request for bid (RFB) that is for special projects.

Buyers prepare their RFQ form, which typically includes date, control number, name of company and buyer, description of goods wanted, quantity sought, any special patterns or dies requirements, any tooling now available by the buying company, delivery destination, special handling and shipment, packaging, delivery date for goods and finally a deadline to receive a reply. Buyers may want to include additional special requests, such as:

a) Request for supplier's blueprints or other documents;
b) Request for alternate proposals;
c) Any special materials or supplies to be used;
d) Any special tests or quality standards.

The buyer lists potential order quantities and asks for price breaks and discounts. By indicating a willingness to consider substitute items, the seller is encouraged to make creative suggestions. Ideas to save money might include grouping of items into blanket orders, packaging or design changes. But, the buyer must make take the initiative to search the market and not wait for a sales pitch.

International purchases require special attention. Unlike a domestic inquiry, additional details need to be given. International codes have to spelled out, along with any special test to which parts will be subjected. The buyer may have to provide the codes themselves as the international supplier may not be familiar with them. Local suppliers know these things from experience, but foreign suppliers may be groping in the dark.

Comparing current quotes with past prices paid and to other competitors' pricing is a fundamental technique of buying value. A chart is prepared showing all suppliers under consideration, price quoted by each, shipping costs, patterns charges, tool cost and any other factors. If all suppliers quoted to identical requirements, the decision is simple. But usually, there are differences of brands, quality, pricing and so on. So, judgement is needed and such analysis clarifies alternatives in deciding the supplier to select.

Supplier Evaluation and Selection Process

One of the key functions of purchasing is to maintain good relations with vendors. A good vendor is an asset to the company. Moreover, just as customer goodwill is considered important, good and firm relationship with vendor also enhances company's capability to satisfy customer needs. Close relationships with vendors are required due to high level of uncertainty in supplying environment. These relationships can be developed on two levels viz.: professional relationship and personal relationship.

(a) By helping the vendor in times of stress and strain with financial and technical help, along with management skills, if required.
(b) Maintaining a healthy and professional relationship by fair negotiations, evaluation and offering fair compensation.

The modern management theory and world class manufacturing calls for a long-term, almost a lifetime, association with the vendors. This also means that there are only a few vendors but they are dedicated to the organization and are a part of the organizational family. Although most organizations carry on the process or programme of vendor evaluation, selection and appraisal continuously, but we classify the activities of purchasing with respect to vendors in three categories to facilitate understanding:-

(i) Vendor selection.

(ii) Vendor rating.

(iii) Vendor development.

An organisation must select suppliers it can do business with over an extended period. The degree of effort associated with the selection relates to the importance of the required good or service. Depending on the supplier evaluation approach used, the process can be an intensive effort requiring a major commitment of resources. We shall now discuss the issues and decisions involved in effectively and efficiently evaluating and selecting suppliers to be part of the purchaser's supply base.

1. Recognize the Need for Supplier Selection

The first step of the evaluation and selection process usually involves recognizing that there is a requirement to evaluate and select a supplier for an item or service. A purchasing manager might begin the supplier evaluation process in anticipation of a future purchase requirement.

2. Identification of Sourcing Requirements

It is necessary to understand the requirements that are critical to a particular purchase, throughout the supplier evaluation and selection process. These requirements differ widely from item to item and are generally determined by the internal and external customers. However, for almost all such evaluations, supplier quality, cost and delivery performance are usually included.

3. Determination of Sourcing Strategy

The purchasing strategy adopted for a particular item or service may not hold good for all types of purchases. There are many decisions that a purchaser initially makes when developing a sourcing strategy. However, these strategies have to be changed as a result of market conditions, user preferences and corporate objectives. The considerations developed during the strategy phase need to be re-evaluated during the supplier selection process. The strategic options greatly influence the supplier selection and evaluation process. The key decisions to be considered are:

a) Single versus multiple supply sources.

b) Short-term versus long-term purchase contracts.

c) Selecting suppliers that provide design support versus those that lack design capability.

d) Full-service versus limited service suppliers.

e) Local versus international suppliers.

4. Identify Potential Suppliers

Purchasers rely on various sources of information when identifying potential sources of supply. The effort which a buyer must put in search for information about the sources of supply is a function of several variables, including how well existing suppliers can satisfy cost, quality or other performance variables. The strategic importance or technical complexity of the purchase requirement also influences the intensity of the search.

Major Sources of Information

a. **Current suppliers** are a major source of information. Buyers often look to existing suppliers to satisfy a new purchasing requirement. The advantage of this approach is that the purchaser does not have to add and maintain an additional supplier. Also, the buyer can do business with an already familiar supplier, which may limit the time and resources required to evaluate the capabilities of a new supplier.

However, the disadvantage of using existing supplier is that a purchasing manager would never know if better suppliers are available without information on other sources. Most organisations, therefore, continuously look for new sources of supply and expand this search to include suppliers from around the world.

Selecting an existing supplier becomes easier if a list of ***preferred supplier*** is maintained. A supplier is designated as a preferred supplier if he consistently satisfies the performance and service standards defined by the buyer. Such a status immediately conveys information about the competency of the supplier.

b. **Sales representatives** of the company also provide valuable sales and marketing information to the purchase department and can be a valuable source of information about potential sources. Even if an immediate need does not exist for a supplier's services, the buyer can record the information for future reference.

c. **Information databases** of suppliers that are capable of supporting an industry or product line, is often maintained by companies. Companies look for information about potential sources in trade journals, financial newspapers, business magazines etc. The use of automated database or data warehouse can easily help identify suppliers potentially qualified to fulfil a requirement. Maintaining a supplier database is particularly important in industries where technology changes rapidly. The database may contain information on current products, the supplier's future technology roadmap, process capability ratios and past performance.

d. **Experience** of personnel having strong knowledge about potential suppliers also serves as a critical source of information. A buyer may have worked within an industry over many years and may be familiar with the suppliers. Experience and knowledge become valuable because it helps purchasing organisations develop an intelligence database about suppliers.

e. **Trade journals** or magazines often present articles about different companies often focusing on a company's technical or innovative development of a material, component, product, process or service. Suppliers also use trade journals to advertise their products or services.

f. **Trade directories** of companies that produce items or provide services within an industry are published by almost all industries. Such directories can be a valuable source of initial information for a buyer who is not familiar with an industry or its suppliers.

5. Sourcing Alternatives

Once the list of potential and current suppliers is put into a database, it is further checked considering the type of supplier a firm wishes to deal with based on the initial sourcing strategy. Major sourcing alternatives include whether to purchase from a:

a) Manufacturer or Distributor;
b) Local or National or International source;
c) Small or Large supplier; and
d) Multiple or Single supplier, for the item.

Buyer's Checklist for Selecting New Suppliers

Before deciding on the "right" supplier, the specific supplier concerns that should be considered are mentioned below. This checklist gives buyers some ideas to build upon. This same list can also be used for supplier evaluation.

A. Reliability

1. Is the supplier reputable, with a proven track record?
2. Have the supplier's ability and integrity been proved by past performance?
3. Is the supplier giving me savings along with product improvements?
4. What is the quality of the supplier's management team?
5. What is the supplier's position in the industry? Is it a product leader?
6. What is the supplier's previous delivery history with the company?

B. Financial and Cost Factors

1. What is the *total cost* of using the supplier's product?
2. How is the product priced and how stable it is?
3. What is the total cost of using the product, including transportation?
4. What is the supplier's financial position and credit rating stability?
5. Does pricing meet company targets?
6. What will be the inventory costs if the supplier's product is not readily

available?

7. Is the supplier willing to negotiate?
8. What, if any, cash discounts are offered?

C. *Technical Capabilities*

1. Will the supplier provide application engineering or design assistance?
2. Will the supplier provide analytical engineering that will help improve the efficiency of my basic processes?
3. Can the supplier handle special needs and designs?
4. Does the supplier contribute to general advancement through basic research?
5. Does the supplier have special technical capability? What has been accomplished recently?
6. What are the operating technology characteristics, such as manufacturing capacity, component design and techniques used?

D. *Delivery and Availability*

1. Will the supplier ensure on-time delivery?
2. Are stocks available locally? On short notices?
3. Does the supplier offer a broad line of commodities?
4. Is the supplier's location an advantage to me?
5. Does the supplier plan shipments to minimize my inventory?
6. Can the supplier be depended upon to provide a steady flow of products or materials?

E. *Buying Convenience*

1. Does the supplier offer a full line of related products?
2. Does the supplier package their product conveniently for my use?
3. Does the supplier have a local sales contact?
4. Are they qualified to help me? Can I call upon specialists for my problems?
5. Will the supplier help me cut acquisition costs such as qualifying visits, telephone calls, lab tests, incoming inspections, spoilage and waste, rejects and complaints?
6. Will the supplier promptly respond in answering queries?

F. *Quality Factors*

1. Quality – does it meet the specification? Will it do so consistently?
2. What is the performance and life expectancy?

3. What quality sampling plans are used?
4. What overall quality control system is in place?

G. Sales Assistance

1. Does the supplier help develop mutual markets? Will they recommend our products?
2. Will the appearance of supplier's product enhance the value of my own product?
3. Will my queries receive personal attention of supplier representatives?

H. After-sales Service

1. Does the supplier have a service shop organisation available when and where I may need it?
2. Is emergency service available?
3. Will renewal parts be available when I need them?
4. Does the supplier provide training and education aids in the use of the product or services provided?

I. Managerial Capabilities

1 Does the management practice long-range planning?
2. Has management committed the supplier to total quality management (TQM) and continuous improvement?
3. Is turnover high among managers?
4. What is the professional experience and educational background of the key managers?
5. Is there a vision about the future direction of the company?
6. Is management customer focused?
7. Is management making the investments that are necessary to sustain and grow the business?
8. Has management prepared the company to face future competitive challenges including providing employee training and development?
9. Does management understand the importance of strategic sourcing?

J. Service Factors

1. Will supplier provide timely information on progress of purchase orders?
2. What is the supplier's labour relations record? Is there a history of strikes?
3. What are the warranties and claims policies?
4. Will the supplier promptly handle rejected materials and credits?

5. What is the supplier's attitude towards our buying organisation?
6. Will the supplier comply with my procedures?
6. Determine Methods of Supplier Evaluation and Selection.

The purchased goods from vendors contribute not only to the company's costs; they also contribute to the quality of the products manufactured by the company. Since the quality of the products manufactured largely depends on the quality of the raw materials, tool, equipment etc. purchased from the vendors, therefore, the quality of the products submitted by vendors is evaluated for making purchasing decisions. For this purpose vendor rating techniques are used; which provide a quantitative measure of the vendor quality. The Supplier Evaluation or Vendor Quality Rating provides a basis for:

1. Measuring how well each vendor is doing, in terms of quality.
2. Comparing various vendors with one another.
3. Judging the progress, or lack of it, of each individual vendor over an extended period of time.
4. For eliminating those vendors who repeatedly fail to meet competitive quality levels.

Most modern organizations do vendor performance appraisal on a continuous basis and call this exercise as Vendor Rating. This vendor rating is done on following characteristics:

1. Delivery (to deliver on time as per order).
2. Quality (to deliver as per quality specifications).
3. Price (to supply material at the lowest possible price).
4. Other factors like:
   - Capability to meet emergency orders.
   - Readiness to try new design and new materials.
   - Ability to supply useful market information.

The National Association of Purchasing Agents has suggested three alternative plans for rating the vendors:

1. **Categorical Method:** This is a non-quantitative system in which buyers hold a monthly meeting to discuss vendors. Based on one's experience suppliers are listed under different categories as: unfavourable, favourable, and superb.

2. **Weighted Point Method:** Each vendor is scored on quality, price and service. These factors are weighted 40, 35 and 25 respectively. A composite rating (on scale of 0 to 100) is then calculated for each vendor.

		Supplier A	*Supplier B*	*Supplier C*
1.	Lots received	60	60	20
2.	Lots accepted	54	56	16
3	Percent accepted=2/1*100	90.0	93.3	80.0
4	Quality rating= 3* 0.40	36.0	37.3	32.0
5	Net price	0.93	1.12	1.23
6	Lowest price*100	100	83	76
7	Net price	35.0	29.1	26.6
8	Price rating= 6*0.35	90%	95%	100%
9	Delivery promises kept	22.5	23.8	25.0
10	Service rating= 8* 0.25	93.5	90.2	83.6
	TOTAL RATING			

Net price= Unit price – Discount + Transportation

Lowest price= minimum price

3. **Cost-ratio Method:** This plan compares vendors on the total cost in terms of money for a specific purpose. Total cost includes price quotation, quality costs, delivery costs, and service costs. The final rating is in rupees of net value cost, which takes into consideration the following three cost ratios:

a) The quality cost ratio reflects the relative cost of quality.
b) The delivery cost ratio reflects the relative cost of placing and receiving an order. It also includes a "promises kept" penalty based on a ranking of past performance of vendors.
c) The service cost ratio reflects the technical, managerial and field service competence of the vendor.

Vendor rating is an important defect prevention device if it is used in an atmosphere of interdependence between vendor and customer. This means that the customer must:

- Make the investment of time, effort and special skill to help the poor vendors improve.
- Be willing to change the specifications when warranted. The customer must search for these situations and change the specifications.

Finally, in the case of consistently poor vendors who cannot respond to help, the vendor rating indicates that such vendors should be dropped.

Vendor Development: signifies making or identifying new vendors. This is a continuous activity of purchasing manager. The major reason for developing new vendors is to build more competition in the supply market. Another reason for buying from a number of sources is to spread the risk of non-availability or shortage of inputs.

Qualification of New Suppliers

Qualification of suppliers is based on a satisfactory assessment of selected criteria that are essentially identical to those quality considerations used when selecting new sources or evaluating current ones.

Before making a major buy, it makes sense to "qualify" any new supplier. When placing a trial order, it is wise to do a source located inspection before the first major shipment. Meeting with quality control and other people who do the job helps gain confidence in their integrity and get their commitment to quality.

Whether to use single or multiple sources is a controversial subject. Some buyers argue that multiple sources reduce risk while increasing costs. Without question, some companies today are using fewer sources based on the philosophy of a monogamous marriage consistent with partnership principles.

A major impetus to single source thrust has been quality legend W. Edwards Deming. One of Deming's 14 points about quality is to have a single supplier. Others have agreed with Deming's position on single sourcing and some American automakers who sole-sourced some items say the practice cuts down on component dimensional variability. They claim to be able to work more closely in meeting design and quality requirements if using fewer suppliers. They also claim it's easier to insist on a process for failure analysis when the supplier has total responsibility.

Single Vendor Development

Japanese companies showed the example that a single supplier can offer many advantages, which multiple suppliers don't offer like:-

1. A close rapport develops between supplier and buyer, which convert into loyalty. This loyalty or relationship can be of great value at difficult times or in crises for the buying company.
2. The close relationship promotes information sharing, which gives buying company an opportunity to gather valuable information of competitors and market trends.
3. Reliability, lack of uncertainty, quick and faithful response to the needs is the advantages of a single vendor.
4. Help in new product development and innovations.
5. This improves quality, reduces inventory and also minimizes purchasing costs.
6. It is easier to work out delivery schedules as may be needed for just-in time (JIT) delivery requirements.
7. Sometimes no one else is willing or able to supply.
8. Concentrating purchases with one good supplier provides advantages of "economy of scale".

9. Requirements may not be large enough to warrant the added expense of testing and inventorying with another supplier.

Yet, when only one source is used, competition is eliminated beyond that which may have existed at the initial point of partner selection. A major deterrent to using maximum economic leverage is when the marketplace is a sole source, or buyers *have not qualified* a second source.

Experience suggests that it is competition that keeps a supplier's performance at the top. Also, the possibilities of a fire, strike, or a new product introduction by another supplier are still other factors to consider.

Single sourcing puts 100 per cent burden on the supplier partner and in practice, once fully understood, the supplying partner will step up to the challenge of true partnership. Some other quality experts might point out that if a backup source is available, each source will feel relief of responsibility.

However, present Indian situation is still in favour of the traditional philosophy of spreading risk with a number of suppliers. Not all buyers embrace the single source philosophy. Most experienced buyers prefer a backup. Typical reactions from buyers have been, "What if my supplier goes on strike, or burns down, or gets flooded out?" Whether to have a backup source or use a single source depends largely on whether there is time to recover from delays or problems. Buying for a high-volume assembly line favours an alternative. If buying for resale or the buyer can wait for new shipments, perhaps a single source is enough. The choice between single supplier and multiple source buying is quite situational. Vendor development is an attempt of both spreading risk, building competition and at the same time establishing a good relationship. Vendor development involves helping vendors by various means such as:

- Lending money for part of his capital, equipment, working capital etc.
- Lending technical help by making company engineers and technicians available to the vendor.
- Help in R&D and in developing new production process.
- Guaranteeing him a certain amount of business.

Arguments for multiple suppliers are:

1. Competitive supply provides leverage to ensure performance at reasonable price levels.
2. Reliability for assurance of supply may be increased.
3. Buyers have greater flexibility should a supplier's quality deteriorate or they fail to maintain delivery schedules.
4. Keeping multiple sources allows the buyer to become knowledgeable about competitive technical innovations. Locked into a supplier who does not innovate could put a company at a great disadvantage.

Clearly a major factor in determining a company's sourcing strategy is the degree of trust in a source and the quality of relationship with the supplier.

Negotiations

Negotiations are an important instrument aiding decision making in purchase. The purpose of negotiations is to obtain the best terms of purchase such as price, discount etc. It is defined as "a conference with a view to compromise or agreement." For negotiation a minimum of two parties are involved viz.: supplier and buyer. Since these two parties are negotiating to get the best terms from the other party, their individual interests are at variance with one another. Ultimately, their objective is to enter into an agreement based on mutually acceptable terms, which will narrow down their individual differences to minimum. The following aspects are important:

1. **Role of Suppliers:** these are to:
   - Submit his lowest priced proposal.
   - Perform the contract on schedule.
   - Co-operate fully with engineering and inspection personnel.
2. **Areas of Negotiation:** these are:
   - Price, terms and conditions of the original contract/new contract.
   - Variation in quantity, specifications and delivery.
   - Price revision under escalation.
   - Facilities to be provided in contracts, on raw materials, tools etc.
   - Unforeseen cost of construction, maintenance and repairs etc.
3. **Role of Buyers:** buyers are looking for suppliers at the minimum available cost. In order to evaluate the cost, there are three common techniques:
   - Quantity discount analysis for complex comparison.
   - Cost analysis for simple comparison.
   - Break-even analysis for internal price analysis.
4. **Qualities of a Good Negotiator:**
   - He must be a clear and rapid thinker.
   - He must express himself well and easily.
   - He must posses the ability to analyse.
   - He must be impersonal.
   - He must be able to consider the other person's point of view.

Storekeeping

Storekeeping refers to the safe custody of all the items of material stocked in the storeroom. The materials carried into the store are to be stored in such a manner that the possibility of their being damaged is reduced and they can be easily located and issued whenever required for use in and out-side the storeroom.

Objectives of Storekeeping

1. **Minimisation of the cost of Production:** Over and above the materials required for production are the costs of storage itself. These include the cost of capital investment in materials and supplies, cost of storage, cost of record-keeping etc. Since these costs influence the cost of production, the objective of storekeeping is to make efforts in the direction of reducing them.
2. **Providing efficient service:** by
   - Making available a balanced flow of right quality and quantity of raw materials, equipment, tools and other components within least possible time.
   - Providing maintenance materials, spare parts, general stores and other materials required by the production department.
   - Receiving from production unit and issuing to the sales unit the finished products.
   - Accepting and storing the scrap and other discarded materials and making arrangements for their disposal.
3. **Establishing co-ordination:** all the departments in the organisation are linked to the stores department. Without the active co-operation of each of them, the smooth and efficient functioning of the stores department cannot be thought of.

The following are the important functions of storekeeping:

- Receipt of materials;
- Storage and preservation;
- Record-keeping; and
- Issue of materials.

Benefits of Successful Storekeeping

1. Location of materials becomes easier, thereby avoiding unnecessary delay and confusion.
2. Smooth running of the production department is ensured because of regular and timely supply of materials.
3. Blocking of capital through over-stocking is avoided.
4. Hold-ups and delays are avoided by ensuring against under-stocking and its resultant disadvantages.
5. Physical verification becomes easier.
6. Accounting of all the materials is facilitated.

7. Minimisation of wastage of time, labour and money due to leakage, pilferage, damage etc.

Stores Accounting

Stores accounting refers to the mathematical process which reveals the quantity, quality and value of stores carried and preserved in a storehouse on a given date relating to a specified period. Material costing gains importance in terms of the valuation of the cost of materials consumed in the process of production as well as in terms of the estimation of the value of materials held in stock. Materials costing shall be discussed under classifications of the receipt of materials, issue of materials and of the stock held at the end of the accounting period. These are as follows:

Costing of the Receipt of Materials

The various elements that can be included in the cost of the materials received are freight charges, insurance, taxes and the price of the material itself.

Prices are often stated in various ways. For costing purposes, the actual cost is worked out by taking price quoted by the supplier as the basis, subtracting the discounts and adding any other expenses not covered. The freight costs incurred in transporting the goods are usually entered under a separate head. Sometimes this cost may be included in the price itself. Goods in transit are usually covered by insurance against damage. All such insurance expenses are calculated and added to the base cost and transportation cost. The costs incurred by way of customs duties, octroi and other such taxes are classified under the miscellaneous head. Such separate classifications give a better framework for cost control.

Costing of Issues to Production

Some of the methods used in the costing of issues to production are as follows:

(1) **First In First Out (FIFO):** the material purchased first is issued first. This is logical in the case of items which deteriorate with time. At the time of issue, the rate pertaining to the time of purchase will be applied.

(2) **Last In First Out (LIFO):** the basic assumption here is that the most recent receipts are issued first. In a period of rising prices, latest prices are charged to the issues, leading to lower reported profits hence saving in taxes.

(3) **Average Cost:** the issues to production department are split into equal batches from each shipment at stock. Here the rate is calculated by dividing the total cost by the number of items. Then, this rate is applied to the issues to production. As more purchases are made, a new average is calculated and this average is applied to the subsequent issues.

(4) **Market Value:** this method is also known as replacement rate costing. The materials that are issued are costed at the market rate prevailing at the time

of issue. The method becomes difficult to manage as it requires continuous monitoring of the market rates for all materials.

(5) **Standard Costs:** here, a standard rate is determined based on detailed analysis of market prices and trends. This standard rate is kept fixed for a period of six months or more. During this period costing is done on the basis of this standard rate, irrespective of the actual rates. At the end of the period, a review is done and fresh standards are set for further period of six months.

Stock Verification

It is the process of physically counting, measuring or weighing the entire range of items in the stores and recording the results in a systematic manner. Stock verification is usually done by the materials audit department and can be carried out periodically or on continuous basis.

Merits of Stores Accounting System

1. Provides protection against:
   - Running short of materials and its consequent disadvantages.
   - Over-stocking and thus running the risk of loss due to fluctuation in prices, deterioration and high carrying cost.
   - Blocking of capital by carrying over unnecessarily large stocks either throughout the year or during a specified period.
2. Settlement of claims from insurance in case of theft, fire, pilferage, obsolescence etc.
3. Detection, localisation, and prevention of waste at every step become easier.
4. Knowledge of good or bad buying, because of availability of reliable statistical information, is possible.
5. A proper and complete record of all receipts, issues and balances is ensured.
6. Actual stock verification becomes less expensive and troublesome.

For Discussion

1. Why do we need vendors? Discuss the factors that are taken into consideration while selecting a vendor.
2. Discuss the process of vendor selection in detail.
3. What is the purpose of Vendor Quality Rating?
4. Discuss the various methods used for rating the performance of the vendors.
5. Japanese companies favour development of a single vendor for the supply of a single product. What are the benefits and limitations of the Single Vendor Concept? Is the concept relevant in Indian conditions?

6. What are the objectives of Storekeeping? What functions need to be performed to accomplish these objectives?
7. What is Stores Accounting? What is the basis for determining the cost of different types of materials?
8. What are the merits of a well-managed Stores Accounting System?

Just-In-Time (JIT)

JIT concept of production was introduced in Japan under the name of Kanban. According to this concept, material and components are supplied to the workstation just at the time they are required for use. It otherwise means whatever materials and components are needed for a shift are received at the beginning of the shift and converted into finished goods, leaving nothing to be carried at the end of the shift. Therefore, JIT emphasizes waste-reduction, total quality control and devotion to the customer.

JIT is a logistic approach, wherein the level of inventory is kept at the bare minimum because they are made to arrive just in time when needed to be used. It means that the various vendors are working in unison with the manufacturing organization as a single team, dedicated to act in unison, wherein the production and supply schedules are matched perfectly and operate in absolute synchronized manner.

JIT means handling the inventory in a much disciplined way. It requires changes in culture. JIT also encompasses the Japanese managerial characteristics, i.e., lifetime employment, implicit control mechanisms, collective decision-making, collective responsibility and holistic concern for employees. JIT applies to all functions of a company and not just the operations. Therefore, JIT can be defined as "a manufacturing system, whose goal is to optimise processes and procedures by continuously pursuing waste reduction and work simplification, improving timeliness, quality productivity and flexibility."

This brings us to the issue of wastes. There are seven kinds of wastes according to Shigeo Shingo, a recognized JIT authority and an Engineer at Toyota Motor Company. Given below are the seven wastes as the target for continuous improvement in production process.

1. *Waste of overproduction*

Companies tend to produce in large volumes if the set-up time between processes is high. The more the production, the higher will be the carrying cost of the excess produced and higher will be the maintenance cost of the inventory. This can be eliminated by reducing set-up times, synchronizing quantities and timing between processes, compacting layout, visibility, and so forth. Make only what is needed now.

2. *Waste of waiting*

If the work across different work stations is unevenly distributed this results in either the machines and workers waiting for the material to arrive or the material itself has to wait for its turn to be processed on the workstations, resulting in wastage in the form of idle time. This can be eliminated through synchronizing workflow as much as possible, and balance uneven loads by flexible workers and equipment.

3. *Waste of transportation*

The more the distance between the different workstations, the higher is handling of material from one place to another, resulting in increased transportation costs and chances of the material getting damaged in transit. This can be avoided by establishing layouts to make transport and handling unnecessary if possible. Then transport and material handling that cannot be eliminated should be rationalized.

4. *Waste of processing itself*

Each step in the production process is expected to add some value to the material. The first question to be addressed is that why this part or product should be made at all, then why each process is necessary? All non-value adding activities should be eliminated from the system.

5. *Waste of stocks*

Stocks are maintained due to uncertainty of demand and lead time. Stocks of finished goods may be maintained in anticipation of demand, since all production cannot be done after the order is received, whereas, stock of raw material is maintained due to uncertainty in lead time. The stocks and resulting waste can be reduced by shortening set-up times and reducing lead times, by synchronizing work flows and improving work skills, and even by smoothing fluctuations in demand for the product. Reducing all the other wastes reduces the waste of stocks.

6. *Waste of motion*

The physical movements of the workers or machines should be closely monitored. Those movements that do no result in any productive output should be eliminated. The motion should be studied for economy and consistency. Economy improves productivity, and consistency improves quality. First improve the motions, then mechanize or automate. Otherwise there is danger of automating waste.

7. *Waste of making defective products*

Production of defective products results in the finished product being rejected by the customer at the same time it may also result in the loss of goodwill for the company. The production process should be developed to prevent defectives from being made so as to eliminate inspection. At each step in the production process, no defects should be accepted and no defectives should be made. The processes are made failsafe to do this. From a quality process, comes a quality product automatically.

American companies seek to eliminate the above mentioned wastes by calling it as Value Added Manufacturing. It is a method that seeks to eliminate wastes in processing adhering to the edict that a stage of the process that does not add value to the product for the customer should be eliminated.

By applying this philosophy many companies are improving their productivity. However, incorporating JIT requires a heavy commitment of time and rigorous discipline upon the organization. Shingo says that it took 29 years to implement the JIT system at Toyota and it will take most other companies almost 10-15 years to obtain similar results.

There are certain cornerstones in the Japanese manufacturing system. According to Professor Robert W Hall of Indiana University, they are:

1. Produce what the customer desires.
2. Produce products only at the rate the customer wants them.
3. Produce with perfect Quality.
4. Produce instantaneously with Zero unnecessary lead time.
5. Produce with no waste of labour, material, or equipment; every move has a purpose so there are zero idle inventories.
6. Produce by methods that allow people to develop.

Development of the JIT Concept

JIT is Japanese management philosophy which has been applied in practice since the early 1970s in many Japanese organizations. It was first developed and perfected within the Toyota manufacturing plants by Taiichi Ohno as a means of meeting consumer demands with minimum delays. For this reason, Taiichi Ohno is frequently referred to as the father of JIT.

The Toyota production plants were the first to introduce JIT. It gained extended support during the 1973 oil embargo and was later adopted by many other organizations. The oil embargo and the increasing shortage of other natural resources were seen as a major impetus for the widespread adoption of JIT. Toyota was able to meet the increasing challenges for survival through an approach to management different from what was characteristic of the time. This approach focused on people, plants and systems. Toyota realized that JIT would only be successful if every individual within the organization was involved and committed to it, if the plant and processes were arranged for maximum outputand efficiency, and if quality and production programmes were scheduled to meet demands exactly.

JIT had its beginnings as a method of reducing inventory levels within Japanese shipyards. Today, JIT has evolved into a management philosophy containing a body of knowledge and encompassing a comprehensive set of manufacturing principles and techniques. JIT manufacturing has the capacity, when properly adapted to the organization, to strengthen the organization's competitiveness in the marketplace substantially by reducing wastes and improving product quality and efficiency of production.

There are strong cultural aspects associated with the emergence of JIT in Japan. The development of JIT within the Toyota production plants did not occur independently of these strong cultural influences. The Japanese work ethic is one of these factors. The work ethic emerged shortly after World War II and was seen as an integral part of the Japanese economic success. It is the prime motivating factor behind the development of superior management techniques that are becoming the best in the world.

In addition, JIT also emerged as a means of obtaining the highest levels of usage out of limited resources available. Faced with constraints, the Japanese worked toward attainment of the optimal cost/quality relationship in their manufacturing processes. This involves reducing waste and using materials and resources in the most efficient manner possible. The input of sustained effort over a long period of time within the framework of continuous improvement is critical. This is achieved by a focus on a continuous stream of small improvements known in Japan as *'Kaizen'* and has been recognized as one of the most significant elements of JIT philosophy.

Furthermore, Japanese firms tend to focus on enhancing the long-run competitiveness rather than emphasizing the realization of short-term profits. They are willing to experience opportunity costs by introducing and implementing innovative ideas within their firms. Stockholders and owners of the companies also encourage the maximization of long-term benefits. This enables them to experience the rewarding long-term profits as a result of their efforts.

Objectives of JIT

The ultimate goal or objective of JIT system is a balanced system, that is one of that achieves a smooth, rapid flow of materials through the system. The idea is to reduce the process time to as low as possible by making best use of the resources. The specific goal or objective is to provide the *right quality level* at the *right place.* JIT tries to build only what internal (employees) and external customers want and when they want it. The supporting goals and objectives of JIT are :

1. Improving sales forecast for production planning so that the suppliers can be better informed about the requirements.
2. Establishing close working relationships with a smaller number of suppliers. JIT can work only when there is mutual cooperation and trust.
3. Setting up effective information systems so that suppliers are immediately informed about any changes in the schedule.
4. Awarding long-term contracts to the suppliers, to give them the confidence to invest in meeting future requirements.
5. Formulating a quality assurance program under which suppliers accept the responsibility for monitoring quality during production.
6. Removing non-value adding activities throughout the whole supply chain.

Key Elements of JIT

JIT manufacturing consists of several components or elements which must be integrated together to function in harmony for its successful implementation. The elements essentially include the human resources and the production, purchasing, manufacturing, planning and organizing functions of an organization. These elements can be grouped together into the above mentioned Toyota production system of people, plants and systems as follows:

People Involvement

Obtaining support and agreement from all individuals involved in the achievement of organizational goals is a fundamental *sine qua non* for JIT success. Obtaining support and agreement requires involving and informing all groups who have an interest in the company. This can significantly reduce the amount of time and effort involved in implementing JIT and can minimize the likelihood of creating and implementation problems. Support and agreement should be obtained from the following groups:

(i) *Stockholders and owners of the company.* Emphasis should be placed on the long-term realization of profit and so short-term earnings should be plowed back into the company to finance the various changes and investment commitments necessary for JIT success. It should be made clear that most of the benefits associated with JIT will only be realized over the long-run.

(ii) *Labour organizations.* All employees and labour unions should be informed about the goals of JIT and made aware of how the new system will affect working practices. This is important in winning the union workers' support to assist with the implementation and to remove potential problems and difficulties. Failure to involve labour organizations will result in a lack of understanding of management motives and causing fear of job loss on the part of the labour. This can lead to impediments such as non-cooperation and resistance to change. Recent research indicates that one possible weakness of JIT is that it may increase the stress placed on workers; this makes the existence of good labour relations essential.

(iii) *Management support.* This involves the support of management from all levels. It also requires that management be prepared to set examples for the workers and initiate the process to change attitudes. Striving for continuous improvement is not only required of the employees on the shop floor, but must also be inherent in management's attitudes.

(iv) *Government support.* Government can lend support to companies wishing to implement JIT by extending tax and other financial incentives. This can provide motivation for companies to become innovative as it bears some of the financial burden associated with the costs of implementing JIT.

Organization theory suggests the hypothesis that people will be more compelled to work toward goals when they are included in the development of the goals. Onto this hypothesis JIT builds the idea of involving employees at different levels in the organization. The introduction of **quality circles** and the concept of **total people involvement** are examples of the avenues available for attempting to maximize people involvement through the use of JIT.

The introduction of changes in an organization has the potential to elicit reactive behaviours from the individuals who may be subjected to these modifications. JIT represents one of these changes and can cause substantial organizational transformations. Although these changes may affect the organization in very positive ways, reactive behaviours such as resisting the change by working against organizational goals may develop. Involving people becomes increasingly important at this point. Communication, training and increasing the values of the workers' jobs can help alleviate reactive behaviours.

Plants

Numerous changes occur about the production plants which encompass plant layout, multi-function workers, demand pull, kanbans, self-inspection, MRP and continuous improvement. Ach of these will be explained separately with relation to how they tie into JIT production.

(i) *Plant layout.* Under JIT production, the plant layout is arranged for maximum worker flexibility and is arranged according to product rather than process. This type of layout requires the use of 'multi-function workers', i.e., the focus shifts towards training workers and providing them with the skills necessary to perform many tasks rather one or two highly specialized tasks.

(ii) *Demand pull production.* The concept of demand pull involves the use of demand for a given product to signal when production should occur. Use of demand pull allows a company to produce only what is required in the appropriate quantity and at the right time.

(iii) *Kanban.* This is a Japanese word meaning signal and is usually a card or tag accompanying products throughout the plant. Indicated on the kanbans is the name or serial number for product identification, the quantity, the required operations and the destination of where the part will travel to. The use of kanbans assists in tying or linking the different production processes together.

(iv) *Self-inspection.* The use of self-inspection by each employee is done to ensure that their production input adds value to the product and is of high quality. Self-inspection allows mistakes and low quality work to be caught and corrected efficiently and at the place where the mistakes initially occur.

(v) *Continuous improvement.* The concept of continuous improvement involves a change in attitudes toward the overall effectiveness of an organization. Continuous improvement is an integral part of the JIT concept an, to be effective, must be adopted by each member of the organization, not only by those directly involved with the production processes. Continuous improvement requires that with every goal and standard successfully met, these goals and standards should be increased but always in a range that is reasonable and achievable. This will allow a company to constantly improve upon its operations, product and ultimately, its customer satisfaction.

Systems

Systems within an organization refer to the technology and processes used to link, plan and co-ordinate the activities and materials used in production. Two such systems are MRP (materials requirement planning) and MRP II (manufacturing resource planning).

MRP is 'a computer-based method for managing the materials required to carry out a schedule.' It is a 'bottom-up' or 'consolidation' approach to planning, i.e., it involves the planning of lower-level products within the product family such as component parts. Planning for MRP can be broken down into two parts. These include a production plan, which is a broad plan indicating the available capacity and the manner in which it is to be allocated about the plant and a master production schedule which is a detailed plan of what products to produce in specified time frames.

MRP II is a computer-based programme which can be used to provide information on financial resources available to carry out the plans of MRP. An example of the information MRP II provides is inventory investment. Other systems within an organization include those that provide linkages with suppliers and assist with the co-ordination of the overall functioning of the organization.

Given the nature of JIT, quality assumes an increasing importance. The use of total quality control is an additional element of JIT and is important in ensuring that the quality standards set for production are achieved. JIT quality involves 'quality at source'. Quality at source means there is an emphasis on producing products correctly the first time. Quality at source contrasts with the traditional 'after the fact' approach to quality or producing the product then inspecting it. This approach does not allow for minimizing inventory levels and rework costs. Thus, it does not tie into the goals of JIT to eliminate wastes.

Advantages of JIT System

1. Reduction of wastes (defects, scrap and rework) and increased ability to remain competitive through customer focus and delivering superior performance of both goods and/or services in terms of cost service and quality.
2. There is a massive reduction in work-in-process, which resultsin lesser space requirements.
3. Stronger and more reliable working relations with suppliers.
4. JIT helps in eliminating non-value adding activities.
5. JIT results in productivity improvements and greater control between various production stages.
6. JIT results in increased flexibility, lower costs and improved quality.

Limitations of JIT

JIT manufacturing requires considerable co-operation between management and workers. It is commonly believed that JIT production system is very efficient, but in due course of time, many demerits have been pointed out, some of these are:

1. Cultural differences have been cited as possible limitation of JIT. The benefit associated with JIT may be culturally bound and somewhat limited to Japanese environment.
2. Loss of individual autonomy is another possible shortcoming of JIT. Reduced cycle time forces the workers to adjust immediately to changes in demand, significantly reducing the idle time of the workers resulting in greater amount of stress and pressure placed upon the workers to perform.
3. The success of JIT production system depends upon co-operation between employer-employee, daily workstation rotation, training of operators for different kinds of jobs and system adaptability to market function etc.
4. There is no safety stock to offset inaccurate demand forecasts.
5. JIT production is effective only when the daily demands are fairly stable.

KANBAN and Pull System

A Kanban system is a system of inventory and production control (pull inventory system), which uses Kanbans as the principal information transmission device. Kanban is a Japanese word meaning 'a signal'. A Kanban is a card or a tag usually attached to work-in-process ports and it is used to facilitate the proper movement of these parts. This movement may be within the same manufacturing plant or between plants.

Functions of the Kanban

The functions of the Kanbans are two-fold:

(i) They are used as a means for process improvement, which helps to reduce the level of in-process inventories.

(ii) The role played by Kanban in production control is to tie the different manufacturing processes together and to ensure that the necessary amount of materials and parts arrive at the appropriate time and place.

The operation of the basic Kanban system can be described using the interchange between a preceding workstation supplying partially processed items or components to a succeeding workstation. Basically, there are two types of Kanbans:

(i) Withdrawal Kanban

(ii) Production Kanban

The 'Withdrawal Kanban' is used to indicate the type and amount of product, which the next process should withdraw from the preceding process.

The 'Production Kanban' specifies the type and quantity of product, which the next process must produce.

A withdrawal Kanban usually includes the following informations:

1. Preceding and succeeding workstations and/or processes.
2. Name and identification number of the item.
3. Quantity in each box or container and its type.
4. Store shelf location.
5. Name or identification number of the final product where this item would be used.
6. Sequence number of Kanban.

Besides these two basic types of Kanbans, several other types of Kanbans are also used, the important ones being supplier Kanban, express Kanban and cart Kanban.

A supplier Kanban is used instead of production Kanban when the preceding workstation is an outside supplier. The supplier is given a fixed delivery frequency.

An express Kanban is used when a subsequent workstation or assembly line is in danger of having to stop due to shortage of one out of many items being used. Express Kanbans are not circulated and are to be used as few times as possible.

A cart Kanban is used for the withdrawal of large items, such as complete engines, where the cart would normally be used to transport the item. After using each engine, the subsequent workstation will send the empty cart to the preceding workstation. The preceding workstation will continue to assemble engines as long as there is at least one empty cart to load.

Rules for Kanban Operation

In order to ensure that the Kanban is being applied properly and is maintaining a smooth and steady production flow, specific rules must be followed. These are:

1. Parts from a downstream process should be obtained from a preceding process in the quantity, type and timing as described on the Kanban. These following steps must occur for this purpose:
   - The Kanban must always be attached to the product;
   - Withdrawal of a product should never occur unless a Kanban is attached; and
   - The number of withdrawals should never exceed the number of Kanbans.
2. The parts should be produced according to the information provided on the Kanbans. Therefore, the quantities produced in the preceding process should match the quantities produced in the subsequent process. The following sub-rules will apply in this regard:
   - Production should never exceed the number of Kanbans;
   - When the manufacturing involves different kinds of parts, the quantity and sequence of their processing should be followed as specified in the preceding operation.
3. If no Kanban is attached to a product, there should not be any production function carried out.
4. In the event that defective items are produced, they should not be transferred to the subsequent process.
5. It should be assured that only 100% quality parts are placed in a container available for use. This will prevent line stoppages from becoming a hindrance to the production process.
6. The number of Kanbans used in the production flow should be minimised. This will prevent the built-up inventory.
7. The use of the Kanban can be applied to follow fluctuations, which exist in the production process. The Kanban can be used to respond to changes in demand by increasing or decreasing the number of units to be produced. Therefore, future changes in demand can be met by levelling the production process.
8. The number of Kanbans used in the production process should be reduced over a period of time. This may connect processes and sources of wastes may surface. Thus, the production process can be streamlined further.

Lean Thinking for the Supply Chain

Although lean thinking is typically applied to manufacturing lean techniques and focus are applicable anywhere there are processes to improve, including the entire supply chain. A lean supply chain is one that produces just what and how much is needed, when it is needed, and where it is needed.

The underlying theme in lean thinking is to produce more or do more with fewer resources while giving the end customer exactly what he or she wants. This means focusing on each product and its value stream. To do this, organizations must be ready to ask and understand which activities truly create value and which ones are wasteful. The most important thing to remember is that lean is not simply about eliminating waste—it is about eliminating waste and enhancing value.

The Concepts of Value and Waste

Value, in the context of lean, is defined as something that the customer is willing to pay for. Value-adding activities transform materials and information into something a customer wants. Non-value-adding activities consume resources and do not directly contribute to the end result desired by the customer. Waste, therefore, is defined as anything that does not add value from the customer's perspective. Examples of process wastes are defective products, overproduction, inventories, excess motion, processing steps, transportation, and waiting.

Consider the non-manufacturing example of a flight to the USA. The value-adding part of that process is the actual flight itself. The non-value-added parts of that process are driving to the airport, parking at the airport, walking to the terminal and then to check-in, waiting in line at check-in, walking to the security check, and so on. Many times the non-value-added time far exceeds the value-added time in this type of process. Where our improvement efforts should be focused—on the non-value-added steps or on making the plane fly faster?

Understanding the difference between value and waste and value-added and non-value-added processes is critical to understanding lean. Sometimes it is not easy to discern the difference when looking at an entire supply chain. The best way is to look at the components of the supply chain and apply lean thinking to each one and determine how to link the processes to reduce waste.

Creating Value

Lean principles focus on creating value by :

1. Specifying value from the perspective of the end customer.
2. Determining a value system by:
    a. Identifying all of the steps required to create value.
    b. Mapping the value stream.
    c. Challenging every step by asking "why" several times.

3. Lining up value creating steps so that they occur in rapid sequence.
4. Creating flow with capable, available, and adequate processes.
5. Pulling materials, parts, products, and information from customers.
6. Continuously improving to reduce and eliminate waste.

The value stream consists of the value-adding activities required to design, order, and provide a product from concept to launch, order to delivery, and raw materials to customers.

"Waste" Reduction

The "Waste" reduction process begins with the question "What can we do to improve?" Some answers may include:

- Stop defective products at their source;
- Flow processes together or change the physical relationship of components of the process;
- Eliminate excess material handling or costly handling steps;
- Eliminate or reduce pointless process steps; and
- Reduce the time spent waiting for parts, orders, other people, or information.

In manufacturing environments, these waste reductions create the benefits of reduced manufacturing cycle time, reduced labour expenditures, improved product quality, space savings, reduced inventory, and quicker response to the customer. When waste is reduced or eliminated across the supply chain, overall cycle time improves, labour and staff costs are reduced, product quality improves, delivery schedules are met, inventories are reduced, and customer lead times are shortened. The net effect is that the entire supply chain is more efficient and responsive to customer needs.

Components of the Lean Supply Chain

Lean Suppliers

Lean suppliers are able to respond to changes. Their prices are generally lower due to the efficiencies of lean processes, and their quality has improved to the point that incoming inspection at the next link is not needed. Lean suppliers deliver on time and their culture is one of continuous improvement.

To develop lean suppliers, organizations should include suppliers in their value stream. They should encourage suppliers to make the lean transformation and involve them in lean activities. This will help them fix problems and share savings. In turn, they can help their suppliers and set continually declining price targets and increasing quality goals.

Lean Procurement

Some lean procurement processes are e-procurement and automated procurement. E-procurement conducts transactions, strategic sourcing, bidding, and reverse-auctions using Web-based applications. Automated procurement uses software that removes the human element from multiple procurement functions and integrates with financials.

The key to lean procurement is visibility. Suppliers must be able to "see" into their customers' operations and customers must be able to "see" into their suppliers' operations. Organizations should map the current value stream, and together create a future value stream in the procurement process. They should create a flow of information while establishing a pull of information and products.

Lean Manufacturing

Lean manufacturing systems produce what the customer wants, in the quantity the customer wants, when the customer wants it, and with minimum resources. Lean efforts typically start in manufacturing because they free up resources for continuous improvement in other areas, and create a pull on the rest of the organization. Applying lean concepts to manufacturing typically presents the greatest opportunity for cost reduction and quality improvement; however, many organizations have received huge benefits from lean concepts in other functions.

Lean Warehousing

Lean warehousing means eliminating non-value-added steps and waste in product storage processes. Typical warehousing functions are :

a) Receiving;
b) Put-away/storing;
c) Replenishment;
d) Picking;
e) Packing; and
f) Shipping.

Warehousing waste can be found throughout the storage process including :

a) Defective products which create returns.
b) Overproduction or over-shipment of products.
c) Excess inventories which require additional space and reduce warehousing efficiency.
d) Excess motion and handling.
e) Inefficiencies and unnecessary processing steps.
f) Transportation steps and distances.

g) Waiting for parts, materials and information.

h) Information processes.

Each step in the warehousing process should be examined critically to see where unnecessary, repetitive, and non-value-added activities might be so that they may be eliminated.

Lean Transportation

Lean concepts in transportation include :

a) Core carrier programs.

b) Improved transportation administrative processes and automated functions.

c) Optimized mode selection and pooling orders.

d) Combined multi-stop truckloads.

e) Cross-docking.

f) Right sizing equipment.

g) Import/export transportation processes.

h) Inbound transportation and backhauls.

The keys to accomplishing the concepts above include mapping the value stream, creating flow, reducing waste-in-processes, eliminating non-value-added activities and using pull processes.

Lean Customers

Lean customers understand their business needs and therefore can specify meaningful requirements. They value speed and flexibility and expect high levels of delivery performance and quality. Lean customers are interested in establishing effective partnerships—they are always seeking methods of continuous improvement in the total supply chain to reduce costs. Lean customers expect value from the products they purchase and provide value to the consumers who they interact with.

Benefits of Lean Systems

Speed and Responsiveness to Customers

Lean systems allow a supply chain to not only to be more efficient, but also faster. As the culture of lean takes over the entire supply chain, all links increase their velocity. A culture of rapid response and faster decisions becomes the expectation and the norm. This does not mean that decisions are made without careful thought. It simply means that a "bias for action" becomes the new corporate culture and anything less will not be tolerated. Slow response or no response becomes the exception, rather than the rule.

Reduced Inventories

In the lean paradigm, inventory is considered waste. Many would argue this point, but manufacturing can take place efficiently with little or no raw material, work-in-process (WIP), or finished goods inventory.

Many companies today produce directly into trailers and maintain no other finished goods inventory. All quality inspections and checks are performed within the process, rather than after production is complete. In this true make-to-order scenario, all goods are shipped directly to the next link in the supply chain when the trailer is full, and overproduction is not possible and cannot be tolerated. No space is designated to store finished goods. The system is not designed to carry them.

Applying one-piece flow and pull systems can reduce WIP dramatically. A Kanban or visual signal for more goods to be moved forward to the next process can accomplish this procedure. Although the ultimate goal is to eliminate WIP, minimal WIP is normally the result. The elimination of bottlenecks is one goal of a lean supply chain, but a bottleneck will always exist to some degree. As a result, WIP must always exist in front of a bottleneck or the bottleneck operation will be starved and will stop.

Raw material inventory is a different matter. Although the leanest organizations have arranged just-in-time deliveries to support manufacturing, this approach requires the absolute highest degree of competency and co-ordination within the supply chain.

Reduced Costs

Traditional mass production tries to minimize unit costs by increasing total production over the life cycle of the product. High development costs are the result of this model. To recover the enormous development and initial capital costs sunk into the product before it was produced; mass producers forecast and run long production cycles for each SKU. Consumer preferences and variety suffer in this scenario. Costs still need to be minimized, but not at the expense of what more sophisticated consumers now demand.

Improved Customer Satisfaction

Lean promotes minimizing new product development time and expense. This delivers the product to market faster, making it easier to incorporate current requirements into the product. Lean also promotes the use of less capital-intensive machines, tools, and fixtures, which results in more flexibility and less initial cost to recover. As a result, product life cycles may be shorter and product developments incorporated in newer versions of the product more frequently. Profitability does not suffer and brand loyalty is increased, as customers prefer to buy products and services from a perceived innovator.

Supply Chain as a Competitive Weapon

A strong supply chain enables the member companies to align themselves with each other and to co-ordinate their continuous improvement efforts. This synthesis enables even small firms to participate in the results of lean efforts. Competitive advantage and leadership in the global marketplace can only be gained by applying lean principles to the supply chain. Thought, commitment, planning, collaboration, and a path forward are required.

Path Forward to a Lean Supply Chain

Lean is a co-operative process for survival and for success. Supply chains that want to grow and continue to improve must adopt lean. Lean concepts require an attitude of continuous improvement with a bias for action. The concepts of lean apply to all elements of the supply chain, including support departments such as product development, quality, human resources, marketing, finance, purchasing, and distribution. The challenge is to bring all of these areas out of their traditional silos and make them work together to reduce waste and create flow. Duplication and a lack of appropriate and timely communication run rampant in these traditional organizations. A lean supply chain is proactive and plans for the unexpected by positioning all resources for effectiveness. Downturns in demand can be addressed without layoffs or significant productivity losses.

Leaning "other" areas presents a larger challenge than it does in manufacturing. Supervisors and factory workers embrace change that results in making their lives less complicated and more successful. In the hierarchy of support areas, it is more challenging for the people to understand how lean can benefit them. The answer is simple: What benefits the organization as a whole benefits the supply chain.

Because the Internet provides us with unprecedented opportunities for sharing information and conducting transactions across the supply chain, companies should have a sense of urgency about adopting lean concepts. But all chain partners have to be on the same playing field, and the lean concept is intended to let everyone reach new levels of efficiency and effectiveness. Supply chain leaders should not delay—it's urgent to act now to implement lean concepts in the supply chain.

For Discussion

1. Explain the Just-in-Time (JIT) system of production. What are the objectives of an ideal JIT system?
2. Trace the development of the concept of JIT.
3. What are the different types of wastes that should be targeted for continuous improvement in the production process?
4. Describe the key elements which must be integrated together for the successful implementation of JIT.

5. Enumerate the advantages and limitations in the implementation of a JIT system.
6. Define the KANBAN system of inventory and production control.
7. What are the functions of the KANBAN? Explain the rules for the operation of a KANBAN system.

Chapter 6

Logistics

The Council of Supply Chain Management Professionals defines logistics management as "that part of Supply Chain Management that plans, implements and controls the efficient, effective forward and reverse flow and storage of goods, services and related information between the point of origin and the point of consumption in order to meet customers' requirements." Logistics, an integral part of the supply chain and logistics networks, systems and management of these operations have become increasingly complex and in multi-channel businesses, logistics management is now responsible to plan for, implement and control:

1. Inbound merchandise from off-shore and domestic vendors to the warehouse.
2. Replenishment of stores by both warehouse operations and vendors.
3. Cross-docking merchandise to stores or directly to the pack line for direct back orders.
4. Outbound small package delivery through zone skipping or vendor drop-shipping.
5. Reverse logistics for single customer returns or to consolidate returns.
6. Other logistics requirements including warehouse-to-warehouse transfers, store-to-store transfers and retail store "sends" directly to the customer.
7. Multi-warehouse logistics, including warehouse vendor receipts and in sophisticated multi-warehouse operations, reception of vendor shipments at the warehouse closest to the vendor and distribution of the inventory to the warehouses and stores.

Logistics is a recent addition in the jargon of integrated business management, formerly with the traditional fields of marketing, finance, production and personnel, although it has been an integral part of these sectors since the Industrial Revolution. Business logistics, physical distribution, materials management, outbound logistics, in-bound logistics, logistics management, supply chain management are only some of the terms being used to define and describe the concept of approximately the same subject– logistics, perhaps due to a rapid change in the scope and wide use of the subject matter.

The term 'Logistics' stems from the Greek word 'Logisticos', meaning 'the science of computing and calculating'. Webster defines logistics as 'the procurement, maintenance and transportation of military materials, facilities and personnel (*Webster's Dictionary*, 1963).'

Military forces used logistics systems and various models during World War II, to ensure that troops and materials were made available at the right place to meet the countries requirements. Hence, from a military point of view, logistics refers to a supportive system, which reflects the practical art of moving armies and materials engaged in combats enemy to achieve the desired results. Today, in the industrial and commercial world, logistics has acquired a wider meaning. Essentially, it covers activities for the material flow from the source to the processing facilities, and subsequent distribution of finished goods from there to the ultimate users.

In 1991, the Council of Logistics Management (CLM) gave a definition as follows:

> *Logistics is the process of planning, implementing and controlling of efficient, effective flow and storage of goods, services and related information from the point of origin to the point of consumption for the purpose of conforming to customer expectations.*

Bowersox and Closs (1996) have given a more systematic definition of logistics management:

> *Logistical Management includes the design and administration of system to control the flow of materials, work-in-process, and finished inventory to support business unit strategy.*

On the basis of above facet of logistics management, a more comprehensive definition of it is:

> *Logistics management refers to designing, developing, producing and operating an integrated system which responds to customer expectations by making available the required quantity of required quality products as and when required to offer the best customer service at the least possible costs.*

This definition implies that an integrated view of a number of activities or functions may be required. Every firm is viewed as a collection of primary and supporting activities. The various decisions in logistics management that need examination for an integrated system are:

1. Product design;
2. Plant location;
3. Choice of markets/sources;
4. Production structure;
5. Distribution/Dealer Network design;

6. Location of warehouses;
7. Plant layout and logistics;
8. Allocation decision;
9. Production planning;
10. Inventory management-stocking levels;
11. Transportation-mode choice, shipment size, routing decision and transport contracting;
12. Packaging;
13. Materials handling; and
14. Warehouse operations.

The key components involved in ensuring an efficient and effective logistics system are:

1. Shippers (users of logistics).
2. Suppliers (of logistics services):
   (a) Carriers (rail, road, water, pipeline rope-way);
   (b) Warehouse providers;
   (c) Freight forwarders; and
   (d) Terminal operators (ports etc.).
3. Government (regulator of logistics).

Four Key Logistics Goals

For the supply chain to be effective in a multi-channel operation, it is necessary for management to meet the following four goals:

1. Increased efficiency.
2. Improved customer service.
3. Increased sales.
4. Improved relationships.

Each of these goals is presented below in terms of definitive and specific objectives required within an operation to help achieve those objectives.

1. Increased Efficiency

To increase efficiency, a company must develop cost-effective transportation modes while reducing its overhead, total inventory and overall cost-per-order processing. Warehouse operations, including processes, layout and flow, can be positively effected by closely working with the transportation provider. A two-way relationship should be established with the transportation carrier to frequently share best practices, issues and opportunities. Conversely, disjointed transportation flow ties up space on the receiving dock. For example, if a product doesn't meet specifications, it must be double-handled, possibly repackaged, stored and shipped back to the source. This process uses extra labour and space. Additionally, lack of a reliable delivery time requires the retailer to carry more inventories, which decreases inventory turns and increases costs for the added storage space.

Ways to improve logistical efficiencies might include:

a) The value-added services like packaging, marking and quality inspection can be performed by the vendor. This improves the chance of catching errors at the source and source-based services speed product flow through the warehouse.

b) The transportation can be built integrally into the warehouse process and layout and making it an afterthought should be avoided. Due consideration has to be given to inbound and outbound conveyances, queuing up shipments by carrier and the capability to pull orders later in the day to increase customer service.

c) Determine if the carriers are able to accommodate business demands, depending on product-type and turnaround time. For example, some multichannel retailers have carriers come into the centre to help load trucks, while other retailers have an in-house office for shipping.

d) Consider whether facilities issues could affect the operation. For instance, limited delivery door access can force companies to rely on their carrier to move a loaded trailer and replace it with an empty one. During peak order shipment periods, this causes down time and an interruption to the workflow when there's no empty trailer ready to load. Additional loading doors could solve this issue.

2. Improved Customer Service

In direct marketing enterprises, fulfilment operations are in partnership with marketing and merchandising. This partnership is like a three-legged table — without all three legs the table cannot stand. Fulfilment operations' inbound and outbound transportation is key to delivering marketing's promise to the customer to get the shipment delivered on time and in good condition. In direct marketing, customer service must be balanced with costs. First, is the cost to acquire a customer which depends on the efficiency of prospecting. This includes the marketing costs, as well as the cost of non-responses. In many businesses, 50 to 70 percent of all first-time buyers do not purchase a second time. Most businesses need a customer to purchase two or three times to break even. The second cost element to consider is the high cost of being on back order.

Returns also cost far more than orders to process and in many businesses, only one-third of the returns are exchanges. Cost of processing a return includes:

a) Original cost of order processing, including indirect and direct labour, credit card processing fees, occupancy costs and phone lines.
b) Prospecting costs to acquire the customer.
c) Cost to process returns and refurbishing items, including indirect and direct labour, occupancy costs.
d) Loss of shipping and handling revenue if refunded from outbound or inbound transaction.
e) Loss of gross margin.
f) Potential loss of customer if shopping or return processing experience is not suitable.

Increases in supply chain efficiency can reduce inventory levels and out-of-stocks. For example, take the radio frequency identification (RFID) used at Wal-Mart. According to Linda Dillman, Wal-Mart's chief information officer, using radio frequency identification has reduced out-of-stock merchandise by 16 percent at participating stores, while improving customer service during the last 4 years. The concentration has been on higher-priced, faster moving products. Additionally, Dillman says, the company can restock RFID-tagged items three times faster than non-tagged items. Wal-Mart has only implemented RFID with about 130 vendors, using 5.4 million tags in the past year, and approximately 1,000 stores are ready to receive RFID product. Getting efficient inbound logistics systems and vendor compliance in place is the first priority. While RFID is in the future for most companies, others need to implement solutions that optimize supply chain efficiency today.

3. Increased Sales

How can inbound and outbound logistics and transportation help a retailer's sales? Several opportunities exist for improving service, and those in turn, can be used to marketing's advantage. Look atinbound and outbound freight as separate operations with separate requirements. Bundle the volumes wherever possible with the carriers, but recognize the differences between the channels.

Inbound logistics

With direct promotions and advertised retail products, maintaining on-time and in-stock position is a must. Sales could be lost withoutan available, reliable source of merchandise. Because it's difficult to project sales, one need to get product quickly and safely into the logistics pipeline. Product damage from inbound transportation can seriously affect product availability and without products to sell, profits decline.

The process starts by tracking what is inbound? Where it is? And when it will be delivered? Direct marketers must notify customers of a possible delay in receiving and, as a result, outbound shipment, or cancel their orders entirely. In addition, warehouses are increasingly becoming the "back room" for specialty store operations in the multi-channel retailing environment. If the product cannot be moved quickly into a retail outlet, this would result in loss of sale. As companies become leaner, transportation becomes even more important to meeting sales goals. Retail customers may substitute another product for what they originally came in to purchase, but in direct promotions the customer is very negative toward substitution.

Outbound logistics

The logistics of delivering to the customer can affect sales if the customer's expectations are not met, for example, with the late delivery of a gift, or a damaged or poor appearance of product upon arrival. If the customer doesn't want the product that arrives, returns increase the cost of operation. Conversely, logistics can factor into a company's marketing plan if transportation costs are under control. Many e-commerce companies offer free shipping and handling. Free shipping has proven to increase sales and average order. Most marketers don't want to give up this source of revenue or offer it only to their best customers or higher-average order buyers. If the company's transportation costs are out of control, it is going to be less willing to offer shipping promotions.

4. Building Relationships

True two-way collaboration between retailer and carrier is a key to the success of overall logistics execution. Measures of success are: total cost, time in transit and responsiveness of the carrier representative. The single-carrier versus multi-carrier philosophy is one of the primary issues that need to be addressed with regard to carrier relations. Using one carrier allows a higher aggregate volume of shipments, which can result in lower negotiated rates. The downside is total dependence on one carrier and the resulting possible problems if there is a carrier service interruption. Both issues should be weighed carefully. A good relationship between the retailer and the carrier representative is vital to making the activity work. Inevitably there will be issues that must be addressed. Trust and a positive attitude can influence how those issues are resolved. Most vendors can meet the technical needs of their business; the difference can be how relationships affect business. It's always more than a matter of cost that breeds success. Merchandisers have the initial primary relationship with vendors in many retail and direct marketing organizations. In re-buying merchandise, this relationship is often delegated to inventory planning or purchasing. In most companies, changes are required in vendor logistics to acquire the blessing of the merchandisers and to achieve vendor compliance. Additionally, gross margin and freight-in are often goals of the merchandising department and the buyers — standards upon which performance objectives and bonuses are evaluated. Obviously, increases in efficiency that yield savings will win partners.

The vendors should be compared using a structured approach. When soliciting bids, the retailer should give carriers as much information about its business requirements as possible. Throughout the bidding process, and later when working with carrier partners, retailers should follow these guidelines:

a) Stay involved with the process.
b) Verify results and reports.
c) Audit bills.
d) Consider the total costs of transportation in your analysis and reviews.
e) Keep options open and treat carrier contracts and relationships as dynamic and evolving not like a fixed three-year arrangement.

In direct retailing businesses, the purchasing and inventory control functions have responsibility for analyzing inventory requirements, purchasing and purchase-order writing, receipt-planning, vendor communication, routing deliveries, improving back orders, co-ordinating required receipts to prevent back orders and stock outs. They are generally good partners with fulfilment in enforcing vendor compliance. In multi-channel and multi-warehouse operations, the purchasing and inventory control departments have the prime responsibility to balance or level inventory between channels, warehouses and stores to optimize sales and profitability.

Features of Logistics Management

1. It ensures a smooth flow of all types of goods such as raw materials, work-in-process and finished goods.
2. It has the ability to meet customer expectations and requirements of goods.
3. It ensures the delivery of quality products.
4. It offers the best possible customer service at the least possible cost.
5. It is an integration of various managerial functions for optimisation of resources.
6. It deals with the movement and storage of goods in appropriate quantity.
7. It enhances productivity and profitability.

Need for Logistics Management

Today's organisations worldwide need logistics management more than ever because of the following reasons:

1. **Competitive Pressures:** During the 1970s, logistics received more attention as a major cost driver to offset the effect of rising interest rates and increasing energy costs. In addition, the logistics cists became more critical for many companies because of globalisation of their business. These developments affected logistics primarily in two ways:

(i) The growth of world-class competitors which has pressurised organisations to differentiate themselves and their product offerings. Logistics enable domestic firms to provide more reliable and responsive service to customers in the local markets than overseas competitors.

(ii) As firms increasingly buy and sell off-shire, the supply chain between the manufacturing firm and its supplier and customer firms becomes longer, costlier and more complex. Hence, in such situations, excellent logistics is necessary to take advantage of global opportunities.

2. **Information Technology :** With the explosion of information technology, organisations gained the ability to better monitor transaction intensive activities such as ordering, transportation (movement) and storage of goods and materials. Computerised quantitative models along with information technology increased the ability to manage material flows and to optimise inventory levels and movements. Profit leverage arising out of the application of logistics resulted in the realisation that logistics can be used as a *strategic weapon* to compete in the marketplace.

3. **Channel Power :** The channel power shifted from manufacturers to wholesalers, distributors and retailers. This has had a major impact on logistics. In major consumer good industries, when competition increases, many suppliers and manufacturers are forced out of competition and a few leading competitors remain in the market. Those who remain are highly competitive and are able to offer very high quality products. Sales of consumer products are determined by what is in stock, and not by what particular brand offered to the customers.

4. **Profit Leverage :** Any amount of money saved in logistics costs has a greater impact on the organisation's profitability than a similar increase in sales revenue. Any savings in logistics costs directly adds to the company's profit. To achieve same amount of profit through sales, a firm has to put more effort and increase sales revenue considerably because profit earned through sales is only a small percent of sales revenue. Therefore, it can be inferred that logistics cost savings have much more leverage than an increase in sales.

Value-Added Role of Logistics

Value of a product can be enhanced by four types of economic utility namely *form utility, time utility, place utility* and *possession utility*. Manufacturing activities provide *form utility* (i.e., converting raw materials into products of required shape and size); logistics activities provide *time utility* and *place utility* (i.e., providing the right product at the right place and at the right time) and marketing activities provide the firm with *possession utility*.

Logistics Costs

Logistics costs are created by logistics activities such as customer service, transportation, warehousing, order processing and information, lot quantity and inventory carrying, which are discussed as follows:

(i) ***Customer Service Level:*** The key cost trade-off resulting from varying levels of customer service is the cost of lost sales. Expenses for customer service support includes the costs of order fulfilment, parts and service support and costs of return goods handling.

(ii) ***Transportation costs:*** These costs are determined by the activity of transporting goods. Costs vary considerably with volume of shipment, weight of shipment, distance between point of origin and destination and also with the mode of transportation chosen (land, air, sea or rail).

(iii) ***Warehousing Costs:*** These costs are due to warehousing and storage activities and also due to warehouse and plant location selection process.

(iv) ***Order Processing/Information Systems Costs:*** These costs are related to activities such as order processing, distribution communications and demand forecasting. Order processing costs include costs or order transmittal, order entry, order processing etc.

(v) ***Lot Quantity Costs:*** These costs are due to procurement and production lot quantities. Lot quantity costs are related to purchasing or production and these costs vary with changes in order size frequency. They include: *(a)* set-up costs, *(b)* capacity lost due to down time during changeover of production set-ups or change over to a new supplier, *(c)* material handling, scheduling, expediting, *(d)* price differentials due to buying in different lot sizes, and *(e)* order costs associated with order placement and follow-up.

(vi) ***Inventory Carrying Costs:*** Logistics activities that cause inventory carrying costs include inventory control, packaging and salvage and scrap disposal. The inventory costs are made up of: *(a)* capital cost or opportunity costs, *(b)* inventory service cost (insurance and taxes on inventory), *(c)* storage space cost, and *(d)* inventory risk cost including obsolescence, pilferage and damage.

Total Logistics Cost

The total cost concept is the key to manage logistics process effectively. The organisation should have the goal of reducing the ***total cost*** of logistics activities rather than merely focusing on each activity in isolation. *For example,* reducing costs in one area, such as transportation, may increase inventory carrying costs because more inventory is needed to cover longer transit times and to balance against greater uncertainty in transit times.

The important elements of logistics cost are:

1. Product inventory at source.
2. Pipeline inventory.
3. Product inventory at warehouses and dealers.
4. Transit losses/insurance.
5. Storage losses/insurance.
6. Handling and warehouse operations.
7. Packaging.
8. Transportation.

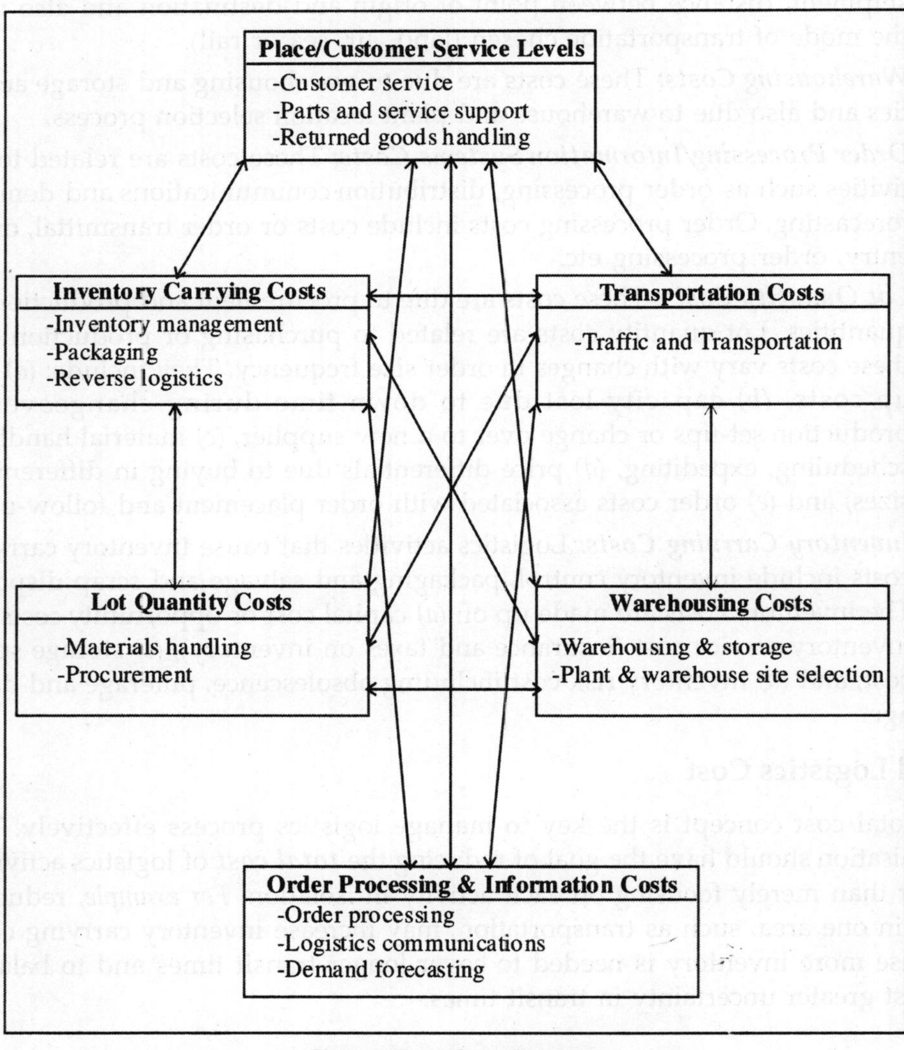

Figure: Total Cost Concept

Models in Logistics Management

1 Forecasting Models

These models allow prediction of demand based on past data or other parameters that are independently available. They enable better planning, given the lead time necessary for response.

2 Mathematical Programming Models

(a) **Location Models:** These models help in planning the optimal location of plants or warehouses, considering the inbound and outbound transportation costs and infrastructure costs at the locations.

(b) **Allocation Models:** These models help in optimally allocating commodities from sources to destinations in a multi-source, multi-destination environment. The costs considered for optimisation are production costs, transportation costs and warehousing costs. The constraints considered can be due to demand, capacity, route restrictions, etc.

(c) **Distribution Network Design Models:** These models are usually comprehensive in nature, deciding between a two, three or even four stage network, location of warehouses and sometimes even the transportation mode choice. The models optimise total distribution costs including transportation, warehousing and handling.

3 Inventory Models

Inventory plays a very key role in logistics management. Issues like shipment size, supplying to one or many points in one shipment, single location vs. multiple location stocking directly relate to inventory and transportation costs. A number of models like the Economic Order Quantity, Economic Batch Quantity, and other lot sizing models are available.

4 Routing Models

These models allow optimal routing on a transportation network from a given source to a destination. The simplest model is called the Shortest Path Problem. When deliveries or collections have to be made from multiple points, the model to use is the Travelling Salesman Problem or the Vehicle Routing Problem.

5 Scheduling Models

These models enable allocation of resources to particular activities. Depending on the criteria of interest and number of resources, the models help evaluate appropriate rules for allocation.

Storage, Warehousing and Distribution Centres

Storages

Storages are the godowns for keeping and storing of raw materials, components, semi-finished goods, tools, maintenance, repairing and operating equipments and supplies related to the production function. The primary use of storages occurs in relation to- and usually in advance of- various production processes. Itis unusual for finished goods in condition to be delivered to customers of a firm to be stored for any length of time. Storage warehouses may be located at any point in a logistics system, but usually have some type of strong location relationship to production facilities, i.e., these storages are generally located near production plants or facilities. Storages are most frequently used by companies for various reasons such as seasonal demand and supply pattern to level out production activities.

Warehouse

Warehouses are the godowns for keeping and storing goods and providing other related services in order to keep traders and or manufacturers to preserve the goods in a scientific and systematic manner so as to maintain their original value, quality and usefulness. The goods may be raw materials, parts, components, in-processes, finished goods, maintenance, repairing and operating supplies or any other items used or sold of a firm. Traditionally, a warehouse was viewed as a storage facility necessary to accomplish basic marketing processes. In supply chain perspective, warehouses perform the storing function, where goods are stored in bulk quantities and from there a new and different small assortment of goods is selected and moved forwards to be dispersed to the next level. Hence, warehouses are generally located near to the market for smooth and quick flow of finished goods to the customers. However, in-plant warehouses store finished goods for the time being till they are transported to warehouses.

Distribution Centre

The distribution centre is a new idea at the advent of logistics and supply chain management, referring to dynamic, full-service warehouse primarily related to the market. It emphasises the movement of goods rather than their storage and other customer-oriented logistical services such as sales, market intelligence, documentation, intact delivery of goods. They may be situated near to the markets and can be termed as centralized warehousing operations that:

(i) Serve regional markets.

(ii) Process and regroup products into customised orders.

(iii) Maintain a full line of products for customer distribution.

(iv) Consolidate large shipments from different production points.

(v) Frequently employ a computer and various materials handling equipment and may be highly automated rather than labour intensive.

Warehousing

A warehouse is typically viewed as a place to store inventory. However, in many logistical system designs, the role of the warehouse is more properly viewed as a switching facility as contrasted to a storage facility. The discussion is relevant for all types of warehouses as well as distribution centers, consolidation terminals, and break bulk and cross-dock facilities. Productivity is the ratio of physical output to physical input. To increase productivity, it is necessary either to obtain greater output with the same input or to maintain existing output with a reduction of input factors.

When business is extremely good and the economy approaches full employment, output per worker-hour falls as marginal productive workers are employed. Warehousing operations get more than their fair share of such new employees because few, if any, skills are required to perform many of the manual tasks. When business activity plummets, union labour contract provisions often prohibit a rapid reduction in payrolls. While not all distribution facilities are unionized, logistics activities have traditionally been a union strength. Although separate productivity figures for warehouse workers are not available, it may be assumed that warehouse labour productivity has lagged most other areas in the private sector.

Let's concentrate on the basic concept and then the definitions propagated by Bombay Warehouse Act, 1959.

1. Warehousing is the function of storing goods to bridge the time gap between their production and demand and thus leads to time and place utility.
2. As a part of marketing strategy, warehousing offers better customer service than competitors who rely on price competition.
3. The creation and strategic location of warehouse are justified if the marginal cost of warehousing is less than marginal revenue.

Definitions as per Bombay Warehouse Act, 1959

"Warehouse means any building structure or other protected enclosure which is used or may be used for the purpose of storing goods on behalf of the depositors but doesn't include cloakroom attached to hotels, railway station and the premises of other public carrier alike."

Depositor means a person who deposits goods with a warehouse for storing in his warehouse and includes any person who lawfully holds the receipt issued by the warehouse in respect of the goods and derives title too by endorsement or transfer from the depositor or his lawful transferee.

Evolution of concept of Warehousing

Manufacturers were able to recognize the fact that the customers' needs should be fulfilled as soon as he asks for a product, in order to retain him. This perspective of storage created a tendency to consider warehouses 'a necessary evil' that added costs to the distribution process and that resulted in creation of operating expenses with little appreciation of the broader logistical spectrum in which warehousing played a vital role. Warehousing capability used to group products into assortments desired by customers was given little emphasis. Internal control and maximum inventory turnover received little managerial attention.

Literature of the early era correctly described the situation. Firms seeking to operate effectively between points of procurement, manufacturing and consumption gave little attention to internal warehouse operations. The establishment of warehouses was essential for survival, but little emphasis was placed on improving storage and handling effectiveness. Engineering efforts were centred on manufacturing problems.

Operation of early warehouses illustrated the lack of concern with material handling principles. The typical warehouse received merchandise by rail or truck. The items were moved manually to a storage area within the warehouse and hand-piled in stacks on the floor. When different products were stored in the same warehouse, merchandise was continually lost. Stock rotation was handled poorly. When customer orders were received, products were handpicked for placement on wagons. The wagons or carts were then pushed to the shipping area where the merchandise was reassembled and hand-loaded onto delivery trucks.

Because labour was relatively inexpensive, human resources were used freely. Little consideration was given to efficiency in space utilization, work methods, or material handling. Despite their shortcomings, these early warehouses provided the necessary bridge between production and marketing.

Following World War II, managerial attention shifted toward increasing warehouse efficiency. Managements began to question the need for so many warehouses. In the distributive industries such as wholesaling and retailing, it was not unusual for every sales territory to have a dedicated warehouse and inventory. As forecasting and production scheduling techniques improved, the need for extensive inventory buildup was reduced. Production became more co-ordinated as time delays during the manufacturing process decreased. Seasonal production still required warehousing, but the overall need for storage to support manufacturing was reduced.

However, changing requirements of the retail environment more than offset any reductions in warehousing gained through manufacturing improvements. The retail store, faced with the necessity of stocking an increasing variety of products, was unable to order in sufficient quantity from a single supplier to enjoy the benefits of consolidated shipment. The cost of transporting small shipments made direct ordering prohibitive. This resulted in a need to utilize warehouses to provide timely and economical inventory assortments to retailers. At the wholesale level of the channel of distribution, the warehouse became a support unit for retailing. Progressive wholesalers and integrated retailers developed state-of-the-art warehouse systems capable of providing necessary retail support.

Improvements in wholesale warehousing efficiency related to retailing were soon adopted in manufacturing. For manufacturers producing products at multiple locations, efficient warehousing offered a method of reducing material and parts storage and handling costs, while optimizing production. Warehousing became an integral part of JIT and stockless production strategies. While the basic notion of JIT is to reduce work-in-process inventory, the concept of manufacturing must be supported by highly dependable delivery. Such logistical support, in a geographically vast country, may be possible only through the use of strategically located warehouses. A basic stock of parts can be staged at a central warehouse, thereby reducing the need to maintain inventory at each assembly plant. Using consolidated shipments, products are purchased and transported to the supply warehouse and then distributed to manufacturing plants as needed. When fully integrated, the warehouse is a vital extension of manufacturing.

On the outbound side of manufacturing, warehouses created the possibility of direct customer shipment of mixed products. The capability to provide product shipments directly from the factory appealed to marketers because it enhanced service capability. For the customer, direct shipments have two specific advantages. First, logistical cost is reduced because full product assortment can be delivered while also taking advantage of the benefits of consolidated transportation. Second, inventory of slow-moving products can be reduced because they can be received in small quantities as part of consolidated shipments. As the level of competition in the marketplace increases, manufacturers capable of rapidly providing direct shipments gain a competitive advantage.

During the 1960s and 1970s, the function of warehousing focused on the application of new technology. Technology based improvements affected almost every area of warehouse operations and created new and better techniques and procedures to perform storage and handling activities. In the 1980s, central focus was on improved configuration of warehouse systems and handling technologies.

During the 1990s, the primary focus of warehousing was flexibility and effective use of information technology. Flexibility is necessary to respond to expanding customer demands in terms of product and shipment profiles. Advanced information technology offers some of this flexibility by allowing warehouse operators to quickly react to changes and measure performance under a wide range of conditions.

Functions of a Warehouse

1. Spot Stock

Stock spotting is most often used in physical distribution. In particular, manufacturers with limited or highly seasonal product lines are partial to this service. Rather than placing inventories in warehouse facilities on a year-round basis or shipping directly from manufacturing plants, delivery time can be substantially reduced by advanced inventory commitment to strategic markets. Under this concept, a selected amount of a firm's product line is placed or "spot stocked" in a warehouse to fill customer orders during acritical marketing period. Utilizing warehouse facilities for stock spotting allows inventories to be placed in a variety of markets adjacent to key customers just prior to a maximum period of seasonal sales.

Suppliers of agricultural products to farmers often use spot stocking to position their products closer to a service-sensitive market during the growing season. Following the sales season, the remaining inventory is withdrawn to a central warehouse.

2. Assortment

An assortment warehouse is one which may be utilized by a manufacturer, wholesaler or retailer to stock product combinations in anticipation of customer orders. The assortments may represent multiple products from different manufacturers or special assortments as specified by customers. In the first case, for example, an athletic wholesaler would stock products from a number of clothing suppliers so that customers can be offered assortments. In the second case, the wholesaler would create a specific team uniform including shirt, pants,and shoes.

The difference between stock spotting and complete line assortment is the degree and duration of warehouse utilization. A firm following a stock spotting strategy would typically warehouse a narrow product assortment and place stocks in a large number of small warehouses dedicated to specific markets for a limited time period. The distribution assortment warehouse usually has a broad product line, is limited to a few strategic locations, and is functional year round.

Assortment warehouses improve service by reducing the number of suppliers that a customer must deal with. The combined assortments also allow larger shipment quantities, which in turn, reduce transportation cost.

3. Mixing

Warehouse mixing is similar to the break-bulk process except that several different manufacturer shipments may be involved. When plants are geographically separated, overall transportation charges and warehouse requirements can be reduced by in-transit mixing. In a typical mixing situation, carloads or truckloads of products are shipped from manufacturing plants to warehouses. Each large shipment enjoys the lowest possible transportation rate. Upon arrival at the mixing warehouse, factory shipments are unloaded and the desired combination of each product for each customer or market is selected.

The economies of in-transit mixing have been traditionally supported by special transportation tariffs that are variations of in-transit privileges. Under the mixing warehouse concept, inbound products may also be combined with products regularly stored in the warehouse. Warehouses that provide in-transit mixing have the net effect of reducing overall product storage in a logistical system. Mixing is classified as a service benefit because inventory is sorted to precise customer specifications.

4. Production Support

The economics of manufacturing may justify relatively long production runs of specific components. Production support warehousing provides a steady supply of components and materials to assembly plants. Safety stocks on items purchased from outside vendors may be justified because of long lead times or significant variations in usage. In these, as well as a variety of other situations, the most economical total cost solution may be the operation of a production support warehouse to supply or "feed" processed materials, components, and sub-assemblies into the assembly plant in an economic and timely manner.

5. Market Presence

While a market presence benefit may not be as obvious as other service benefits, it is often cited by marketing managers as a major advantage of local warehouses. The market presence factor is based on the perception or belief that local warehouses (and presumably local inventory) can be more responsive to customer needs and offer quicker delivery than more distant warehouses. As a result, it is also thought that a local warehouse will enhance market share and potentially increase profitability. While the market presence factor is a frequently discussed strategy, little solid research exists to confirm its actual benefit impact.

Benefits of Warehousing

Benefits realized from strategic warehousing are classified on the basis of economics and service. From a conceptual perspective, no warehouse should be included in a logistical system unless it is fully justified on a cost-benefit basis. While there is some overlap, the major warehouse benefits are reviewed individually.

(A) Economic Benefits

Economic benefits of warehousing result when overall logistical costs are directly reduced by utilizing one or more facilities. It is not difficult to quantify the return on investment of an economic benefit because it is reflected in a direct cost-to-cost trade-off. For example, if adding a warehouse to a logistical system will reduce overall transportation cost by an amount greater than the fixed and variable cost of the warehouse, then total cost will be reduced. Whenever total cost reductions are attainable, the warehouse is economically justified. Four basic economic benefits are consolidation, break bulk and cross-dock, processing/ postponement, and stockpiling. Each is discussed and illustrated.

(i) Consolidation

Shipment consolidation is an economic benefit of warehousing. With this arrangement, the consolidating warehouse receives and consolidates materials from a number of manufacturing plants destined to a specific customer on a single transportation shipment. The benefits are the realization of the lowest possible transportation rate and reduced congestion at a customer's receiving dock. The warehouse allows both the inbound movement from the manufacturer to the warehouse and the outbound movement from the warehouse to the customer to be consolidated into larger shipments.

In order to provide effective consolidation, each manufacturing plant must use the warehouse as a forward stock location or as a sorting and assembly facility.

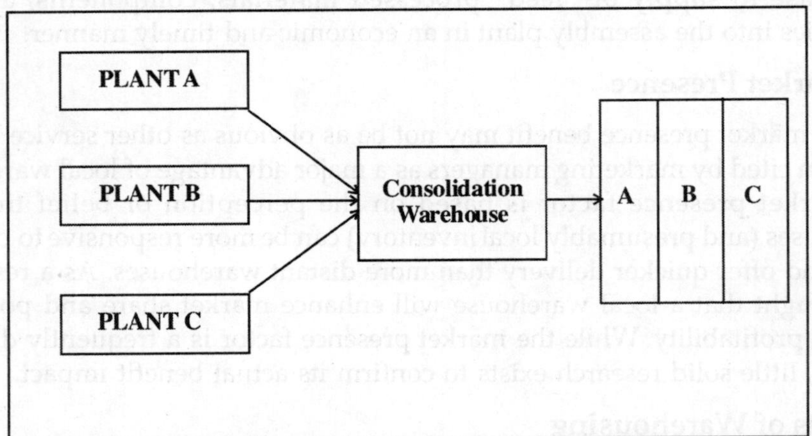

The primary benefit of consolidation is that it combines the logistical flow of several small shipments to a specific market area. Consolidation warehousing may be used by a single firm, or a number of firms may join together and use a for-hire consolidation service. Through the useof such a program, each individual manufacturer or shipper can enjoy lower total distribution cost than could be realized on a direct shipment basis individually.

(ii) Break Bulk and Cross-Dock

Break bulk and cross-dock warehouse operations are similar to consolidation except that no storage is performed. A break bulk operation receives combined customer orders from manufacturers and ships them to individual customers. The break bulk warehouse or terminal sorts or splits individual orders and arranges for local delivery. Because the long-distance transportation movement is a large shipment, transport costs are lower and there is less difficulty in tracking.

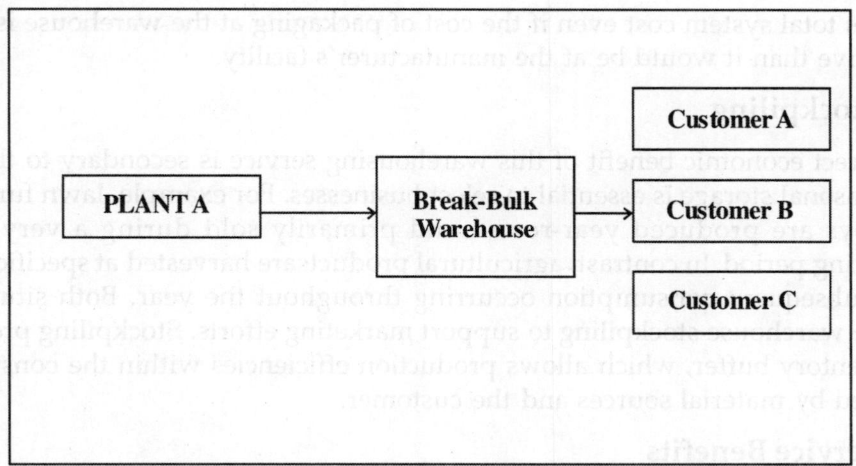

A cross-dock facility is similar except that it involves multiple manufacturers. Retail chains make extensive use of cross-dock operations to replenish fast-moving store inventories. E.g. Full trailer-loads of product arrive from multiple manufacturers. As the product is received, customer either sorts it if it is labelled or allocated to customers. If it has not been labelled, product is then literally moved "across the dock" to be loaded into the trailer destined for the appropriate customer. The trailer is released for transport to the retail store once it has been filled with mixed product from multiple manufacturers. The economic benefits of cross-docking include full trailer movements from manufacturers to the warehouse and from the warehouse to retailers, reduced handling cost at the cross-dock facility since product is not stored, and more effective use of dock facilities because all vehicles are fully loaded, thus maximizing loading dock utilization.

(iii) Processing/Postponement

Warehouses can also be used to postpone or delay, production by performing processing and light manufacturing activities. A warehouse with packaging or labelling capability allows postponement of final production until actual demand is known. For example, vegetables can be processed and canned in "Brights" at the manufacturer. Brights are cans with no pre-attached labels. The use of Brights for a private label product means that the item does not have to be committed to a specific customer or package configuration at the manufacturer's plant. Once a specific customer order is received, the warehouse can complete final processing by adding the label and finalizing the packaging.

Processing and postponement provides two economic benefits. *First,* risk is minimized because final packaging is not completed until an order for a specific label and package has been received. *Second,* the required level of total inventory can be reduced by using the basic product (Brights) for a variety of labeling and packaging configurations. The combination of lower risk and inventory level often reduces total system cost even if the cost of packaging at the warehouse is more expensive than it would be at the manufacturer's facility.

(iv) Stockpiling

The direct economic benefit of this warehousing service is secondary to the fact that seasonal storage is essential to select businesses. For example, lawn furniture and toys are produced year-round and primarily sold during a very short marketing period. In contrast, agricultural productsare harvested at specific times with subsequent consumption occurring throughout the year. Both situations require warehouse stockpiling to support marketing efforts. Stockpiling provides an inventory buffer, which allows production efficiencies within the constraints imposed by material sources and the customer.

B Service Benefits

Service benefits gained through warehouses in a logistical system may or may not reduce costs. When a warehouse is primarily justified on the basis of service, the supporting rationale is an improvement in the time and place capability of the overall logistical system. For example, placing a warehouse in a logistical system to service a specific market segment may increase cost but might also increase market share, revenue, and gross margin. At a conceptual level, a service-justified warehouse would be added if the net effect was profit-justified. At an operational level, the problem is how to measure the direct revenue impact.

Warehousing Alternatives

Here we focus on the options of private, public, and contract warehousing. A *private warehouse* facility is owned and managed by the same enterprise that owns the merchandise handled and stored at the facility. A *public warehouse,* in contrast, is operated as an independent business offering a range of services–such as storage, handling, and transportation–on the basis of a fixed or variable fee. Public warehouse operators generally offer relatively standardized services to all clients. *Contract warehousing,* which is evolving from the public warehouse segment, provides benefits of both the private and public alternatives. Contract warehousing is a long term, mutually beneficial arrangement which provides unique and specially tailored warehousing and logistics services exclusively to one client, where the vendor and client share the risks associated with the operation. Important dimensions that differentiate contract warehousing operators from public warehouse operators are the extended time frame of the service relationship, tailored services, exclusivity, and shared risk. The benefits of private, public, and contract warehouse options are as follows:

1. Private Warehouses

A private warehouse is operated by the firm owning the product. The actual facility, however, may be owned or leased. The decision as to which strategy best fits an individual firm is essentially financial. Often it is not possible to find a warehouse for lease that fits the exact requirements of a firm. For example, a warehouse requires substantial material-handling activities. Existing or leased facilities may not be adequately designed. As a general rule, an efficient warehouse should be planned around a material-handling system in order to encourage maximum efficiency of product flow.

Real estate developers are increasingly willing to build distribution warehouses to firms' specifications on a leased basis. Such custom construction is available in many markets on lease arrangements as short as five years.

Benefits of Private Warehousing

The major benefits of private warehousing include control, flexibility, cost, and other intangible benefits. Private warehouses provide more control since the enterprise has absolute decision-making authority over all activities and priorities in the facility. This control facilitates the ability to integrate warehouse operations with the rest of the firm's internal logistics process.

Private warehousing is usually considered less costly than public warehousing because private facility costs do not have a profit mark-up. As a result, both the fixed and variable cost components should be less. This perceived benefit, however, may be misleading since public warehouses often are more efficient or may operate at lower wage scales. It is important to develop an accurate assessment of total warehouse-related costs prior to making a decision regarding warehouse strategy.

Finally, private warehousing has some intangible benefits, particularly with respect to market presence. A private warehouse with a firm's name on it may produce customer perceptions of responsiveness and stability. This perception sometimes provides a firm with a marketing advantage over other enterprises.

2. Public Warehouses

Public warehouses are used extensively in logistical systems. Almost any combination of services can be arranged with the operator either for a short-term or over a long duration. A classification of public warehouseshas been developed. On the basis of the range of specialized operations performed, they are classified as:

(i) General merchandise,

(ii) Refrigerated,

(iii) Special commodity,

(iv) Bonded, and

(v) Household goods and furniture.

Each warehouse type differs in its material handling and storage technology because of the product and environmental characteristics.

3. Contract Warehouse

Contract warehouse combines the best of both private and public warehouse. The long-term relationship and shared risk will result in lower cost than typical public warehouse arrangement although minimum fixed assets are required for facilities. At the same time, contract warehouse operations can provide benefits of expertise, flexibility, and economies of scale by sharing management, labour, equipment, and information resources across a number of clients.

Contract warehouse operators are also expanding the scope of their services to include other logistics activities such as transportation, inventory control, order processing, customer services, and return processing. There are contract warehouses capable of assuming total logistics responsibility for enterprises that desire only to manufacture and market.

Factors in the Location of a Warehouse

1. Number of geographical locations of the market targeted by the firm. If markets are located close to the production plant of the company, then it is always better to serve from the in-plant warehouse. In the case of wide and diversified markets, the company has to have decentralised warehouses.
2. If the company has multiple production plants and they are near the different target markets, then it is suggested to operate from the in-plant warehouses.
3. Transportation infrastructure facilities also determine the number and location of warehouses. These include quality and availability of vehicles, quantity to be transported, transit time etc.
4. Nature and quality of goods to be stored is another factor. Highly seasonal goods need to be stored in bulk quantity for a specific time period. In such a situation, decentralised warehouses should be hired.
5. In case of strong brand loyalty among customers who can wait for the product during a stock out situation, the firm can have a centralised and limited number of warehouses.
6. When a firm is not financially strong enough, it is suggested to have a limited number of public warehouses to reduce costs.
7. If a management wants to use customer service as means of competitive advantage, then the firm should have decentralised warehouses near the market so that the customer can be served better and market dominance can be maintained.

Elements of Warehousing Costs

There are basically three types of warehousing costs:

1. **Warehousing Infrastructural Development Costs,** which includes:
   (a) Costs of procurement of storage space;

(b) Handling and transfer cost;

(c) Administrative cost; and

(d) Costs incurred in direct and indirect physical facilities.

2. **Working Capital Costs** include the cost of working capital involved in the goods stored in warehouse as inventory.

3. **Miscellaneous Costs** include:

(a) Tax to be paid;

(b) Insurance paid for covering risks; and

(c) The risk of product obsolescence or deterioration.

Obstacles to Co-ordination in a Supply Chain

The Bullwhip Effect

Supply chain co-ordination improves if all stages of the chain take actions that together increase total supply chain profits. Supply chain co-ordination requires each stage of the supply chain to take into account the impact its actions have on other stages.

A lack of co-ordination occurs either because different stages of the supply chain have objectives that are conflicting or because information moving between stages is delayed and distorted. Different stages of a supply chain may have conflicting objectives if each stage has a different owner. As a result, each stage tries to maximize its own profits, resulting in actions that often diminish total supply chain profits. Today, supply chains consist of stages with many different owners. For example, Ford Motor Company has thousands of suppliers, and each of these suppliers has many suppliers in turn. Information is distorted as it moves across the supply chain because complete information is not shared between stages. This distortion is exaggerated by the fact that supply chains today produce a large amount of product variety. For example, Ford produces many different models with several options for each model. The increased variety makes it difficult for Ford to co-ordinate information exchange with thousands of suppliers and dealers.

Many firms have observed the *bullwhip effect*, in which fluctuations in orders increase as they move up the supply chain from retailers to wholesalers to manufacturers to suppliers. The bullwhip effect distorts demand information within the supply chain, with each stage having a different estimate of what demand looks like. The result is a loss of supply chain co-ordination.

Causes of Bullwhip Effect

Any factor that leads to either local optimization by different stages of the supply chain, or an increase in information delay, distortion, and variability within the supply chain, is an obstacle to co-ordination. The major obstacles or the causes of bullwhip effect can be divided into the following categories:

1. **Incentive Obstacles** occur in situations when incentives offered to different stages or participants in a supply chain lead to actions that increase variability and reduce total supply chain profits. For example, if the compensation of a transportation manager at a firm is linked to the average transportation cost per unit, the manager is likely to take actions that lower transportation costs even if they increase inventory costs or hurt customer service.

   Improperly structured sales force incentives are a significant obstacle to co-ordination in a supply chain. In many firms, sales force incentives are based on the amount the sales force sells during an evaluation period of a month or a quarter. The sales typically measured by a manufacturer are the quantity sold to distributors or retailers (sell-in), not the quantity sold to final customers (sell-through).

2. **Information Processing Obstacles** occur in situations when demand information is distorted as it moves between different stages of the supply chain, leading to increased variability in orders within the supply chain. When stages within the supply chain make forecasts that are based on orders they receive, any variability in customer demand is magnified as orders move up the supply chain to manufacturers and suppliers. In supply chains that exhibit the bullwhip effect, the fundamental means of communication between different stages are the orders that are placed. Each stage views its primary role within the supply chain as one of filling orders placed by its down stream partner. Thus, each stage views its demand as the stream of orders received and produces a forecast based on this information. The lack of information sharing between stages of the supply chain magnifies the bullwhip effect. E.g. a retailer such as Wal-Mart may increase the size of a particular order because of the planned promotion. If the manufacturer is not aware of the planned promotion, it may interpret the larger order as a permanent increase in the demand and place orders with suppliers accordingly. The manufacturers and suppliers thus have a lot of inventory right after Wal-Mart finishes its promotion.

3. **Operational Obstacles** occur when actions taken in the course of placing and filing orders lead to an increase in variability. When a firm places orders in lot sizes that are much larger than the lot sizes in which demand arises, variability of orders is magnified up the supply chain. Firms may order in large lots because there is a significant cost associated with placing, receiving, or transporting an order. The bullwhip effect is magnified if replenishment lead times between stages are long.

4. **Pricing Obstacles** arise when the pricing policies for a product lead to an increase in variability of orders placed. Lot-size based quantity discounts increase the lot-size of orders placed within the supply chain. Trade promo-

tions and other short-term discounts offered by a manufacturer result in forward buying, by which a wholeseller and retailer purchases large lots during the discounting period to cover demand during future periods. Forward buying results in large orders during the promotion period followed by very small orders after that.

5. **Behavioural Obstacles** are problems in learning within the organisation that contribute to the bullwhip effect. These problems are often related to the way the supply chain is structured and the communication between different stages. Some of the behavioural obstacles are as follows:
   a) Each stage of the supply chain views its actions locally and is unable to see the impact of its actions on other stages.
   b) Different stages of the supply chain react to the current local situation rather than trying to identify the root causes.
   c) Based on local analysis, different stages of the supply chain blame each other for the fluctuations, with successive stages in the supply chain becoming enemies rather than partners.
   d) No stage of the supply chain learns form its actions over time because the most significant consequences of the actions, any one stage takes, occur elsewhere. The result is viscious cycle in which actions taken by a stage create the very problems that the stage blames on others.
   e) A lack of trust among supply chain partners causes them to be opportunistic at the expense of overall supply chain performance.

Impact of Bullwhip Effect

1. The bullwhip effect increases the manufacturing cost in the supply chain. A firm can respond to the increase variability by either building excess capacity or holding excess inventory, both of which increase the manufacturing cost per unit produced.
2. The bullwhip effect increases inventory cost in the supply chain. To handle the increased variability in demand a firm has to carry a higher level of inventory than would be required in the absence of bullwhip effect. As a result, inventory costs in the supply chain increase. The high levels of inventory also increase the warehousing space required and thus the warehousing cost incurred.
3. The bullwhip effect increases replenishment lead times in the supply chain. The increased variability as a result of the bullwhip effect makes scheduling much more difficult compared to a situation with level demand.
4. The bullwhip effect increases transportation cost in the supply chain. The transportation requirements over time are correlated with the orders being filled. As a result of the bullwhip effect, transportation requirements fluctu-

ate significantly over time. This raises transportation cost because surplus transportation capacity needs to be maintained to cover high-demand periods.

5. The bullwhip effect increases labour costs associated with shipping and receiving in the supply chain. Labour requirement for shipping fluctuate with orders. A similar fluctuation occurs for the labour requirements for receiving at distributors and retailers. The various stages have the option of carrying excess labour capacity or varying labour capacity in response to the fluctuation ion orders. Either option increases the total labour cost.

6. The bullwhip effect hurts the level of product availability and results in more stock outs in the supply chain. The large fluctuations in orders make it harder to supply all retailer and distributor orders on time. This increases the likelihood that retailers will run out of stock, resulting in lost sales for the supply chain.

Mechanisms to Counter the Bullwhip Effect

1. Managers can improve co-ordination within the supply chain by aligning goals and incentives so that every participantin supply chain activities works to maximize total supply chain profits.
2. Managers can achieve coordination by improving the accuracy of information available to different stages in the supply chain.
3. Managers can help dampen the bullwhip effect by improving operational performance and designing appropriate product rationing schemes in case of shortages.
4. Managers can diminish the bullwhip effect by devising pricing strategies that encourage retailers to order in small lots and reduce forward buying.
5. Sharing of accurate information that is trusted by every stage results in a better matching of supply and demand throughout the supply chain and a lower cost. A better relationship also tends to lower the transaction cost between supply chain stages.

For Discussion

1. Define logistics. What are the key decision areas in the Logistics Management function?
2. Discuss the various decisions in logistics management that need examination for an integrated system.
3. Why do organizations manage the logistics function? Discuss the need for logistics management.
4. Describe the various elements of logistics cost.
5. What do you understand by a Warehouse? Trace the evolution of the concept of Warehousing.

6. Describe the Economic Functions of a warehouse.
7. What are the various warehousing alternatives available to an organization? Highlight the benefits of efficient warehousing.
8. Discuss the major factors to be considered in the location of a warehouse.
9. What is outsourcing? Why do organizations outsource?
10. What is Bullwhip Effect? What are the major obstacles to co-ordination in a supply chain?
11. How do organizations suffer due to lack of co-ordination in a supply chain? Discuss the mechanisms to counter the Bullwhip Effect.

Outsourcing

The increasing prevalence of outsourcing has led to it being considered central to the strategic development of many organizations. Outsourcing is increasingly being employed to achieve performance improvements across the entire business. For example, one particular growth area has been the externalization of Information Technology (IT). Another area of the business that is also increasingly being outsourced is the human resource function. The outsourcing decision can often be a major influence on the profitability and competitive position of the organization. However, many organizations possess a limited understanding of outsourcing and in particular the potential benefits and risks and how they should be managed.

An Overview of the Outsourcing Concept

Outsourcing involves the sourcing of goods and services previously produced internally within the sourcing organization from external suppliers. The term outsourcing can cover many areas, including the outsourcing of manufacturing as well as services. The term 'outsourcing' is most commonly used in relation to the switching of the supply of product or service activities to external suppliers. Outsourcing can involve the transfer of an entire business function to a supplier. Alternatively, outsourcing may lead to the transfer of some activities associated with the function whilst some are kept in-house. Outsourcing can also involve the transfer of both people and physical assets to the supplier. Outsourcing is not just a straightforward financial or purchasing decision. In many cases, outsourcing is a major strategic decision that has implications or the entire organization. The evaluation and management of the outsourcing process involves a number of important elements. A starting point in the evaluation process involves analyzing whether outsourcing an activity is appropriate for the organization. This involves considering issues such as the capability of the organization in the activity relative to competitors, the importance of the activity to competitive advantage, the capability of suppliers to provide the activity, the level of risk in the supply market, potential workforce resistance and the impact upon the employee morale. Where the decision to outsource has been made, a number of important issues have to be considered including supplier selection, contract negotiation and the transitioning of assets to the supplier. Significant attention should also be given to managing the relationship with the supplier to ensure that outsourcing meets its intended objectives.

A term often used in the context of outsourcing is vertical integration. Vertical integration refers to the level of ownership of activities either *backward* (for example, component manufacture or inbound logistics) into the supply chain or *forward* (for example, distribution or after sales-service) towards the customer or end user of the product or service.

Vertical integration is similar to the outsourcing concept in that it is concerned with the decision on whether to perform an activity internally or source it from an external supplier. Another term that is often used in a manufacturing context is 'make-or-buy', which has been around for many years.

The application of the outsourcing concept involves an analysis of whether outsourcing is appropriate for the organization and, if so, how the outsourcing process should be managed.

Organizations have always employed external product and service providers to carry out a range of business activities such as catering, security, distribution, accounting, and information technology. However, many organizations are increasingly outsourcing a wider range of activities and a greater level of the value associated with these activities.

The Emergence of Outsourcing

After the Second World War, businesses sought diversification in order to achieve scale and protect profits. In the 1970s and 1980s, organizations found themselves struggling to compete in a more global environment because of their lack of agility, caused by over-complex and over-staffed management structures. To resolve this, many large companies developed a strategy of focusing on their core business. This meant selling off some non-core activities, but also identifying those non-critical processes that could be outsourced. Meanwhile, transportation deregulation occurred across the Western world, making it much easier and more attractive for companies to contract out their road freight transport function. In many countries external purchases of freight transport services had been constrained by government controls on the capacity of the road haulage industry.

The growth in contracting out cannot, however, simply be attributed to deregulation because the move away from in-house transport did not accelerate until the general change in managerial attitudes to contracting out that occurred in the late 1980s. At this time, companies also began to contract out other physical distribution activities such as warehousing and materials handling.

Outsourcing was not officially identified as a business strategy until 1989. During the 1990s businesses, by now under cost pressures, reviewed their core competencies and as a result outsourced more and more activities. In logistics this was mostly confined to outsourcing dedicated distribution and transportation activities, but gradually other logistics services were outsourced, including stock control, order processing and return operations.

The Logistics Service Provider and 3PL

As globalization began to dawn, freight forwarders began to emerge to support the increased movement of goods across the world. Transportation and distribution companies began to see an opportunity to operate warehouses and other part of the logistics process. The term 'logistics' started to be used in the early 1990s, and haulage and distribution companies reinvented themselves as 'logistics providers'. It was around this time that industry coined the name '3PL'.

In the late 1990s, with the advancements of information technology (IT) and globalization impacting on more businesses, logistics service providers broadened their service offerings and reinvented themselves yet again, this time positioning themselves as providers of supply chain management. Subsequently all industry sectors across the world have seen the benefits of outsourcing some or all of their logistics or supply chain activities.

External Drivers of Growth of Logistics Outsourcing

As well as a number of internal company-related drivers for logistics outsourcing, typically categorized as organizational, financial, service and physical, there are also several external drivers that have helped to accelerate the growth of outsourcing. They are now discussed in detail:

Globalisation

Perhaps the most prominent factor has been the increase in the number of companies operating in the global marketplace. This necessitates a broader perspective than when operating as an international company, which may include amongst others, attributes such as global branding, global sourcing, global production, centralisation of inventories and the centralisation of information. All of these aspects serve to emphasize the added difficulty of operating effectively in a global environment. Logistics and supply chain networks have become far more complicated and meeting the need to plan and manage logistics as a complete and integrated system has become far more difficult. Because of this, the best solution for a global company is very often to outsource its logistics operations. The types of services required by global companies are much more sophisticated than those that have been traditionally offered by 3PLs. These include, for example:

- *Manufacturing support*: undertaking or supporting sourcing, managing procurement, owning finished products, completing light manufacturing and assembly activities;
- *Origin management:* managing vendors, purchase orders, in-country collections, order consolidation;

- *Freight management:* managing and coordinating global freight movements, covering all different major modes of transport;
- *Destination management:* managing down stream operations, port to distribution delivery, deconsolidation, customs brokerage, demurrage, quality checking;
- *Contract distribution:* the more traditional aspects of storage and delivery and certain value-added elements such as inventory management, distribution center management, pre-retailing, reverse logistics, retail delivery, home delivery.

Complexity

Linked closely to the globalisation of business is the increase in the complexity of supply chain management. As already indicated, globalisation almost certainly leads to greater complexity, which in turn provides some significant implications for logistics operations. These include extended supply lead times, production postponement with local added value, complicated node management, multiple freight transport options, extended and unreliable transit times and the need for greater visibility in the supply chain.

In order for a manufacturer or retailer to succeed in this new, more complex, environment, many companies choose to outsource their supply chain management. This reflects one of the key business reasons for outsourcing logistics, which is to concentrate on core competencies or key business areas; however, the need to do this is very much involved with the increased complexity of logistics and supply chain management.

Emerging Markets

In the current business environment there are some very significant regional market developments. The most important is probably the opening of China and India. There are obvious implications for logistics regarding the flow of products out of the Far East, whether raw materials, components or finished goods and the inward flow of mainly finished goods into the Far East. There are significant implications for logistics as a result of these long and unsophisticated supply chains. One solution that many companies adopt is to outsource these operations. Key reasons for this include the difficulty of setting up in-house operations in these regions and the risk of investing in organizations and structures that may not see the growth in supply and demand that is initially forecast.

Another important area for change and growth is Eastern Europe, which has seen significant developments in the relocation of low-cost manufacturing and also opportunities for new markets and a growth in demand. Here, the main issues for logistics are the poor transport infrastructure, the inexperienced and untrained labour market and the lack of guaranteed product flows. Thus, there are good reasons for manufacturers and retailers to avoid the high risk and high cost of setting up in-house logistics facilities.

Outsourcing Operations

As a result of the fast growth in the use of outsourcing and the robust competition between the various third party companies, there are now many different distribution and distribution related services on offer. It is useful to be aware of the breadth of services that are available and to be able to select those that are most appropriate for a user company. As well as the standard tyoes of operations involved in the warehousing and the transport of goods, such as storage, picking and final delivery, there are also many other operations that can be outsourced, such as the repacking of goods or a return operation. One very important decision that must be made by any company that is contemplating outsourcing as an option is whether to outsource a part of the operation or the complete operation as a whole. This is the decision whether to use a multi-user style of operation or a dedicated operation.

As already indicated, there is a vast choice of different operations and services that can be outsourced. A good way to understand the opportunities available is to consider a typical logistics structure as shown in the figure below. This represents the theoretical physical flow, storage and manufacture of a product all the way through from the supplier of a raw material to the delivery of finished goods to the final customer.

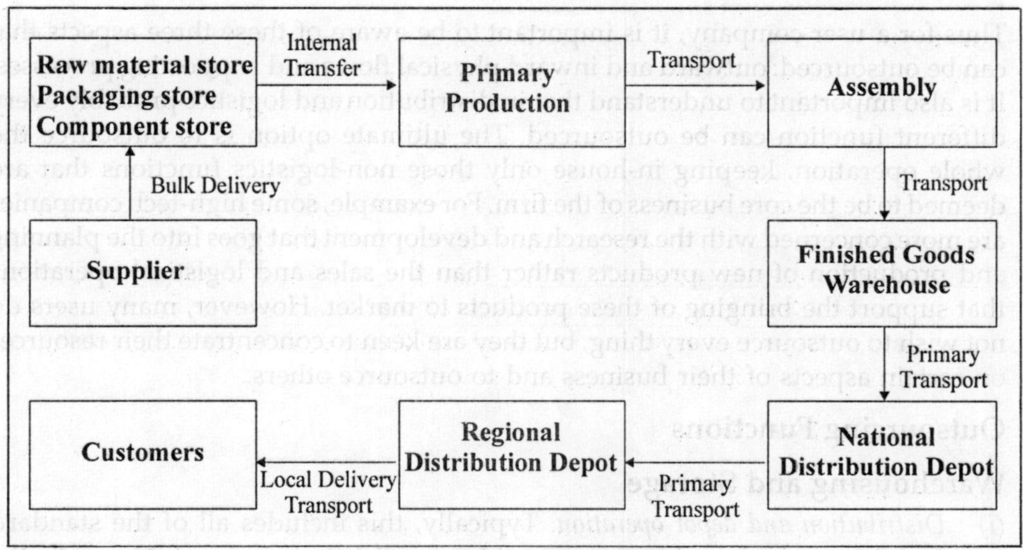

Functions to be Outsourced

Many companies so not actually fulfill all of the many physical logistics functions that are represented in the diagram, but some fast-moving consumer goods (FMCG) manufacturers fit into this model. The key point to appreciate is that any of these functions could be outsourced to a third-party contractor.

In addition to the physical logistics functions that are shown in the figure above, there are also many supporting processes for these functions which could also be outsourced, not forgetting any opportunities to outsource reverse-logistics flows of product. Thus, decisions to outsource should cover the three main alternatives:

- Physical logistics/delivery operations;
- Logistics processes;
- Reverse-logistics flows.

These broad aspects will be broken down further and further discussed in detail. One example, however, is the process of customers or end users ordering goods. This might include the following elements, some or all of which might be outsourced:

- Order receipt;
- Telesales;
- Credit control;
- Customer enquiries;
- Stock availability;
- Stock allocation.

Thus for a user company, it is important to be aware of these three aspects that can be outsourced: outward and inward physical flows and supporting processes. It is also important to understand that in distribution and logistics probably every different function can be outsourced. The ultimate option is to outsource the whole operation, keeping in-house only those non-logistics functions that are deemed to be the core business of the firm. For example, some high-tech companies are more concerned with the research and development that goes into the planning and production of new products rather than the sales and logistical operations that support the bringing of these products to market. However, many users do not wish to outsource every thing, but they are keen to concentrate their resources on certain aspects of their business and to outsource others.

Outsourcing Functions

Warehousing and Storage

(i) *Distribution and depot operation.* Typically, this includes all of the standard functions to be found in the operation of a distribution depot. Normally the complete set of functions is outsourced, including goods inward, reserve storage, pick, pack and consolidation for delivery. This is because it is difficult to only partially outsource such a physically sensitive operation. However, the boundary between outsourcing and own operation may well concern the asset ownership. Thus, as previously indicated, the ownership fot eh building could be kept in-house while all other assets (people, equipment and so on) might be outsourced or *vice versa.*

(ii) *Excess storage.* This was probably the original form of outsourcing, where externally owned general warehouses were used to store, in particular, goods that could not be stored in a company's own warehouse because of a lack of space. It is typically used if large orders are received or if goods must be stockpiled for a particular event or season.

(iii) *Cross-docking* is often used to enable customer orders to be consolidated from goods that are sourced from a number of different locations. As physical deliveries from these sources occur, orders are immediately assembled and on completion the final customer deliveries are made. These operations use a lot of physical space and need to be carefully co-ordinated for both in-bound and out-bound movements. Some third-party companies have the facilities and expertise to undertake this.

(iv) *Transhipment.* This is similar to cross-docking, but trans-shipment often refers to the sorting and onward delivery of ready-picked orders. Some third-party providers operate satellite depots in rural or geographically peripheral areas that can collect ready-picked small orders from different companies' distribution depots and then tranship these at their satellite depots to provide consolidated deliveries to local delivery points.

(v) *Break bulk.* Examples of break bulk operations are where containers or full vehicle loads are received from abroad for final delivery in a country. The loads are broken down into individual orders by the operator and then dispatched as required to the appropriate delivery points. This might for inward bound raw materials for company's manufacturing sites, or for finished goods that need to be delivered to retailers or end users.

Stock and Inventory

(i) *Inventory management.* Linked very closely to the storage operations previously described, this includes the additional responsibility of the management of all the stock and inventory that is held, covering elements such as stock control, stock replenishment, stock rotation, obsolescence and other related activities.

(ii) *Specific stock responsibility.* Many companies like to have full control and vision of their finished goods inventory, but there are situations when the control and management of certain types of inventory can be outsourced. Good examples are spares inventory, packaging and unit loads.

Transport

(i) *Primary transport (trunking, linw-haul).* The focus on primary transport is often one of cost reduction. It is seldom regarded as an activity that 'adds value' to an operation because there is no direct link to the final customer or retail store. Primary transport is all about moving the product at minimum cost, which generally involves using as large a vehicle as possible and making sure that the vehicle is filled to capacity. These movements usually consist of delivery to a single drop point.

(ii) *Secondary transport.* Usually involves direct contact with the customer or end user. These are, therefore, what are known as 'customer facing' logistics operations and they can be an important part of the customer service element of logistics strategy. As such, cost reduction is not the main operational criterion as it is with primary transport. Many customers have very restricted delivery windows (the time in which delivery may be made). This makes the accurate scheduling of secondary vehicle very important. Service is usually critical. In particular, inventory reduction in retail stores and the increase of store selling space and elimination of stock rooms make timely delivery essential.

Secondary transport operations are thus both service and cost-sensitive and require particular skills for planning and management, as well as some fairly substantial financial investment. For these reasons, most companies now outsource their secondary transport operations to medium and large third-party service providers.

(iii) *Collections.* Normally, distribution operations are planned and designed to provide a one-way flow of physical product that is delivered to customers. Vehicles, unit loads, handling equipment, schedules and the like may be inappropriate for items to be returned or collected via the out-bound delivery system. Thus many types of collection operations (damaged product, packaging, unit loads) are often outsourced.

(iv) *Fleet management.* Many companies see the day-to-day management of a vehicle fleet as a specialist technical operation – sometimes described as mobile asset management. Thus, although they may schedule and manage the vehicles and drivers to give them control of their delivery operations, they may choose to outsource the management of the fleet (maintenance, legal responsibility and so on) to a third-party company.

(v) *Contract hire.* A classic opportunity for third-party providers is the provision of vehicles and/or drivers to supplement own-account fleets when they require additional resources. This might be to cover breakdowns, holidays, seasonal demand increases and similar factors.

Packaging and Unitization

(i) *Packaging.* There are various opportunities for companies to outsource packaging operations. These are normally where special requirements make it difficult for the packaging to be undertaken in-house. A typical example is packaging product for export, which might be undertaken more cost effectively of a specialist export contractor is used.

(ii) *Labeling and product preparation.* Many products are delivered to retailers from their suppliers without specific price information as an integral part of each individual item. This information often needs to be added before the goods are displayed in store. Some products may also need to be presented in a special selling unit in the store. Although shop staff can undertake this work, there has been a move to ensure that all products are sales-ready before they enter the store; the idea is to simplify the store operation so that all effort is concentrated on selling items rather than preparation work. Thus, many companies (and this may be the suppliers or the retailer) now outsource these type of operation to a third party.

(iii) *Unit loads.* For operations that use a large number of unit loads (pallets, roll-cages and the like), it is important to have close management and control. This is often for reasons of both cost and supply. The cost reasons are to minimize costs by monitoring units and reusing them as often as possible (thus keeping capital costs down by avoiding the need for the regular purchase of new units). Supply reasons are to ensure a constant availability of units at the end of the production process. This is an operation that is sometimes outsourced.

For Discussion

1. What do you understand by the term outsourcing? Why do companies outsource?
2. Trace the evolution of the concept of outsourcing.
3. Discuss the role of 3PL service providers in outsourcing.
4. What are the critical factors that drive the growth of logistics outsourcing?
5. Describe the functions of SCM that are outsourced?

Materials Handling

The handling of products is a key to warehouse productivity for several important reasons. First, the relative number of labour hours required to perform material handling creates a vulnerability to any reduction in the output rate per labour hour. Warehousing is typically more sensitive to labour productivity than manufacturing since material handling is highly labour-intensive.

Second, the nature of warehouse material handling is limited in terms of direct benefits gained by improved information technology. While computerization has introduced new technologies and capabilities, the preponderance of material handling requires significant manual input.

Third, until recently, warehouse material handling has not been managed on an integrated basis with other logistical activities, nor has it received a great deal of top management concern. Finally, automation technology capable of reducing material handling labour is only now beginning to reach full potential.

Within the warehouse system, material handling is the prime consumer of labour. The application of labour to product selection and handling represents one of logistics highest personnel cost components. The opportunity to reduce this labour intensity and improve productivity lies with emerging handling technologies. In logistics, the primary emphasis is placed on material and product in-bound and out-bound flows rather than inventory storage. The warehouse represents the primary arena for material handling operations. Therefore, warehouse design is an integral aspect of overall handling efficiency and is also of vital concern in obtaining increased labour productivity.

First, this chapter introduces issues related to managing the warehouse in terms of handling and storage requirements. Handling requirements are discussed as they pertain to receiving, in-storage handling, and shipping. Storage requirements are presented for both planned and extended storage.

Next, the chapter provides an overview of material handling in terms of basic to special requirements. Degrees of automation are discussed along with levels of flexibility. Finally, the chapter describes how warehouse design and operations affect material handling. It focuses on considerations for receiving, storage, shipping, and order selection. The operations discussion emphasizes the activities and the options for material-handling automation.

Managing the Warehouse Resource

The warehouse contains materials, parts, and finished goods on the move. Operating procedures consist of breaking bulk and regrouping merchandise in accordance with customer requirements. The objective is to efficiently move large quantities of inventory into, and specific customer orders out of, the warehouse. The ideal arrangement would be for products to arrive and depart the warehouse during a single working day.

This section describes basic handling and storage requirements, discusses alternative material-handling technologies, and presents the steps to plan a warehouse.

The functions performed in a warehouse are classified as movement and storage. Movement is emphasized; storage is secondary. Within these two broad categories, movement is divided into three activities and storage into two activities.

Handling Requirements

The primary handling objective in a warehouse is to sort in-bound shipments according to precise customer requirements. The three handling activities are receiving, in-storage handling, and shipping. Each is discussed below:

(1) Receiving

Merchandise and materials typically arrive at the warehouse in larger quantities than when they depart. The first handling activity required is unloading the transportation vehicle. In most warehouses, unloading is manual. Limited automated and mechanized methods have been developed that are capable of adapting to varying product characteristics. Generally, one or two people unload a shipment. The product is hand-stacked on pallets or slip sheets to form a unit load for movement efficiency. In some cases, conveyors are employed to unload more rapidly. Larger types of merchandise may be unloaded directly from the car or truck to be moved into the warehouse. Containerized or unit-load shipments dramatically reduce unloading time.

(2) In-storage Handling

In-storage handling consists of all movement within a warehouse facility. Following product receipt, it is necessary to transfer merchandise within the warehouse to position it for storage or order selection. Finally, when an order is received, it is necessary to accumulate the required products and to transport them to a shipping area. The two types of in-storage handling are transfer and selection.

There are at least two and sometimes three transfer movements required within a typical warehouse. The merchandise is first moved into the building and placed at a designated storage location. The inbound movement is handled by forklift trucks when pallets or slip-sheets are used or other mechanical traction for larger unit loads. A second internal movement may be required prior to order assembly depending on the operating procedures of the warehouse. When products are required for order selection, they are transferred to an order selection or picking area. When the merchandise is physically large or bulky, such as a stove or washing machine, this second movement may be omitted. In the final transfer, the assortment of products required for a customer shipment is moved from the warehouse to the shipping dock.

Selection is the primary function of the warehouse. The selection process groups materials, parts and products into customer orders. It is typical for one section of the warehouse to be established as a selection area to minimize travel distance. The typical selection process is co-ordinated by a computerized control system. The primary focus for warehouse automation is the selection process. Various forms of automation are discussed later in this chapter.

(3) Shipping

Shipping consists of checking and loading orders onto transportation vehicles. As in receiving, shipping is manually performed in most systems. Shipping with units loads is becoming increasingly popular because considerable time can be saved in vehicle loading. A unit load consists of grouped products, while a dead-stack or floor-stack load consists of boxes loaded directly from the floor. A checking operation is required when merchandise changes ownership as a result of shipment. Checking generally is limited to carton counts, but in some situations a piece-by-piece check for proper brand, size, and so on, is necessary to ensure that all items ordered by the customer are being shipped.

Storage Requirements

The warehouse performs two types of storage:

1. Planned
2. Extended

Planned Storage

As previously noted, primary emphasis is placed on product flow in the warehouse. Regardless of inventory turnover velocity, all goods received must be stored for at least a short time. Storage for basic inventory replenishment is referred to as planned storage. Its duration varies in different logistical systems depending on performance cycles. Planned storage must provide sufficient inventory to fulfil the warehouse's function within the logistical system.

Extended Storage

Extended storage, a somewhat misleading term, refers to inventory in excess of that planned for normal warehouse operation. In some special situations, storage may be required for several months prior to customer shipment. A warehouse may be used for extended storage for other reasons as well. In controlling and measuring warehouse performance, care should be taken to separate inventory turnover according to the type of storage used.

The basic nature of some products, such as seasonal items, requires that they be stored to await demand or to spreadsupply across time. Extensive storage needed to match supply and demand results in very little turnover. One justification of warehousing is to accommodate seasonality in the logistical system. Other extended storage rationales include erratic demand items, product conditioning, speculative purchases, and discounts.

When a product has erratic demand fluctuations, it may be necessary to carry additional supplies or safety stocks to satisfy customer service standards. An example is air-conditioners. Because air-conditioners are expensive items, dealers prefer to carry small inventories. When a period of high temperature begins, manufacturers have limited time to distribute additional units.

Product conditioning is sometimes required (such as to ripen bananas), and this can be accomplished at the warehouse. Food distribution centres typically have ripening rooms to hold items until they reach peak quality.

The warehouse may also contain goods purchased for speculative purposes. The degree to which this activity takes place will depend on the specific materials and industries involved. For example, it is not unusual to store grain for this reason.

The warehouse often is used to realize special discounts. Early purchase discounts may justify extended storage. The purchasing manager may be able to realize a substantial reduction during a specific period of the year. Under such conditions, the warehouse holds inventories in excess of planned storage. Manufacturers of fertilizer, toys, and lawn furniture often attempt to shift the warehousing burden to customers by offering off-season storage allowances.

Basic Handling Considerations

Material handling in the logistics system is concentrated in and around the warehouse facility. A basic difference exists in the handling of bulk materials and master cartons. Bulk handling is a situation where protective packaging at the master carton level is unnecessary. Specialized handling equipment is required for bulk unloading, such as for solids, fluids, or gaseous materials. The following discussion focuses on master carton handling within the logistical system.

Over the years a variety of guidelines have been suggested to assist management in the design of material handling systems. These are representative:

1. Equipment for handling and storage should be as standardized as possible.
2. When in motion, the system should be designed to provide maximum continuous product flow.
3. Investment should be in handling rather than stationary equipment.
4. Handling equipment should be utilized to the maximum extent possible.
5. In handling equipment selection, the ratio of deadweight to payload should be minimized.
6. Whenever practical, gravity flow should be incorporated in system design.

Handling systems are classified as:

1. Mechanized;
2. Semi-automated;
3. Automated; and
4. Information-directed.

A combination of labour and handling equipment is utilized in mechanized systems to facilitate receiving, processing, and/or shipping. Generally, labour constitutes a high percentage of overall cost in mechanized handling.

Automated systems, in contrast, attempt to minimize labour as much as practical by substituting capital investment in equipment. An automated handling system may be applied to any of the basic handling requirements depending on the situation.

When selected handling requirements are performed, using automated equipment and the remainder of the handling is completed on a mechanized basis, the system is referred to as semi-automated.

An information-directed system uses computers to maximize control over mechanized handling equipment. Mechanized handling systems are the most common. However, the use of semi-automated and an automated system is rapidly increasing. As noted earlier, one factor contributing to low logistical productivity is that information-directed handling has yet to achieve its full potential.

Mechanized Systems

Mechanized systems employ a wide range of handling equipment. The types of equipment most commonly used are:

1. Forklift trucks;
2. Walkie-rider Pallet trucks;
3. Towlines;
4. Tractor-trailer devices;
5. Conveyors;

6. Carousels; and
7. Pick-to-light systems.

1. Forklift Trucks

Forklift trucks can move loads of master cartons both horizontally and vertically. A pallet or slip sheet forms a platform upon which master cartons are stacked. A slip sheet consists of a thin sheet of material such as solid fiber or corrugated paper. Slip sheets are an inexpensive alternative to pallets and are ideal for situations when product is handled only a few times. A forklift truck normally transports a maximum of two unit loads (two pallets) at a time. However, forklifts are not limited to unit-load handling. Skids or boxes may also be transported depending on the nature of the product.

Many types of forklift trucks are available. High-stacking trucks, capable of up to 40 feet of vertical movement, pallet-less side-clamp versions and trucks capable of operating in aisles as narrow as 56 inches, can be found in logistical warehouses. Particular attention to narrow-aisle forklift trucks has increased in recent years, as warehouses seek to increase rack storage density and overall storage capacity. The forklift truck is not economical for long-distance horizontal movement because of the high ratio of labour per unit of transfer. Therefore, forklifts are most effectively utilized in shipping and receiving, and to place merchandise in high cube storage. The two most common power sources for forklifts are propane gas and electricity Many forklift operations are utilizing new forms of communication technology to increase their productivity. For example, radio frequency data communication (RFDC) is utilized to speed load put away and retrieval assignments for forklift truck operators in warehousing, manufacturing, and distribution operations. Instead of following handwritten or pre-printed instructions, workers receive their assignments through either handheld or vehicle-mounted RF terminals. Use of RF technology provides real-time communication capability to central data processing systems, and when combined with bar code scanning of cartons and pallets, it allows forklift truck operators to receive and update item status inquiries, material orders and movements, and inventory adjustments.

2. Walkie-Rider Pallet Trucks

Walkie-rider pallet trucks provide a low-cost, effective method of general material-handling utility. Typical applications include loading and unloading, order selection and accumulation, and shuttling loads over longer transportation distances throughout the warehouse. Electricity is the typical power source.

3. Towlines

Towlines consist of either in-floor or overhead-mounted drag devices. They are utilized in combination with four-wheel trailers on a continuous power basis. The main advantage of a towline is continuous movement. However, such handling devices do not have the flexibility of forklift trucks. The most common application of towlines is for order selection within the warehouse. Order selectors place merchandise on a four-wheel trailer, which is then towed to the shipping dock. A number of automated decoupling devices have been perfected that route trailers from the main line to selected shipping docks.

A point of debate involves the relative merits of in-floor and overhead towline installation. In-floor installation is costly to modify and difficult to maintain from a housekeeping viewpoint. Overhead installation is more flexible, but unless the warehouse floor is absolutely level, the line may jerk the front wheels of the trailers off the ground and risk product damage.

4. Tow Tractor with Trailers

A tow tractor with trailer consists of a driver guided power unit towing a number of individual four-wheel "trailers" that hold several palletized loads. The typical size of the trailers is 4 by 8 feet. The tow tractor with trailer, like the towline, is typically used to support order selection. The main advantage of tow tractor with trailers is flexibility. It is not as economical as the towline because it requires greater labour participation and is often idle.

Considerable advancements have been made in automated-guided vehicle systems (AGVS). These are discussed under semi-automated material handling.

5. Conveyors

Conveyors are used widely in shipping and receiving operations and form the basic handling device for a number of order selection systems.

Conveyors are classified according to:

(1) Power;

(2) Gravity; and

(3) Roller or belt movement.

In power systems, the conveyor uses a drive chain from either above or below. Considerable conveyor flexibility is sacrificed in such power configuration installations.

Gravity and roller or belt systems permit the basic installation to be modified with minimum difficulty. Portable gravity-style roller conveyors are often used at the warehouse for loading and unloading and, in some cases, are transported on over-the-road trailers to assist in unloading at the destination.

6. Carousels

A carousel operates on a different concept than most other mechanized handling equipment. It delivers the desired item to the order selector by using a series of bins mounted on an oval track. The entire carousel rotates and brings the desired bin to the operator. A wide variety of carousels are available. The rationale behind carousel systems is to shrink order selection labour requirements by reducing walking length/ paths and time. Carousels, particularly modern stackable or multi-tiered systems, also significantly reduce storage floor requirements.

7. Pick-to-Light Systems

Technology has also been applied to carousel systems in an application known as "pick-to-light". In these systems, order selectors pick designated items and put them directly into cartons from carousel bins or conveyors. A series of lights or a "light tree" in front of each pick location indicates the number of items to pick from each location. The light system may also be used to indicate when a carton is ready to move on. In systems where an item is picked to fill multiple orders, "soft bars" show the order selector how many items are needed in a carton, since each carton typically represents a separate order. Some carousel systems also utilize computer-generated pick lists and computer-directed carousel rotation to further increase selection productivity. These systems are referredto as "paperless picking" because no paperwork exists to slow down employee efforts.

The types of mechanized material-handling equipment discussed are basic samples of the wide range available for use. Most systems combine different types of handling devices. For example, forklift trucksmay be used for vertical movements while tow tractor with trailers and walkie-rider pallet trucks are used for horizontal transfers.

Semi-automated Handling

The semi-automated system supplements a mechanized system by automating specific handling requirements. Thus, the semi-automated warehouse is a mixture of mechanized and automated handling. Typical equipments utilized in semi-automated warehouses are automated-guided vehicle systems, computerized sorting, robotics, and various forms of live racks.

1. Automated-Guided Vehicle

The automated-guided vehicle system (AGVS) performs the same type of handling function as a mechanized tow tractor with trailer or rider pallet truck. The essential difference is that an AGVS does not require an operator. It is automatically routed and positioned at the destination without operator intervention.

Typical AGVS equipment relies on an optical or magnetic guidance system. In the optical application, tape is placed on the warehouse floor, and the equipment is guided by a light beam that focuses on the guide path. A magnetic AGVS follows an energized wire installed in the floor. The primary advantage is the elimination of a driver. Newer AGVs use video and information technology to follow paths without the need of fixed tracks. Contemporary AGVS are smaller, simpler, and more flexible than their predecessor systems of the 1980s.

2. Sortation

Automated sortation devices are typically used in combination with conveyors. As products are selected in warehouse and conveyed out, they must be sorted to specific shipment docks. In order to operate the automated sortation systems, the master carton must have a distinguishing code. These codes are read by optical scanning devices and automatically routed to the desired location. Most controllers are able to be programmed to permit a customized rate of flow through the system to meet changing requirements.

Automated sortation provides two primary benefits. The first is obvious reduction in labour and the second benefit is a significant increase in speed and accuracy.

High speed sortation system can divert and align packages at rate exceeding one package per second. In these systems, packages are diverted to the desired destination and can be positioned to accommodate unit loading.

3. Robotics

The robot is a human-like machine that can be programmed by microprocessors to perform one or a series of activities. The appeal of robotics lies in the ability to program the robot to function as an expert system capable of implementing decision logic in the handling process. The popularity of robotics resulted from their widespread adoption in the automotive industry during the early 1980s to replace selected manual tasks. However, a warehouse provides a different type of challenge than a typical manufacturing plant. In warehousing, the goal is to accommodate the exact merchandise requirements of a customer's order. Thus, warehouse specification can vary extensively from one customer order to the next and results in far less routine activities than typically found in manufacturing.

The primary use of robotics in warehousing is to break down and build unit loads. In the breakdown process, the robot is programmed to recognize stocking patterns and place products in the desired position on a conveyor belt. The use of robots to build unit loads is essentially the reverse operation.

Another prime potential use of robotics in warehousing occurs in environments where humans find it difficult to function. Examples include high noise areas and extreme temperature environments like cold-storage freezers.

Significant potential exists to use robots in a mechanized warehouse to perform selected functions. The capability to incorporate artificial intelligence–in addition to their speed, dependability, and accuracy makes robotics an attractive alternative to traditional manual handling methods.

4. Live Racks

Live Racks Storage Design, in which product flows forward to the desired selection position, is a commonly used device to reduce manual labour in warehouses. The typical live rack contains roller conveyors and is constructed for rear loading. To complete the installation, the rear of the rack is elevated higher than the front, causing a gravity flow forward. When unit loads are removed from the front, all other loads in that specific rack automatically move forward.

Live racks are a prime example of incorporating gravity flow into material - handling system design. The use of the live rack replaces the need to use fork trucks to reposition unit loads. A significant advantage of this form of storage is the automatic rotation of product that results from rear loading of a live rack. Rear loading facilitates "first-in, first-out" management of inventory. Applications of gravity flow racks are extremely diverse. For example, such racks are utilized to "stage", or store and position, fresh biscuits or bread for bakery manufacturers on individual pallet loads in preparation for shipping. Flow-rack staging is also typically utilized for automotive seats in JIT systems.

Automated Handling

For several decades the concept of automated handling has been long on potential and short on accomplishment. Initial efforts directed toward automated handling concentrated on order selection systems at the master carton level. Recently, emphasis has switched to Automated High-rise Storage and Retrieval Systems (ASRS). Each is discussed in turn after a brief review of automated handling concepts.

Potential of Automation

The appeal of automation is that it substitutes capital investment in equipment for labour required in mechanized handling systems. In addition to using less direct labour, an automated system operates faster and more accurately. Its shortcomings are the high degree of required capital investment and the complex nature of development and application.

To date, most automated systems have been custom-designed and constructed for each application. The six guidelines previously noted for selection of mechanized handling systems are not applicable to automated systems. For example, storage equipment in an automated system is an integral part of the handling capability and can represent as much as 50 percent of the total investment. The ratio of deadweight to payload has little relevance in an automated handling application.

Although computers play an important part in all handling systems, they are essential to automated systems. The computer provides programming of the automated selection equipment and is used to interface the warehouse with the remainder of the logistical system. The warehouse control system is vastly different in automated handling. One factor that prohibited rapid development of automated systems was the high cost of minicomputers. Breakthroughs in microprocessors have eliminated this barrier.

Order Selection Systems

Initially, automation was applied to master carton selection or order assembly in the warehouse. Because of high labour intensity in order selection, the basic objective was to integrate mechanized and automated handling into a total system.

The initial concept was as follows. An automated selection device was preloaded. The device itself consisted of a series of racks stacked vertically. Merchandise was loaded from the rear and permitted to flow forward in the "live" rack on gravity conveyors until stopped by a rack door. Between or down the middle of the racks, power conveyors created merchandise flow line, with several flow lines positioned above each other, one at each level of rack doors.

Upon receipt of an order, the information system that controlled distribution operations generated sequenced instructions to trip the rack doors, which allowed the desired merchandise to flow forward onto the powered conveyors. The conveyors, in turn, transported merchandise to an order-packing area for shipment. Product was often loaded sequentially so that it could be unloaded in the sequence in which it would be used.

When compared to modem applications, these initial attempts at automated package handling were highly inefficient. Considerable labour was required during the merchandise input and output phase and the automated equipment were expensive. Applications were limited to merchandise of extremely high value or situations where working conditions justified such investment. For example, these initial systems were adopted widely for frozen food order selection.

Substantial advancements have been made recently in automated selection of case goods. The handling of fast-moving products in master cartons can be fully automated from the point of merchandise receipt to placement in over-the-road trailers. Such systems use an integrated network of power and gravity conveyors linking power-motivated live storage. The entire system is controlled by a computer coupled with the inventory and order processing control systems of the warehouse facility.

Upon arrival, merchandise is automatically routed to the live storage position, and inventory records are updated. Upon order receipt, merchandise is pre-cubed to vehicle size and scheduled for selection. At the appropriate time, all merchandise is selected in loading sequence and automatically transported by conveyor to the loading dock. In most situations, the first manual handling of the merchandise within the warehouse occurs when it is stacked into the transport vehicle.

The solution of the input/output interface problem and the development of sophisticated control systems resulted in a highly effective and efficient package handling system. Such systems are common today.

The Automated High-Rise Storage and Retrieval System (ASRS)

The concept of automated unit-load handling using high-rise storage has received considerable attention recently. The high-rise concept of handling is fully automated from receiving to shipping. Four main components constitute the basic system: storage racks, storage and retrieval equipment, input/output systems, and control systems.

The name high-rise derives from the physical appearance of the vertical storage rack. It is made of steel and can be up to 120 feet high. When one considers that the stacking height of palletized cartons in a mechanized handling system is normally 20 feet, the potential of high-rise storage is clear.

The typical high-rise facility consists of rows of storage racks, separated by aisles running from 120 to over 800 feet. Primary storage and retrieval is completed within these aisles. The storage and retrieval machine travels back and forth in an aisle. Its primary purpose is to move products in and out of storage. A variety of storage and retrieval equipment is available. Most machines require guidance at the top and bottom to provide the vertical stability necessary for high-speed horizontal movement and vertical hoisting. Horizontal speeds range from 300 to 400 feet per minute (fpm) with hoisting speeds of up to 100 fpm or more.

The initial function of the storage and retrieval equipment is to reach the desired storage position rapidly. A second function is to deposit or retract a load of merchandise. For the most part, load deposit and retraction are achieved by shuttle tables, which can enter and exit from the rack at speeds up to 100 fpm. Since the shuttle table moves only a few feet, it must be able to accelerate and stop rapidly.

In some installations, the storage and retrieval machine can be moved between aisles by transfer cars. Numerous transfer arrangements and layouts have been developed. Such transfer units may be dedicated or non-dedicated. The dedicated transfer car is always stationed at the end of the aisle in which the storage and retrieval equipment is working. The non-dedicated transfer car works on a number of aisles and retrieves product on a scheduled basis to achieve maximum equipment utilization. The decision as to whether or not to include aisle-to-aisle transfer in a high-rise storage system rests with the economics of throughput rate and number of aisles included in the overall system.

The input/output system in high-rise storage is concerned with moving loads to and from the rack area. Two types of movement are involved. First, loads must be transported from receiving docks or production lines to the storage area. Second, within the immediate peripheral area of the racks, loads must be positioned for entry or exit. The greatest potential handling problem is in the peripheral area. A common practice is to assign pickup and discharge stations capable of staging an adequate supply of loads to each aisle, in order to fully utilize the storage and retrieval equipment. For maximum input/output performance, the normal procedure requires that different stations for transfer of inbound and outbound loads be assigned to the same aisle. The pickup and discharge stations are linked to the handling systems that transfer merchandise to and from the high-rise storage area.

The control system in high-rise storage is similar to the automated order selection systems described earlier. In the case of high-rise storage, considerable sophistication in programming and control measurement is required to achieve maximum equipment utilization and rapid command cycles. Recent advancements in the speed and cost of microprocessors have resulted in computers being fully dedicated to the ASRS.

In addition to scheduling arrivals and location assignments, the control system handles inventory and stock rotation. When orders are received, the command control system directs the retrieval of specified unit loads. From the outbound delivery stations, the unit load flows by power and gravity conveyor to the appropriate shipping dock. While retrieval and outbound delivery are being accomplished, all the paperwork necessary to initiate product shipment is completed.

An innovative application of ASRS technology is found in the United States automotive industry. In Toledo, Ohio, the Chrysler Corporation manufactures vehicle bodies for both pickup trucks and jeeps at one plant. As manufacturing is completed, two SR machines pick up each body in sequence and load it onto canvas-sided over-the-road trailers to transport the vehicle bodies to a second Chrysler plant four miles away, where final assembly is completed. At the second plant, two SR machines take over to co-ordinate the JIT staging and delivery of the vehicle bodies to the appropriate assembly lines for each model.

These examples are typical of ASRS currently operating in a variety of industries. They are designed to increase material handling productivity by providing maximum storage density per square foot of floor space and to minimize the direct labour required in handling. The highly controlled nature of the system combines reliable pilferage-free and damage-free handling with extremely accurate control.

Information-Directed Systems

The concept of information-directed handling is relatively new and is still in the testing process. The idea is appealing because it combines the control of automated handling with the operational flexibility of mechanized systems.

The information-directed system uses mechanized handling equipment. The typical source of power is the forklift truck. In layout and design, the warehouse facility is essentially the same as any mechanized operation. The difference is that all fork-truck movements are directed and monitored by the command of a microprocessor.

In operation, all required handling movements are fed into the computer for analysis and equipment assignment. A computer is utilized to analyze handling requirements and to assign equipment in such a way that direct movement is maximized and deadhead movement is minimized. Work assignments are provided to individual forklift trucks by terminals located on the truck. Communication between the computer and the truck uses radio frequency (RF) waves with antennae located on the forklifts and high up in the warehouse. Less exotic applications use computer-generated movement printouts picked up at selected terminal locations throughout the warehouse. Information-directed handling has noteworthy potential in that selected benefits of automation can be achieved without substantial capital investment.

Information-directed systems can also increase productivity by tracking material handler performance and allowing compensation to be based on activity level. The main drawback is the flexibility of work assignments. As a specific forklift truck proceeds during a work period, it may be involved in loading or unloading several vehicles, selecting many orders, and completing several handling assignments. The wide variety of work assignments increases the complexity of work direction and can decrease performance accountability.

Special Handling Considerations

As expected, the primary objective of material movement is for merchandise to flow in an orderly and efficient manner from manufacturer to point of sale. However, material handling systems must also be capable of handling reverse merchandise flows within the logistical network.

For a variety of reasons, merchandise may be recalled by or returned to a manufacturer. Normally such return flows are not of sufficient quantity or regularity to justify mechanized movement. Therefore, the only convenient method for processing reverse flows of merchandise is manual handling. To the degree practical, material-handling design should consider the cost and service impact of reverse logistics. Such flows often involve pallets, cartons, and packaging materials, as well as damaged, dated, or excess merchandise. In addition, ecological pressure to eliminate non-disposable containers will increase the quantity of returnable containers moving through the logistical system. Overall logistical systems design in many industries will require the ability to handle two-way movement efficiently.

Best Practices in Material Handling and Put-away

Most distribution professionals understand that it is not enough to know how their company performs year over year; they must also continue to improve their performance in order to stay ahead of their competition. Today's companies are in an environment where their customers continue to demand more - instant availability, error free service, and customized products - all at a lower cost. That is why many professionals look to adopt best practices as a way to drive improvement.

Here we review key elements of the material handling and put-away processes. Material handling and the put-away function encompass all the processes that support the movement of material from the receiving area to the point of use or the storage location. Some of the common practices that best-in-class companies use, within their warehouse, to drive high productivity and lower costs shall be highlighted here.

Material handling — managing the movement of products throughout the warehouse — can be as basic as using lift trucks and pallet jacks and as complex as employing fully automated systems that are made up of customized conveyor systems, automated guided vehicle systems (AGVS) and automated storage systems.

Material handling can be enhanced when warehouse automation is used in line with well thought out put-away processes. Best practice companies put in place flexible and efficient material handling processes that use appropriate automation and technology tools to meet the needs of their current and forecasted business. Common material handling automation includes radio frequency equipment in fork trucks and portable/hand held RF devices that direct warehouse personnel, automated conveyor systems with sorters and diverters and automated storage and retrieval systems (AS/RS). Let's take a closer look at some of these automation options.

RF equipment: Employing RF terminals in lift trucks and portable RF devices, which can be carried by employees, will boost productivity while reducing data entry errors. These devices when integrated with the warehouse management system (WMS) can send product movement tasks to the employees and give information about the product that needs to be moved. Typically, systems are designed to work with bar coded labels or RFID tags.

Automated conveyor systems: An automated conveyor system with sorters and diverters will route product to the appropriate put-away zones, reducing travel time and handling. Productivity and labour costs can be significantly improved by automation if the transit time from receiving areas to storage zones is considerable or when product is moved and stored in case-size lots.

Automated storage/retrieval systems: AS/RS benefits might include maximized storage space, increased put-away productivity, reduced warehouse labour and improvements to put-away accuracy. AS/RS technology is especially effective when working with narrow aisles and extremely high racks found in some larger high volume distribution centres (DC). While AS/RS solutions are capital intensive, they can be tremendously cost-effective in the correct applications.

Put-away Practices

Put-away is the process of moving material from the dock and transporting it to a warehouse's storage, replenishment, or pick area. Best-practice companies manage the put-away area by calculating resource and space requirements based on expected receipts and current backlogs. Best practice is to put away product the same day it is received, because not doing so affects space, causes congestion, increases transaction errors, and makes product more susceptible to damage. In a busy warehouse, it is easy to let product put-away fall behind other tasks such as picking, replenishment, shipping, and loading. But pulling away resources from put-away tasks can affect fill rates by not having product in pick racks. This can bring about congestion in staging areas that overflow into aisles. Delaying put-away may also result in product damage as the merchandise is moved, again and again, to make way for higher priority receipts. Proper staffing of the put-away team will support down stream processes of picking and shipping, and in the long run lead to better customer order fill rates.

The put-away process is typically managed by one of, or a mix of, the following methods; staging product from the receiving area, based on the purchase order, based on the part number, or based on a put-away zone or by using direct delivery (put-away) to the storage location. The most efficient practice is to put-away directly from receipt to its final location and is often the primary method used in best practice companies. This process uses the least space for staging and product is handled less and ready for use sooner. Direct put-away programs require a more sophisticated WMS system that has the ability to assign locations from an ASN or upon receipt to the dock. Assigning locations and using direct put-away can be optimized by the use of automated conveyor systems that are capable of sorting and diverting materials by zone and location.

Best practice companies also use their warehouse management system (WMS) to manage travel time from receiving to storage areas, pick locations and replenishment areas; so that the best put-away route can be selected. The end result is put-away travel paths that are sequenced based on the shortest route for the product in the load, with reduced aisle conflicts and congestion. Many WMS programs also support task interleaving; most best-practice companies make use of this capability in their warehouses to reduce non-productive travel time. The put-away process is critical and significantly affects overall warehouse efficiency.

Best-practice companies identify products using some form of bar code or RFID label. Product identification labels, zone or location labels and pallet license plates should all be utilized in the put-away process. Both bar code and RFID can work equally as well to identify product, with barcode labels far more common in today's warehouses. The advantage of RFID is that it works better in harsh environments, it has a fast read from almost any position, and the tag can hold a lot of information that can be changed as the product flows through the warehouse.

Barcode labels however have been used for years, successfully, to identify and manage the flow of materials in the warehouse.

Many companies have some type of process to manage expedited materials once they have been received. In a manual process the product might be flagged as "hot" and placed in a special "expedite" staging area, so that the put-away team can move the product to the required location as quickly as possible. This can be a hit or miss arrangement and is less than effective. In the Best-Practice Companies, the cross-docking process is managed by the WMS system. Cross-docking, as it relates to put-away and material handling, is the process of moving specific products to support an open order or replenishment request, with minimal handling and delay. The WMS system flags the product for cross-docking by matching it to an open order or replenishment requirement, at the time of receipt, or when the advance ship notice (ASN) is received. The product may still end up in a special staging area but the system is keeping track of it and will prioritize it over other material. The task to move the material is sent to the lift truck or hand held RF device for movement directly to the point of use. This is a far more effective system to get priority product moved.

Good housekeeping must be part of any best-in-class warehouse, as best practice processes cannot succeed in a workplace that is cluttered, disorganized, or dirty. Poor workplace conditions lead to waste, product damage, and safety issues; such as extra motion to avoid obstacles, time spent searching for things, delays due to defects, machine failures, or accidents. Establishing basic workplace conditions is an essential first step in creating a safe and productive warehouse environment.

For Discussion

1. What do you understand Materials Handling? What are the primary Materials handling objectives of a warehouse?
2. What is the basis for classification of the Materials Handling System?
3. What are the types of equipment most commonly used in Mechanized Systems?
4. Discuss the use of semi-automated handling in a warehouse.
5. What is the relevance of Automated Handling in modern business?
6. What do you understand by ASRS Systems?

Transportation

Transportation refers to the movement of product from one location to another as it makes its way from the beginning of a supply chain to the customer's hands. Transportation plays a key role in every supply chain because products are rarely produced and consumed in the same location. Transportation is a significant component of the cost most supply chains incur. With the growth in e-commerce and the associated home delivery of products, transportation costs have become even more significant in retailing. From the book industry to the grocery industry, on-line firms are delivering products in small packages to the customer's home instead of full trucks to a retail outlet. As a result, transportation cost is a larger fraction of the delivered cost of products sold on-line.

Transport Functionality and Principles

Transportation is one of the most visible element of logistics operations. As consumers, we are accustomed to seeing trucks and trains moving products or parked at a distribution facility. While this experience provides a good visual understanding of transportation elements, it does not allow the necessary depth of knowledge to understand transportation's role in logistics operations. This foundation is established here by reviewing functionality provided by transportation and the underlying principles of transport operation.

Transport Functionality

Transportation functionality provides two major functions:

1. Product movement; and
2. Product storage.

Product Movement

Whether the product is in the form of materials, components, assemblies, work-in-process, or finished goods, transportation is necessary to move it to the next stage of the manufacturing process or physically closer to the ultimate customer. A primary transportation function is product movement up and down the value chain. Transportation utilizes temporal, financial, and environmental resources, it is important that items be moved only when it truly enhances product value.

The major objective of transportation is to move product from an origin location to a prescribed destination while minimizing temporal, financial, and environmental resource costs. Loss and damage expenses must also be minimized. At the same time, the movement must take place in a manner that meets customer demands regarding delivery performance and shipment information availability.

Product Storage

A less common transportation function is temporary storage. Vehicles make rather expensive storage facilities. However, if the in-transit product requires storage but will be moved again shortly (e.g., in a few days), the cost of unloading and reloading the product in a warehouse may exceed the per unit cost of the product itself. A second method to achieve temporary product storage is diversion. This occurs when an original shipment destination is changed while the delivery is in transit. Traditionally, the telephone was usedto direct diversion strategies. Today, satellite communication between enterprise headquarters and vehicles more efficiently handles the information.

There are two fundamental principles guiding transportation management and operations. They are Economy of scale and Economy of distance.

Economy of scale

It refers to the characteristic that transportation cost per unit of weight decreases when the size of the shipment increases. For example, truckload (TL) shipments (i.e., shipments that utilize the entire vehicle's capacity) cost less per pound than less-than-truckload (L TL) shipments (i.e., shipments that utilize a portion of vehicle capacity). It is also generally true that larger capacity transportation vehicles such as rail or water are less expensive per unit of weight than smaller capacity vehicles such as motor or air. Transportationeconomies of scale exist because fixed expenses associated with moving a load can be spread over the load's weight. As such, a heavier load allows costs to be "spread out", thereby decreasing costs per unit of weight. The fixed expenses include administrative costs of taking the transportation order, time to position the vehicle for loading or unloading, invoicing, and equipment cost.

Economy of distance

It refers to the characteristic that transportation cost per unit of distance decreases as distance increases. For example, a shipment of 800 miles will cost less than two shipments (of the same combined weight) of 400 miles. Transportation economy of distance is also referred to as the tapering principle since rates or charges taper with distance. The rationale for distance economies is similar to that for economies of scale. Specifically, the relatively fixed expense incurred to load and unload the vehicle must be spread over the variable expense per unit of distance. Longer distances allow the fixed expense to be spread over more miles, resulting in lower overall per mile charges.

These principles are important considerations when evaluating alternative transportation strategies or operating practices. The objective is to maximize the size of the load and the distance that it is shipped while still meeting customer service expectations.

Participants in Transportation Decisions

Transport transactions are often influenced by five parties: the shipper (the original party), the consignee (destination party or receiver), the carrier, the government, and the public.

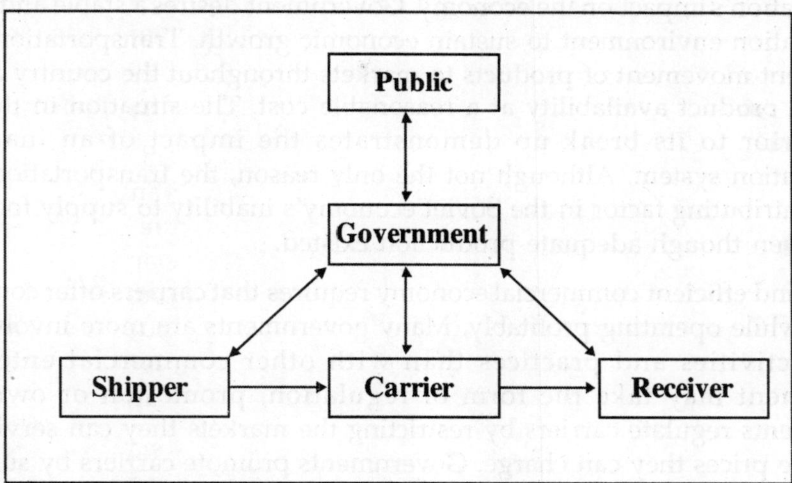

Relationship between the shipper, the consignee, and the public

Above Figure illustrates the relationship between these parties. They may be related by ownership in some situations, such as when company-owned vehicles are used to transport goods between two company locations. In many cases, however, the parties are independently owned and operated. In order to understand the complexity of the transportation environment, it is necessary to review the role and perspective of each party.

Shippers and Consignees

The shipper and consignee have the common objective of moving goods from origin to destination within a prescribed time at the lowest cost. Services include specified pickup and delivery times, predictable transit time, zero loss and damage, as well as accurate and timely exchange of information and invoicing.

Carriers

The carrier, as the intermediary, takes a somewhat different perspective. Carriers desire to maximize their revenue associated with the transaction while minimizing the costs necessary to complete the transaction. The perspective suggests that a carrier wants to charge the highest rate that the shipper (or consignee) will accept and minimize the labour, fuel, and vehicle costs required to move the goods. To achieve this objective, the carrier desires flexibility in pickup and delivery times to allow individual loads to be consolidated into economic moves.

Government

The government maintains a high interest level in the transaction because of transportation's impact on the economy. Government desires a stable and efficient transportation environment to sustain economic growth. Transportation enables the efficient movement of products to markets throughout the country and thus promotes product availability at a reasonable cost. The situation in the Soviet Union prior to its break-up demonstrates the impact of an inadequate transportation system. Although not the only reason, the transportation system was a contributing factor in the Soviet economy's inability to supply food to the market even though adequate production existed.

A stable and efficient commercial economy requires that carriers offer competitive services while operating profitably. Many governments are more involved with carrier activities and practices than with other commercial enterprises. Involvement may take the form of regulation, promotion or ownership. Governments regulate carriers by restricting the markets they can service or by setting the prices they can charge. Governments promote carriers by supporting research and development or by providing rights-of-way such as roadways or air traffic control systems. In countries like the United Kingdom or Germany, some carriers are owned by the government, which maintains absolute control over markets, services, and rates. Such control allows government to have a major influence on the economic success of regions, industries or firms.

The Public

The final participant, the public, is concerned with transportation accessibility, expense and effectiveness, as well as environmental and safety standards. The public ultimately determines the need for transportation by demanding goods from around the world at reasonable prices. While minimizing transportation cost is important to consumers, trade-offs associated with environmental and safety standards also require consideration. The effects of air pollution and oil spills remain a significant transportation issue even though there have been tremendous strides in pollution reduction and consumer safety during the past two decades. The cost of reducing the risk of environmental or vehicle accidents is passed on to consumers, who must collectively judge how much safety is necessary.

The transportation relationship is complex because of the interaction between the parties. This leads to frequent conflicts between parties with micro interest shippers, consignees, and carriers–as well as parties with a macro interest-government and the public. These conflicts have led to duplication, regulation, and restrictions of transportation services.

The success and failure of any business activity is largely dependent on the final travel of outputs from the point of production to the point of final consumption at an economy of scale. There are a lot of transport benefits to an economy, mainly divided in two broad categories, namely; economic and non-economic.

Economic Benefits

1. Transportation makes products available to the final consumer, i.e., it serves not only existing demand, but also stimulates new demand by extending the variety of goods available anywhere and everywhere.
2. It facilitates production by moving different means of production, i.e., raw materials, machines, tools, men etc., to places of production where these are best-suited.
3. It is also considered as a key agency for the promotion of planned development, i.e., regional economic disparities can be removed by way of transport.
4. Transport provides ample opportunity for acceleration of employment and income, which in turn, create demand for consumer goods.

Non-Economic Benefits

Non-economic benefits of transport may be judged by its great contribution towards social, political as well as cultural integration of mass population of any country with different moods, languages, castes, creeds and traditions. Transportation brings people of different regions at a common platform with the common social make-up of the community.

Transportation plays a very strategic role in the success of any logistical system and co-ordinated and efficient supply chain performance, because:

a) It ensures speedier and timely physical movement of goods from point of inception to point of consumption;
b) It creates core competency by preventing stock out and customer annoyance;
c) It provides protective storage during transit;
d) It ensures cost-efficient better customer service; and
e) It fulfils specific service requirements of the corporate enterprises for

improvement of logistical capabilities and harmonious supply chain relationships.

Transport Infrastructure

Transportation infrastructure consists of the rights-of-way, vehicles, and carrier organizations that offer transportation services on a for-hire or internal basis. The nature of the infrastructure also determines a variety of economic and legal characteristics for each mode or multimodal system. A mode identifies the basic transportation method or form.

Model Characteristics

The five basic transportation modes are rail, highway, water, pipeline, and air. The relative importance of each mode can be measured in terms of system mileage, traffic volume, revenue, and the nature of traffic composition. Each mode is discussed with respect to these measures.

1. Rail Network

Historically, railroads have handled the largest number of tonne-miles. As a result of the early establishment of a comprehensive rail network connecting almost all cities and towns, railroads dominated intercity freight tonnage until after World War II. This early superiority resulted from the capability to transport large shipments economically and to offer frequent service, which gave railroads a somewhat monopolistic position. However, with the advent of serious motor carrier competition following World War II, the railroads' share of revenues and tonne-miles started to decline.

The capability to efficiently transport large tonnage over long distances is the main reason railroads continue to handle significant intercity tonnage and revenue. Railroad operations incur high fixed costs because of expensive equipment, right-of-way (railroads must maintain their own track), switching yards, and terminals. However, rail experiences relatively low variable operating costs. The replacement of steam by diesel power reduced the railroads' variable cost per tonne-mile, and electrification offers potential for more reductions. New labour agreements have reduced workforce requirements, further decreasing variable costs.

2. Motor Carriers

Highway transportation has expanded rapidly since the end of World War II. To a significant degree the rapid growth of the motor carrier industry results from door-to-door operating flexibility and speed of intercity movement.

Motor carriers have flexibility because they are able to operate on all types of roadways. In comparison to railroads, motor carriers have relatively small fixed investments in terminal facilities and operate on publicly maintained highways. Although the cost of license fees, user fees, and tolls is considerable, these expenses are directly related to the number of over-the-road units and miles operated. The variable cost per mile for motor carriers is high because a separate power unit and driver are required for each trailer or combination of tandem trailers. Labour requirements are also high because of driver safety restrictions and the need for substantial dock labour. In comparison to railroads, motor carriers are best suited to handle small shipments moving short distances.

The characteristics of motor carriers favour manufacturing and distributive trades, short distances and high-value products. Motor carriers have made significant inroads into rail traffic for medium and light manufacturing. Because of delivery flexibility, they have captured almost all freight moving from wholesalers or warehouses to retail stores. The prospect for maintaining stable market share in highway transport remains bright.

The primary difficulties relate to increasing cost to replace equipment, maintenance, driver wages, and platform and dock wages. Although accelerating labour rates influence all modes of transport, motor carriers are more labour-intensive, which causes higher wages to be a major concern. To counteract this trend, carriers have placed considerable attention on improved line-haul scheduling that bypasses terminals, computerized billing systems, mechanized terminals, tandem operations that pull two or three trailers by a single power unit, and utilization of coordinated inter-modal systems. These enhancements reduce labour intensity and, thus cost.

Specialty carriers include package haulers such as Federal Express and United Parcel Service. These firms focus on specific requirements of a market or product. Despite the aforementioned problems, it is quite apparent that highway transportation will continue to function as the backbone of logistical operations for the foreseeable future.

3. Water Transport

Water is the oldest mode of transportation. The original sailing vessels were replaced by steamboats in the early 1800s and by diesel power in the 1920s. A distinction is generally made between deep-water and navigable inland water transport.

The main advantage of water transportation is the capacity to move extremely large shipments. Water transport employs two types of vessels. Deep-water vessels, which are generally designed for ocean and Great Lakes use, are restricted to deep-water ports for access. In contrast, diesel-towed barges, which generally operate on rivers and canals, have considerably more flexibility.

Water transport ranks between rail and motor carrier in respect to fixed cost. Although water carriers must develop and operate their own terminals, the right-of-way is developed and maintained by the government and results in moderate fixed costs compared to rail and highway. The main disadvantages of water transport are the limited range of operation and speed. Unless the origin and destination of the movement are adjacent to a waterway, supplemental haul by rail or truck is required. The capability of water to carry large tonnage at low variable cost places this mode of transport in demand when low freight rates are desired and speed of transit is a secondary consideration.

Typical inland water freight includes mining and basic bulk commodities such as chemicals, cement, and selected agricultural products. In addition to the restrictions of navigable waterways, terminal facilities for bulk and dry cargo storage and load-unload devices limit the flexibility of water transport. Labour restrictions on loading and unloading at docks create operational problems and tend to reduce the potential range of available traffic. Finally, a highly competitive situation has developed between railroads and inland water carriers in areas where parallel routes exist.

4. Pipelines

It operates on a twenty-four hour basis, seven days per week and is limited only by commodity changeover and maintenance. Unlike other modes, there is no empty "container" or "vehicle" that must be returned. Pipelines have the highest fixed cost and lowest variable cost among transport modes. High fixed costs result from the right-of-way, construction and requirements for control stations, and pumping capacity. Since pipelines are not labour-intensive, the variable operating cost is extremely low once the pipeline has been constructed. An obvious disadvantage is that pipelines are not flexible and are limited with respect to commodities that can be transported: only products in the form of gas, liquid, or slurry can be handled.

5. Air Transport

The newest but least utilized mode of transport is air freight. Its significant advantage lies in the speed with which a shipment can be transported. A coast-to-coast shipment *via* air requires only a few hours contrasted to days with other modes of transportation. One prohibitive aspect of air transport is the high cost. However, this can be traded-off for high speed, which allows other elements of logistical design, such as warehousing or inventory, to be reduced or eliminated.

Air transport still remains a potential opportunity than a reality. Although the mileage is almost unlimited, air freight accounts for significantly less than 1 percent of all intercity ton-miles. Air transport capability is limited by lift capacity (i.e., load size constraints) and aircraft availability. Traditionally, most intercity air freight utilized scheduled passenger flights. While this practice was economical, it resulted in a reduction of both capacity and flexibility. The high cost of jet aircraft, coupled with the erratic nature of freight demand, has limited the assignment of dedicated planes to all-freight operations.

However, premium air carriers such as Federal Express and United Parcel Service

Overnight provide dedicated global freight operation. While this premium service was originally targeted at documents. It has expanded to include larger parcels. For example, both United Parcel and Federal Express have extended their air freight service to include overnight delivery from a centralized distribution centre located at their air hub. This is an ideal service for firms with a large number of high-value products and time-sensitive service requirements.

The fixed cost of air transport is low compared to rail, water and pipeline. In fact, air transport ranks second only to highway with respect to low fixed cost. Airways and airports are generally developed and maintained with public funds. Likewise, terminals are normally maintained by local communities. The fixed costs of air freight are associated with aircraft purchase and the requirement for specialized handling systems and cargo containers. On the other hand, air freight variable cost is extremely high as a result of fuel, maintenance, and the labour intensity of both in-flight and ground crews.

Factors in Selection of Transportation Mode

1. The strengths and weaknesses of the company in terms of marketing, financial and production resources.
2. The prevailing market characteristics, including the competitive scenario, geographical and territorial structure.
3. Braved equity of company's products in the eyes of customers to bear with a stock out situation.
4. Product features and suitability to various modes of transportation such as weight, size, shape, etc.
5. Quantity to be transported each time.
6. Distance to be covered.
7. Total transportation cost of various modes of transportation.

Transport Economics

Transport economics and pricing are concerned with the factors and characteristics that determine transport costs and rates. To develop an effective logistics strategy and to successfully negotiate transport agreements, it is necessary to understand the economies of industries.

Firstly, we will discuss the factors that influence transport economics. Then, secondly, the factors that influence the cost structure and finally, the rate structures that form the foundation for actual customer charges.

Economic Factors

Transport economics is influenced by several factors. While not direct components of transport rate tables, each factor is considered when developing rates. The specific factors are:

a. Distance:

Distance has a major influence on transportation cost since it directly contributes to variable cost, such as labour, fuel, and maintenance. First, the cost curve does not begin at the origin because there are fixed costs associated with shipment pickup and delivery regardless of distance. Second, the cost curve increases at a decreasing rate as a function of distance. This characteristic is known as the tapering principle, which results from the fact that longer movements tend to have a higher percentage of intercity rather than urban miles. Intercity miles are less expensive since more distance is covered with the same fuel and labour expense as a result of higher speeds and also because frequent intermediate stops typical of urban miles add additional loading and unloading costs.

b. Volume:

The second factor is load volume. Like many other logistics activities, transportation scale economies exist for most movements. Transport cost per unit of weight decreases as load volume increases. This occurs because the fixed costs of pickup and delivery as well as administrative costs can be spread over additional volume.

c. Density:

Since vehicle labour and fuel expenses are not dramatically influenced by weight, higher density products allow relatively fixed transport costs to be spread across additional weight. As a result, these products are assessed lower transport costs per unit of weight. In general, logistics managers attempt to increase product density so that more can be loaded in a trailer to better utilize capacity. Increased packaging density allows more units of product to be loaded into the fixed cube of the vehicle. At a certain point, no additional benefits can be achieved through increased density because the vehicle is fully loaded.

For example, from a capacity perspective, liquids such as beer or soda "weigh out" a highway trailer when it is about half-full. As such, the weight limitation is reached before the volume restriction is met. Nevertheless, efforts to increase product density will generally result in decreased transportation cost.

d. Handling:

Special handling equipment may be required for loading or unloading of trucks, railcars or ships. Furthermore, the handling cost is also affected by the manner in which products are physically grouped together (e.g. taped, boxed or palletized), for transport and storage.

e. Liability:

Liability includes six product characteristics that primarily affect risk of damage and the resulting incidence of claims. Specific product considerations are:

1. Susceptibility to damage;
2. Property damage to freight;
3. Perishability;
4. Susceptibility to theft;
5. Susceptibility to spontaneous combustion or explosion; and
6. Value per pound.

Carriers must either have insurance to protect against possible claims or accept responsibility for any damage. Shippers can reduce their risk, and ultimately the transportation cost, by improved protective packaging or by reducing susceptibility to loss or damage.

f. Market Factors:

Finally, market factors, such as lane volume and balance, influence transportation cost. A transport lane refers to movements between origin and destination points. Since transportation vehicles and drivers must return to their origin, either they must find a load to bring back ("back-haul") or the vehicle is returned empty ("deadhead"). When deadhead movements occur, labour, fuel, and maintenance costs must be charged against the original "front-haul" move. Thus, the ideal situation is for "balanced" moves where volume is equal in both directions. However, this is rarely the case because of demand imbalances in manufacturing and consumption locations. Demand directionality and seasonality result in transport rates that change with direction and season. Logistics system design must take this factor into account and add back-haul movement where possible.

Cost Structures

The second dimension of transport economics and pricing concerns the criteria used to allocate cost components. Cost allocation is primarily the carrier's concern, but since cost structure influences negotiating ability, the shipper's perspective is important as well. Transportation costs are classified into a combination of categories.

a. Variable Costs

Variable costs are those costs that change in a predictable, direct manner in relation to some level of activity during a time period. Variable costs can be avoided only by not operating the vehicle. Aside from exceptional circumstances, transport rates must at least cover variable costs. The variable category includes direct carrier costs associated with movement of each load. These expenses are generally measured as a cost per mile or per unit of weight. Typical cost components in this category include labour, fuel, and maintenance.

b. Fixed Costs

Fixed costs are those costs that do not change in the short-run and must be covered even if the company is closed down (e.g., during a holiday or a strike). The fixed category includes carrier costs not directly influenced by shipment volume. For transportation firms, fixed components include terminals, rights-of-way, information systems, and vehicles. In the short-term, expenses associated with fixed assets must be covered by contributions above variable cost on a *per* shipment basis. In the long-term, the fixed cost burden can be reduced somewhat by the sale of fixed assets; however, it is often difficult to sell rights-of-way or technologies.

c. Joint Costs

Joint costs are unavoidable expenses created by the decision to provide a particular service. For example, when a carrier elects to haul a truckload from point A to point B, there is an implicit decision to incur a joint cost for the back-haul from point B to point A. Either the joint cost must be covered by the original shipper from A to B or a back-haul shipper must be found. Joint costs have significant impact on transportation charges because carrier quotations must include implied joint costs based on considerations regarding an appropriate backhaul shipper and/or back-haul charges against the original shipper.

d. Common Costs

This category includes carrier costs that are incurred on behalf of all shippers or a segment of shippers. Common costs, such as terminal or management expenses, are characterized as overhead. These are often allocated to a shipper according to a level of activity like the number of shipments handled (e.g., delivery appointments). However, allocating overhead in this manner may incorrectly assign costs. E.g. a shipper may be charged for delivery appointments when it doesn't actually use the service (such as when the shipper's deliveries are unloaded on an "as available" basis).

Pricing Strategies

a. Cost-of-Service Strategy

The cost-of-service strategy is a "build-up" approach where the carrier establishes a rate based on the cost of providing the service plus a profit margin. For example, if the cost of providing a transportation service is Rs. 200 and the profit mark-up is 10 percent, the carrier would charge the shipper Rs. 220. The cost-of-service approach, which represents the base or minimum transportation charge, is a pricing approach for low-value goods or in highly competitive situations.

b. Value-of-Service Strategy

Value-of-service is an alternative strategy that charges a rate based on perceived shipper value rather than the cost of actually providing the service. For example, a shipper perceives transporting 1,000 kg of electronic equipment as more critical or valuable than 1,000 kg of coal since the equipment is worth substantially more than the coal. As such, a shipper is probably willing to pay more to transport it. Carriers tend to utilize value-of-service pricing for high-value goods or when limited competition exists.

Value-of-service pricing is illustrated in the premium overnight carrier market. When Federal Express first introduced overnight delivery, there were few competitors that could provide the service, so it was perceived by shippers as a high-value alternative. They were willing to pay $ 22.50 to obtain the value of an overnight shipment. Once competitors such as UPS and the United States Postal Service entered the market, rates dropped to current discounted levels of $5 to $ 10 per package. This rate decrease is more in line with the actual cost for the service.

c. Combination Strategy

The combination strategy establishes the transport price at some intermediate level between the cost-of-service minimum and the value-of-service maximum. In standard practice, most transportation firms use such a middle value. Logistics managers must understand the range of prices and the alternative strategies so that they can negotiate appropriately.

Rating

a. Class Rates

In transportation terminology, the price in rupees and paisa per hundredweight to move a specific product between two locations is referred to as the rate. The rate is listed on pricing sheets or computer files known as tariffs. The term class rate evolved from the fact that all products transported by common carriers are classified for pricing purposes. All products legally transported in interstate commerce can be shipped *via* class rates.

b. Commodity Rates

When a large quantity of a product moves between two locations on regular basis, it is common practice for carriers to publish a commodity rate. Commodity rates are special or specific rates published without regard to classification. The terms and conditions of a commodity rate are usually indicated in a contract between the carrier and the shipper. E.g. Exception Rates or exceptions to the classification, are special rates published to provide shippers lower rates than the prevailing class rate. The original purpose of the exception rate was to provide a special rate for a specific area, origin-destination, or commodity when either competitive or high volume movements justified it. A limited service rate is utilized when a shipper agrees to perform services typically performed by the carrier, such as trailer loading, in exchange for a discount. A common example is a shipper load and count rate, where the shipper takes responsibility for loading and counting the cases.

Not only does this remove the responsibility for loading the shipment from the carrier, but it also implies that the carrier is not responsible for guaranteeing the number of cases transported. Another example of limited service is a released value rate, which limits carrier liability in case of loss or damage. Normally, the carrier is responsible for full product value if loss or damage occurs in transit. The quoted rate must include adequate insurance to cover the risk. Often it is more effective for manufacturers of high-value product to absorb the risk in return for lower transportation rates. Limited service is used when shippers have confidence in the carrier's capability, and cost can be reduced by eliminating duplication of effort or responsibility.

c. Special Rates and Services

A number of special rates and services provided by for-hire carriers are available for logistical operations. Several important examples are discussed:

(i) **Freight-All-Kinds (FAK) Rates :** as indicated earlier, freight-all-kinds rates are important to logistics operations. Under FAK rates, a mixture of different products is transported under a generic rating. Rather than determine the classification and applicable rate of each product, an average rate is applied for the total shipment. In essence, FAK rates are line-haul rates since they replace class, exception or commodity rates. Their purpose is to simplify the paperwork associated with the movement of mixed commodities and thus lower the costs. As such, they are of particular importance in physical distribution.

(ii) **Local, Joint, Proportional, and Combination Rates :** numerous special rates exist that may offer transportation savings on specific freight movements. When a commodity moves under the tariff of a single carrier, it is referred to as a local rate or single-line rate. If more than one carrier is involved in the freight movement, a joint rate may be applicable even though multiple carriers are involved in the actual transportation process. Because some motor and rail carriers operate in restricted territory, it may be necessary to utilize the services of more than one to complete a shipment. Utilization of a joint rate can offer substantial savings over the use of two or more local rates.

(iii) **Proportional rates :** offer special price incentives to utilize a published tariff that applies to only part of the desired route. Proportional provisions of a tariff are most often applicable to origin or destination points outside the normal geographical area of a single-line tariff. If a joint rate does not exist and proportional provisions do, the strategy of moving a shipment under proportional rates provides a discount on the single-line part of the movement, thereby resulting in a lower overall freight charge.

(iv) **Combination rates :** are similar to proportional rates in that two or more rates may be combined when no published single-line or joint rate exists between two locations. The rates may be any combination of class, exception and commodity rates. The utilization of combination rates often involves several technicalities that are beyond the scope of this discussion. Their use substantially reduces the cost of an individual shipment. In most cases that involves regular freight movements, the need to utilize combination rates is eliminated with publication of a thorough rate. A thorough rate is a rate that applies from origin to destination for a shipment.

(v) **Transit Services :** transit services permit a shipment to be stopped at an intermediate point between its initial origin and final destination for unloading, storage, and/or processing. The shipment is then reloaded for delivery to the final destination. Typical example of transit services are milling for grain products and processing for sugar beets. When transit privileges exist, the shipment is charged a through rate from origin to destination plus a transit privilege charge. Transit services are typically performed by railroads. From the viewpoint of the shipper, the use of this specialized service is restricted to specific geographical areas once the product enters into transit service.

Therefore, a degree of flexibility is lost when the product is placed in transit because the final destination can be altered only at significant added expense or, at the least, with loss of the thorough rate and assessment of the transit charge. Finally, the utilization of transit privileges increases the paperwork of shippers in terms of both meeting railroad record requirements and ultimately settling the freight bills. The added cost of administration must be carefully weighed in evaluating the true benefits gained. During the last decade railroads have generally discouraged use of transit services.

(vi) **Diversion and Re-consignment :** for a variety of reasons, a shipper or consignee may desire to change route, destination or even consignee once a shipment is in transit. This flexibility can be extremely important, particularly with regard to the transportation of food and other perishable products where markets quickly change. It is a normal practice among certain types of marketing intermediaries to purchase commodities with the full intention of selling them while they are in transit. Diversion consists of changing the destination of a shipment prior to its arrival at the original destination. Re-consignment is a change in consignee prior to delivery.

(vii) **Split Delivery :** a split delivery is desired when portions of a shipment need to be delivered to different facilities. Under specified tariff conditions, pickup and delivery can be extended to points beyond the initial destination. The payment is typically structured to reflect a rate as if the shipment were going to the farthest destination. In addition, there is a charge for each delivery stop-off.

(viii) **Demurrage and Detention** : demurrage and detention are charges assessed for retaining freight cars or truck trailers beyond specified loading or unloading time. The term demurrage is used by railroads for holding a railcar beyond forty-eight hours before unloading the shipment. Motor carriers use the term detention to cover similar delays. In the case of motor carriers, the permitted time is specified in the tariff and is normally limited to a few hours.

(ix) **Accessorial Services** : in addition to basic transportation, motor and rail carriers offer a wide variety of special or ancillary services that can aid in planning logistical operations.

Carriers may also offer environmental services and special equipment. Environmental services refer to special control of freight while in transit, such as refrigeration, ventilation, and heating. For example, in the summer, Hershey's typically transports its chocolate and confectionery products in refrigerated trailers to protect them from high temperature levels. Special equipment charges refer to the use of equipment that the carrier has purchased for the shipper's economy and convenience. For example, specialized sanitation equipment is necessary to clean and prepare trailers for food storage and transit when the trailer has been previously utilized for non-food products or commodities.

Where Are You on the Transportation Best-Practice Continuum?

The supply chain has become a place for many new and creative ideas and the focus for business differentiation and efficiency. According to one recent study, 80% of CEOs said supply chain management was *important or very important* for the success of their company. But to win in the trenches, it takes a company that can execute key operational tactics at their best. A transportation framework has been developed to allow shippers to align their transportation operation with their supply chain strategy and overall business objectives. This framework allows shippers to take their improvement to the next level.

The new framework divides transportation management into six process areas made up of six activities:

1. Carrier Management;
2. Load Planning and Optimization;
3. Preparing and Executing Shipments;
4. Shipment Monitoring;
5. Freight Payment and Audit; and
6. Performance Monitoring.

Core to this new transportation management framework is flexibility to align transportation tactics with your company's business strategy. Therefore, the model does not profess that there is one right answer that fits all situations. Instead the model helps shippers tie their transportation management process activities to their business strategy.

In August 2005, FedEx studied the financial results of 197 publicly held companies. The transportation managers of 100 of these companies were then surveyed on how they perform fifty-two different transportation activities found in the transportation management framework. Following is a brief explanation of the findings of the study and some examples of the tactics used by leading companies. Understanding each process area, one can use the assessment tools to help identify opportunities for improving the transportation activities.

Process Area 1: Carrier Management

Carrier management is the set of activities shippers employ to identify and procure the best modes, best carriers for each mode and best rates. The leading companies here tend to manage all in-bound and out-bound freight with carrier partners that are selected through a formal, detailed process. Best practices include collaboration between shippers and carriers that leads to better overall performance for both parties.

Process Area 2: Load Planning and Optimization

Load planning and optimization is the creation of efficient transportation plans that allow shippers to reduce costs and improve service. Use of a transportation management system (TMS) is typical for leading companies. The optimization capabilities of a TMS selects the best option for a shipment based on preset criteria, including cost, transit time, and overall mode. Leading companies also use a longer planning horizon, allowing orders to be evaluated for combination with others, allowing for example a mode shift from parcel to less than truckload (LTL).

Process Area 3: Shipping Execution

Optimal plans must be supported by effective operations in the shipping office, on the dock, and in the yard. Getting the right shipment on the right carrier's truck at the right time takes flawless planning. A Transportation Benchmark study showed that companies with a strategic transportation plan often had higher customer service level and lower transportation costs than those without such a plan. Leading companies use electronic data interface/interchange (EDI) and other communications to tender shipments, set and confirm pickup appointments and submit shipping documentation to their carriers. This is one of the win-win areas as carriers will recognize the efficiency in making pickups and deliveries at a well-scheduled dock.

Process Area 4: Shipment Monitoring

Shipment visibility throughout an organization, notjust in shipping, is paramount to a responsive customer-centric company. Leading companies are incorporating real-time updates from their carriers into their own systems, giving visibility throughout their organizations. This makes the shipping department more efficient as they spend less time on requests for tracking and proof-of-delivery information. Leading carriers are also providing proactive notifications of a shipment's status. These updates can be routine as when a shipment delivers or a warning that a shipment's delivery is in jeopardy due to a delay—for example, it is stopped for customs inspection.

Process Area 5 : Freight Pay and Audit

Transaction-heavy processes, such as audit and freight pay, are ideal for automation. Recent technology developments and large shipper's scale have begun to drive efficiencies in freight-payment processes. Leading companies manage rates for all ship points from a central location and re-rate the invoices when received to compare invoice amounts to contracts terms. Without automated systems, re-rating high volumes would not be practical. Smaller shippers that want the assurances of re-rates but don't have the volume to warrant a system can look to third-party service providers.

Process Area 6 : Performance Measurement and Management

The old adage "if you're not measuring it, you can't manage it" certainly holds true for transportation. You need to know how good you are before you can decide how good you can be. Performance measurement requires combining internal data from your company with data from your carrier to create a scorecard. The scorecard usually includes internal process measures such as per cent of requested ship dates attained, per cent of shipments moving on planned mode (or inversely how often expedited transportation was required), and transportation cost as a percent of sales. Measures of the carrier performance may include on-time performance, transit time by lane, and claims as a per cent of shipments, or as a percent of transportation cost.

For Discussion

1. Explain the major functions performed by transport operations.
2. Who are the key participants in a transportation decision? Discuss the role of each.
3. What are the economic and non-economic benefits of transportation to an economy?
4. Discuss the role of transportation in the success of any logistical system.
5. Describe the various modes of transportation available in a logistics system along with their benefits and limitations.
6. Highlight the key factors taken into consideration in the selection of a mode of transportation.
7. Identify the various elements of transportation costs.
8. Discuss the various factors influencing transport economics.
9. What are the various transportation pricing strategies?

Packaging

Packaging refers to a container in which the product reaches the end use consumer. It is a part of the presentation of the product and stays right till the customer takes it from the retail store. It should not be confused with packing. Packing refers to the external protective covering used for the safe transportation of the goods to the importer. For example, plastic box used to pack a set of embroidered handkerchiefs is an example of packaging. On the other hand, the corrugated fireboard boxes, which are used for packing the plastic boxes for their safe transportation to the importer in the foreign country, would represent packing.

Packaging plays a very important role in the marketing of a product; it is a part of the augmented product. The augmented product is that part of the product which deals with adding new features to the basic product in order to exceed the customer expectations. These features take the form of packaging, delivery arrangements, warehousing, customer advice etc., in order to add value to the product. As a matter of fact, the competition between the exporters at the foreign market place is not in relation to the core product or its basic tangible features but it is about the augmented product. For instance, an expensive chessboard offered to a customer wrapped in the old newspaper is very likely to lose out to an identical chessboard set neatly presented in a nice matching box. In the latter case, the packaging makes it a more valuable product and offers more 'value' to the customer.

Functions of Packaging

Packaging of goods for exports performs the following functions:

1 The product is broken down into saleable units in terms of size or weight or any other dimension relevant to that product.

2 It protects the product during transportation, storage, display and use.

3 It conveys a message about handling of the product to the transporters / buyers during transport, storage, display and use.

Packaging Design

The design of the packaging should be developed very carefully to ensure that:

1. Proper protection is provided to the product.
2. The product is environment-friendly to produce and dispose off.
3. It is safe to handle during transportation.
4. It is economical to produce, handle and store.
5. It is very attractive when displayed.
6. It is convenient and safe to use in compliance with the relevant standards of the target export market.

It should be understood that primary packaging of the product performs the function of the silent sales man. It should appeal to the prospective consumer and satisfy his desire to use a better quality product. The total package design (comprising of material, size, shape, colour, text, graphics and logo) should be such that it provides:

A. Proper perception and expectations about the product.
B. Convenience and efficiency in use.
C. It should be faultless.

The exporter should also keep in mind the product and the targetted group of customers while designing the primary packaging of the product.

Packaging Materials

There are various types of materials available for packaging of the goods. These materials are paper, plastics, wood, cardboard etc. Selection of the packaging materials should be made keeping in view primarily the specifications given by the importer because he has to plan further for consumer packaging of the goods. Broadly, the selection of the packaging materials would depend upon the following factors:

1. Product characteristics;
2. Transportation and storage methods;
3. Climate, culture; and
4. Standards and environmental considerations.

The type and quality of the packaging is specific to the given product. For example, certain products such as garments, shoes, textiles etc., are sold to the consumers without any packaging. They are usually displayed without any packaging at the retail stores. Such goods do not require very expensive packaging. The exporters have to ensure that the packaging used by them should be such that it prevents the products from getting dirty. These goods are often packaged in polyethylene bags.

Cardboard boxes are used for the packaging of items such as sets of glasses or tableware, decoration with several delicate parts, pairs of candle holders, glass vases, delicate statuettes etc., to ensure that they are not damaged and their appearance is not spoiled during handling and display.

Expensive products and gift items such as jewellery require a high standard of packaging. In fact, the more expensive or exclusive the product, the more justified high quality and more expensive the packaging is.

Kinds of Packaging

Depending on the use of packaging materials, the packaging for export products can be classified into the following categories:

1. Plastic packaging.
2. Paper-based packaging.
3. Combined plastic and cardboard packaging.
4. Miscellaneous packaging.

Plastic Packaging

The various kinds of plastic materials are used for packaging of the export products. The most common plastic materials used for packaging are polyethylene (PE) and polypropylene (PP). Polyethylene film has two main varieties of consumer packaging namely, low density polyethylene (PE-LD) film and high-density polyethylene (PE-HD).

PE-LD film is used for making plastic bags, shrink wrapping and stretch wrapping. This film is very useful to provide protection against moisture and dirt. It does not, however, provide any mechanical protection. The exporters can use the plastic bags made of PE-LD films for wrapping articles to package products like T-shirts, table cloths, napkins, leather hand bags etc. These products are placed inside the plastic bags, which are transparent and are suited for retail display. In shrink-wrapping, a specially treated film is loosely wrapped around the product(s) and then shrunk with heat to form a tight package. This kind of wrapping is suitable for solid products like sets of drinking glasses, a group of egg-cups etc.

In stretch wrapping, a thin film is tightly wound around the product, often in several layers. When the wrap is completed, the stretched film tries to return to its original size, thereby holding the product or group of products tightly in place.

PE-HD also used for making plastic bags because it provides better resistance against moisture and fats than PE-LD. PE-HD is more expensive than the PE-LD.

Both the forms of plastic films are environment-friendly as they are easy to recycle.

The PP films are stronger than the PE films. It is better to use bags made of PP films for packaging textiles and garments as these can be printed or can be used in plain form as well. PP films are better than PE films in terms of providing better moisture protection but these films are more expensive. Another alternative to PP films is polyvinyl chloride (PVC) material. But from environmental point of view, PVC materials should not be used, as these are not recyclable.

Plastic boxes can be used especially as retail packages for jewellery and other small, precious products. They are also well-suited to add appeal to products such as embroidered handkerchiefs or tablecloths, souvenir dolls, etc. They come in square, oval or round shapes; printed or plain.

Paper-Based Packaging

Paper-based materials are used as wrapping, as paperboard cartons or corrugated fibreboard boxes. The various types of paper can be coated with plastics, waxed or treated with anti corrosion agents. Paper is either produced from virgin wood fibres or recycled fibres. The former is stronger than the latter.

Paper wrappings provide protection against dust and light, but do not provide mechanical protection.

Paper absorbs moisture when the surrounding air is more humid than the paper, and it gives up, moisture when the surroundings are drier. Thus, paper wrappings can be used to some extent as moisture protection inside the packages as well to slow down the harmful effect of moisture in the air. One should use tissue paper instead of newspaper to protect the surface of products.

Paperboard folding cartons

Folding cartons made of different paperboard qualities can be used as retail packaging for variety of reasons. Folding cartons are economical; they can be shaped in almost unlimited number of ways; they can be printed very decoratively; properly designed cartons provide mechanical protection to products; they protect products against dust and light, and are easy to handle in retail shops. The most important property of such cartons is their stiffness.

Paperboard cans

The paperboard can is a form of paper-based retail packaging, which is quite inexpensive and is used to pack different types of products. These cans can be lined inside with aluminium foil or plastic films to provide additional protection against humidity. Such cans are used for packaging toys, puzzles, games, tennis balls and other sports goods.

Combined Plastic and Cardboard Packaging

There are three main types of packaging that combine paperboard and plastic materials. These are as follows:

1. Skin packaging,
2. Blister packaging, and
3. Plastic bags with a paperboard card.

These packages are used mainly for retail packaging of pens, small toys, gift items, lightweight souvenir articles. This type of packaging has several advantages: the product is visible through the plastic; the paperboard card can be printed to provide information and to add sales appeal; especially small products are not lost or stolen easily.

Skin packaging

Skin packaging is a form of packaging where the product is first placed on a paperboard card with heat seal coating. It is suitable for products, which need protection against moisture and are not very heavy or expensive. It is however, not suitable for products which are sensitive to heat.

Blister packaging

In this form of packaging, the product is first placed into a pre-formed plastic blister. Then a paperboard card is attached to it. Blister packaging can be used for a variety of products such as toys, pens, textile articles and decorations etc. It should not be used for those products, which are too delicate as there is always some space for movement inside the blister. This might damage the delicate product.

Plastic bag with paperboard card

In this form of packaging, a paperboard card is attached to the plastic bags through a hole in the bag. This adds sales appeal to plain plastic bags and is always very cost-effective. The paperboard card can be printed on adding information and attraction. The plastic bags can be made of any materials but PP film should be preferred in the interest of better product presentation.

Miscellaneous Packaging

Exporter can make use of wood, textiles, straw, leaves or any other locally available materials for packaging of the goods. Specially made wooden boxes can be used to package traditional ceramics, woodcarvings, various gift items, pieces of jewellery etc. If wooden packaging is used as a gift or retail package, it has to be made with as much care as the product itself. This means that it should be smooth, clean, and dry, with any hinges or locks well made and functioning. It is also important to pack the product with sufficient cushioning material into a wooden package, so that the product is not damaged during transport. Before using wood as packaging material, one should always check, whether there are any regulations concerning the treatment or certification of wooden materials.

Paperboard cartons or boxes can be covered or lined with cloth to give them a more decent appearance. Bags made of jute, cotton, velvet or other fabric could be used for the packaging of products, which do not need much protection. Baskets made of local materials can also provide very attractive packaging for handicraft products.

Preparing for Packaging

Packaging affects the image of the product and in turn would affect the purchase decision of the buyer. Exporter should ensure the use of quality packaging material for packaging of the product. Quality packaging plays a very important role in creating the image of a country. The transformation of the image of Japan as a supplier of industrial goods owes to quality packaging; so is true for South Korea, Singapore and Hong Kong.

Packaging has two components namely, technical and promotional

1. The technical aspect of packaging is concerned with protection of the product from moisture, heat, scratches, mechanical shocks and so on. The exporter can ensure technical protection by using appropriate plastic materials, paper and the cushioning materials.
2. The promotional aspect of packaging is concerned with creating sales appeal through packaging by making use of traditional patterns/designs of the country and by way of illustration of the item using a combination of two or three colour. The following steps should be taken to prepare the product for packaging:

Clean all the products so that they are completely free of dust, dirt or fingerprints. It is especially important to remove fingerprints from polished metal surfaces, as fingerprints may cause corrosion and stains. Dry those products, which are, stains affected by humidity. The drying should be done just before packing so that the humidity in the air cannot penetrate the products again. Such products are: articles made of wood, straw, paper, leather, and all textiles and garments. In the case of painted or lacquered products, it is important to ensure that the paint is completely dry before packing. Make sure that all parts of the product are there and that articles in sets are complete. Make sure that possible stickers or other product labels are correct and that they are fastened so that removal of the labels by the end consumer does not damage the product.

While preparing for packaging of the export products, the exporter should aim at ensuring efficient packaging. It minimizes the use of packaging materials and optimizes on the container space. Besides, it should facilitate:

a. Product identification.
b. Handling, storage and display of the goods.
c. Price markings, tags and bar codes.
d. Opening of the package.
e. Disposability of transport and surrounding materials.

Principles governing packaging

The exporter should observe the following principles while planning for packaging of the export products:

1. There should be no compromise on the protective capacity of the packaging.
2. It is good to save on packaging costs but it should not result in any possible loss of sales, profit and goodwill due to rejection by the buyer.
3. The exporter should anticipate the risks to the health of the consumers due to the use of inferior packaging.

Packing of Goods

As explained above, packing of goods is concerned with placing the goods in protective external covering to ensure their safe transportation. Packing is a vital part of successful export operation as it facilitates transportation of goods economically over long-distances; and their sales on arrival at the destination. It plays an important role in improving the perception of 'value' of the product. A clean, correctly marked package, i.e., easy to handle, gives the impression of good quality of the product and its exporter too. The package should be treated as the business card of the exporter. Thus, the objective of packing the goods for export should be to make packing 'as good as necessary, and as economically as possible'.

Need for Packing: Risks in the Chain of Transportation

The need for packing arises due to the fact that there are many stresses and risks involved during the transportation of goods from the exporter to the importer. These risks can be better understood if one knows the links involved in the chain of transportation of goods to their destination. The various steps involved in the transportation of goods are as follows:

1. Stacking and storage of goods in the factory while waiting for loading on the truck or freight container. The risk involved at this stage is that if the boxes are weak then they may not endure stacking of more boxes on each other and as a consequence, there could be possible damage to the boxes on the ground. Such possibilities are very strong in the case of cardboard boxes. If there is a visible damage to the boxes before they leave the exporter's premises, they will certainly not endure the vibrations and shocks during transportation caused by bumps or pot holes on the roads etc.

2. The boxes are loaded onto the truck and are transported by road to the nearest airport/seaport. At this stage, the possible risk of damage to the goods may be caused because of vibrations and shocks arising due to bad road conditions. It should be ensured that the boxes in the truck are not able to move inside and there are no empty spaces in the truck otherwise, bumps in the roads or sudden brakes would cause serious damage to the goods.

3. The boxes are unloaded and are stored at the airport/seaport for custom clearance before being loaded on to the plane/container/ship. At this stage, manual unloading and handling, breakage or damage due to humidity causes the possible risk of the damage to the goods by insects or rodents.

4. The goods are packed into the freight container or loaded on the plane/ship. The possibility of damage to the goods is again caused due to poor handling, and stacking of the goods. If the container is not properly inspected, cleaned and repaired, there is risk of damage to the goods by insects or rodents. The risk of damage to the goods is often multiplied if the goods are sent as loose cargo, i.e., not in a freight container.

5. Sailing of the ship to the port of destination: During sailing, the goods may be damaged due to stormy weather, waves, heaves, twists and turns.

6. Unloading of the containers at the port of discharge. If the boxes have not been secured properly, some boxes may fall out when the doors are opened - risk 01 damage of products and risk of injury to the person opening the cargo. Manual handling during unloading holds risks of its own.

7. The palletized goods are transferred with a forklift truck to a warehouse. If the goods are sent to retail shops, they are either transferred as pallet loads or as individual packages. There is no special risk involved at this stage.

The main point here is that transport, handling and storage are always more stressing and rougher than the packer thinks. This should be kept in mind all the time when selecting packing for goods.

Although sea transport is considered to be the roughest mode of transport, one should not forget that risks are also involved in air transport. Even if air freight takes less time and is generally not as rough as the sea freight, there are very rough points, such as the landing of the aircraft and the handling of the goods on the ground before they are loaded and de-loaded into the aircraft.

Thus, the exporter should plan for packing of the goods keeping in view the risks involved in different stages in the transport chain from exporter's country to the importer's country.

Functions of Packing

The various functions of packing are as follows:

- It holds the product for the total duration of the transport and distribution chain.
- It protects the product from getting broken or being otherwise spoilt, from the time of manufacturing until the product reaches its final user.
- It makes the transport and handling of the product as easy as possible. The boxes that are easy and quick to handle would be more competitive than others in Europe because manual handling is costly there.
- It informs various people in the transport and distribution chain about the 'identity', destination of the product, and how it should be handled and stored, recycled or disposed off. If the product is sold in a retail package, this has to contain information related to the product, its producer and its handling.
- It is also the task of the packing department to make the transport and distribution of the product economical. This requirement means that the total cost has to be considered - not only the price of the packing. Total cost includes all costs from the time when the product is manufactured until the product reaches the end-user and the empty package is recycled or disposed off. When goods arrive at their destination, packing appeals to the buyer. Untidy, damaged or dirty looks lowers value,esteem of the product & manufacturer as well.

Dimensions of the Packing Boxes

The exporters should ascertain as to how the export boxes are handled in the importing country. This would help the exporter in planning for the dimensions of the boxes for packing of the export cargo. For example, in Europe, the pallets of the standard sizes are used for storage of the export boxes. The two main sizes of standard pallets are: 1200 x 1000 mm and 1200 x 800 mm. The shelves in warehouses are fitted to hold these two sizes of the pallets.

In order to fit cartons on the standard pallets economically, boxes and crates should be based on a module of 600 x 400 mm. This basic module fits the standard pallets economically and without wasting (expensive) space. From a practical standpoint, dimensions should be 550 x 330 mm (length x width). Ideal size to be followed is 800 x 600 x 300 to 800 mm, i.e., (length x width x height). The dimensions have to be smaller, because if the boxes land over the pallet edge, the boxes, especially corrugated fibre board boxes, will be damaged. Warehouse damage and difficulties will follow if the load packed on a pallet is larger than the pallet deck.

The basic module is the cornerstone of distribution and handling in Europe. Pallets, warehouse shelves and even retail shop shelves follow a basic module, its multiple & sub-multiple, they are easy, economical to handle and store. The exporter can use this vital information about the dimensions of the boxes to gain an edge over their competitors in the market.

Transportation of Goods: Types of Packing Boxes

Depending on its usage export boxes use different types from available packing material and are classified as:

1. Corrugated fibreboard boxes;
2. Wooden boxes and crates; and
3. Miscellaneous boxes such as gunny bags or-steel drums.

Corrugated Fibreboard Boxes

Corrugated fibreboard boxes are the most commonly used boxes for the transport packing of the goods for export. These boxes are used for large number of products such as fresh fruits and vegetables; consumer-packed manufactured goods; handicrafts; garments; household appliances; leather goods and so on. Such boxes are equally good for export both by air and sea. The advantage of these boxes is that these can be tailor made even to the smallest possible sizes.

The different types of corrugated fibreboard boxes are as follows:

1. Single faced board.
2. Double faced board (Single wall).
3. Double faced board (Double wall).

Single faced board: More than 90% of all the corrugated boxes are made of single wall or double faced board. The single wall double faced is used for heavy weight products. Preferably a cardboard box should weigh about 30 kg and should never exceed 50 kg in weight. Mechanical handling enabled boxes be used for carrying any excess weight.

Transport boxes can also be made of solid fibreboard. Exporters utilize the advantage of using fibreboard as it is easy to manufacture and can be economically coated with various materials which offers maximum resistant against moisture.

Wooden Boxes and Crates

Though corrugated fibreboard boxes or the solid fibreboard boxes have replaced wooden boxes for most products, yet wooden boxes and crates remain important alternatives for transport packing for export. This is particularly true for heavy and vulnerable products. The dimensions of the boxes should be decided keeping in view the need for safe transportation of the export product.

The exporter should consider the following point as regards the selection of wood for making the boxes:

1. Wood density: It is an important factor as it determines the strength of the wood and how it holds the nails. One should use wood with the densities varying between 350 kg per cubic meter and 650 kg per cubic meter, as it will have sufficient mechanical strength. Higher the density of wood, higher the strength and *vice versa.*

2. Moisture content: The moisture content of the wood used for packing should be around 20% as it would protect the wood against decay by mould and from any other kind of fungus. If the moisture content is more than 20%, then the wood should be dried up before making the boxes.

3. Quality of the wood: It depends on the number of knots, splits, decay or grain irregularities present in the wood. The wood with faults in the form of knots, splits, and decay or grain irregularities should not be used for transport packing for export.

4. Type of nails: Quality nails having high maximum holding power, i.e., grooved or threaded ones should be used. It should also be ensured that correct number of nails is driven in the wood allowing for proper spacing between two nails.

Miscellaneous Boxes

Sometimes, steel drums or the jute bags can also be used for export packing. For example, liquids can be exported in the steel drums and agricultural items can be transported in jute bags.

Cost of Packing

Quality standard sized packing materials ensures and avoid breakage & damage to products thereby increasing profits for an exporter, cuts down unnecessary losses. This has no bearing or selling price.

It is thus, more economical to use packing of sufficient quality rather than using too cheap packing. There is no need to overdo in the quality of packing, as it would be expensive. It is desirable to economize on the cost of packing without compromising with the quality of packing. Identifying the points where scrap and waste is created and then respond appropriately to reduce the cost can do this. The various stages for the economy in packing cost are as follows:

Purchase of standard packing materials and boxes

1. Use standard materials with standard dimensions to economise on the packing cost. The supplier should always be given sufficient time for delivery of the supplies required for packing.
2. Better quality packing material minimizes damages and in turn helps in increasing the demand for the goods as the perception about the reliability of

the exporter increases to deliver the goods in safe and sound condition.

3. Importers requisitions, export market requirements, especially with regard to environmental regulations should be accounted for & considered before ordering packages or printing on the boxes by a exporter.
4. The packing materials should be used as economically as possible, the exporter should plan in such a manner that maximum number of packages can be taken from a given quantity of packaging/packing material. This can be achieved by taking the assistance of the packaging professionals. A tightly fitting package is always considered the most economical package.
5. Trained packing staff, waste management of packing material will reduce packing cost considerably.

Marking on the Export Boxes

Proper identification, correct handling and delivery to the consignee ensures marking a important part of the logistics for transportation of the goods to the buyer. Marking on the export boxes not only ensures safe transportation and delivery but also helps proper handling of the cargo by the attending people.

Types of Marking

There are three different types of markings namely:

1. Shipping marks.
2. Information marks.
3. Handling marks.

Shipping marks contain all the information, which is necessary to deliver the boxes to its correct destination. These marks are the same as given on the transport documents.

Information marks provide additional necessary information as regards buyer's code number, quantity, dimensions and information for storage of the boxes. This information need not be given on the transport document.

Handling marks are the instructions given on the boxes for their proper handling at different stages during the transport chain starting with warehousing/storage of the goods in the factory of the exporter through the business premises of the importer. These marks are generally given in pictorial form.

All the three types of marks should be written at the appropriate place on the boxes to avoid any kind of confusion and to make sure correct handling and delivery of the goods.

The markings on the export boxes for sea shipments and air shipments are different from each other. Internationally recommended shipping marks as used in sea shipments consist of following four points and should be placed in the middle of the at least two sides of the box. These informations are as follows:

1. Short name of the buyer.
2. Reference number agreed to between the exporter and the importer.
3. Destination, i.e., the port of discharge.
4. Box number/total number of boxes in the shipment.

As far as handling marks are concerned, these should be used only when they are really needed. For example, there would be no need for handling marks in the case of boxes containing textiles, handicrafts, leather goods, furniture items etc. In case it is necessary to indicate the handling marks, then such marks should be stated on all sides of the boxes.

The use of handling marks does not actually guarantee that the boxes are handled correctly. Nevertheless, their use offers two advantages namely: First, they at least allow the goods to be handled correctly. Secondly, if handling marks have not been used when required, insurance will not cover the loss caused by incorrect handling.

For shipment by air, the International Air Transport Association's (IATA) standardized format label to be pasted on the export boxes. The mandatory information points relate to:

1. The name of the airline.
2. The airway bill number.
3. Destination in the form of three-letter IATA code for transport, e.g., DEL for Delhi.
4. Total number of boxes included in the shipment and the box number e.g., 3/25. This indicates that this box number is 3 and the total number of boxes is 25.

Essential Features of Marking

Effective marking on the export boxes for transportation should be big, bold and brief. The exporter should ensure that the markings are:

1. Legible i.e., it should be possible to read the markings from a distance. The exporters should preferably use the colour black for this purpose.
2. Durable i.e., the exporter should use ink that is permanent, water proof and resistant to humidity, sunlight and friction. It should be ensured that the marks do not fade away or are smudged.
3. Visible i.e., the marks should be placed on at least two sides of the boxes, front and back.
4. Communicative i.e., the markings should convey the message as clearly as possible and it should be as short as possible. One may use pictorial forms if possible. Handling marks should be placed on the extreme left and right position of the box.

Environmental Requirements

There is a growing awareness among the consumers in the developed markets of the world, in particular, the European markets to protect their environment from the ill-effects of pollution. They are of the view that they must take care of their environment so that the future generations can enjoy a decent life. Consequently, the consumers demand environmentally sound products and hold the manufacturers accountable for their actions and products. Appreciating this concern of the consumers regarding environment, even the manufacturers have begun to find ways and means to satisfy the customers in this regard. For example, the manufacturers in Germany have set up a Dual System under which the manufacturers contribute towards funding of a system for recycling of the packaging waste materials. Thus, the manufacturers who contribute to this system permit their customers to return the packaging material to them for their recycling. Under this system, the manufacturers are allowed to use a label called the Green Dot (●). If a product has this label then it implies that the customer can return the packaging material to the retail store, which, in turn, returns it to the manufacturer for recycling. This system is now being enforced as part of the EU Directive on Packaging and Packing. A similar system is in place in the Netherlands amongst the manufacturers of electrical appliances. These trends are indicative of the responsibility that the manufacturers realize to protect their environment. Exporters must understand these trends, as importers will pass on these demands to them. Thus, they (exporters) can gain a competitive edge if the products and or the packaging used are environment-friendly. In fact, an environment-friendly image and substance of the product is fast becoming a very important marketing asset. In sum and substance, it means using re-usable or recyclable materials for the product, during the production process and for packaging and packing.

The regulations and requirements as regards environment protection keep on changing. It would be in the interest of the exporters to ascertain these requirements of the target markets of planning for production and introduction of the product in the foreign markets. Therefore, exporters should always ask the importers about the up-to-date requirements. The main thrust of the environmental requirements is that:

1. The amount of packing used should not be more than what is essential for safe transport and distribution.
2. All packages, materials and accessories should preferably be recyclable. For instance, adhesive tape made of PVC should not be used for corrugated boxes because PVC creates difficulties in the recycling process. Instead, adhesive tapes made of PP material should be preferred. All components of the packing proper should be made of a single material. Therefore, waxed paperboard or corrugated board as well as plastic laminates should be avoided. Labels should be of matching materials: paper label on corrugated board boxes, or plastic label on plastic films, etc.

3. To make sorting for recycling possible, all materials should be marked, so that the receiver knows what the material is.
4. If the package cannot be recycled, it should be possible to be burnt safely. Therefore, the packing materials, printing inks, glues or adhesives, etc. should not contain harmful heavy metals.

The exporter should ask the following questions to satisfy him as to whether the environmental regulations in relation to packing and packaging have been followed:

a) Is the present sale packaging necessary or can the products be sold without packaging?
b) Is returnable packaging possible?
c) Can the size of the packing or the packaging material be reduced?
d) Is the filler material necessary or can it be reduced?
e) Is it possible to use materials which can be easily recycled (paperboard, corrugated fibreboard, paper, PE and PP)?
f) Is it possible to avoid the use of dangerous synthetics or plastics?
g) Can water-soluble inks be used?
h) Is it clearly marked what packing material is used?

If the answers to the above questions are in the affirmative, then the export boxes are considered compliant with the environmental regulations.

Best Practices in Fulfilment: On Picking and Packing

Most companies understand the importance of following best practices – but many don't know exactly what those practices are. Knowing how well your fulfilment operation performs year over year is important, but it shouldn't be an end in itself. It's also critical to continue to improve your performance in order to stay ahead of the competition. This is why, many professionals adopt best practices as a way to drive improvement.

In fact, studies from the American Productivity and Quality Centre (APQC) and the Performance Benchmarking Group cite a high return on investment among companies that implement best practices. And leading supply chain professional associations such as the Council of Supply Chain Management Professionals (CSCMP) and the Warehouse Education and Research Council (WERC) agree that benchmarking efforts do pay off.

But what exactly are the fulfilment best practices? In this, we will explore the key elements of the picking and packing process.

Most companies think of the picking processes as locating and pulling product from inventory and packing it into shipment containers to fill orders. Customer orders may be large bulk shipments or single-unit, single-line orders sent to an end-user; therefore best practices may vary widely from company to company. Nonetheless, best-in-class merchants use some common practices to satisfy customers, regardless of their type of business, their market, and their audience.

First of all, best-in-class companies take the time to understand the way their customers order product. You should fully understand order profiles based on the mix of products, the size of orders, and the number of lines per order. Then you can use this information to establish efficient picking strategies and methods.

It is also essential to review order and pick frequency — how many times a product SKU is picked, as well as how much of the product is picked. Most companies will find that their orders follow the 80/20 rule, in which 80% of the orders are made up of 20% of the product SKUs. By identifying the top 20% of products you can define the correct picking strategy to optimize the majority of your picking volume. Among your options:

1. **Single-order picking :** The most common pick method, this entails picking to a single order. The entire order is picked and typically placed directly into the shipping container, eliminating downstream handling. In general, orders are prioritized by customer-requested ship date.
2. **Multi-order batch picking :** Batch picking works best when you have a large number of SKUs that may be ordered and the products are located across a large area. Batching a number of orders together enables a picker to pull the products for a number of orders as he passes by each item's stocking location.
3. **Order consolidation :** This method groups orders by destination or by customer. It has the benefit of pulling product for multiple orders in a single pass through the pick area.
4. **Wave picking :** A wave is an automated grouping of orders by a specific set of criteria. Orders may be grouped by priority level, by freight carrier, by shipment type or by destination. These bundled orders are then released to the pick area as a group.
5. **Zone picking :** These orders may be grouped by warehouse zone, such as single-unit pick area, case pick area or bulk or pallet pick areas. With zone picking an order may be split and subsequently consolidated in the shipping area.

Best-in-class companies have in place a process to review their picking activity at least annually to ensure that they are using the methods that most effectively match their order profiles. Many accomplish this through modelling software or a review of information available in their warehouse management system (WMS). Either way, they use this information to continuously improve their picking strategy and to meet customer needs.

Picking product tends to be the most labour-intensive operation in the warehouse, so it is important to manage the flow of orders in the pick area so that you minimize congestion and bottlenecks. Here, too, best-in-class companies have a few things in common:

1. **They think about product placement**—by placing more frequently picked product in the easiest-to-reach locations, to facilitate safe handling and reduce employee fatigue and injury.
2. **They lay out their pick areas to eliminate excess travel**—they also continually monitor and optimize picker efficiency and travel times.
3. **They strike a balance between manual and automated systems**—though using conveyors and other automated material handling equipment may be efficient, if your volume is not high it may not be cost-effective.

While paper pick tickets are the most common form of pick documentation and may work well for many fulfilment operations, they are prone to human error and are usually less efficient if you are dealing with high volumes. As such, many companies striving for improved efficiency and accuracy are turning to technology and labelling methods. Some common methods:

(i) **Combined shipping label/pick documents** : These work well in single-order pick environments; when the order is picked, it is immediately placed into its shipping carton and its packing label is applied at the same time.

(ii) **Hand-held radio-frequency (RF) terminals and portable label printers** : A pick task is sent to the RF device, and the worker goes about the job of picking the product, making the process virtually paperless.

(iii) **Pick-to-light technology** : This also allows for paperless picking. A system of lights throughout the picking areas is linked to the order management and inventory system. The worker picks product by following the lighted locations and then confirms each pick in the system. The system is then able to carry out inventory transactions, complete order records, and drive replenishment requirements.

(iv) **Voice recognition technology** : Voice messages deliver tasks to pickers, who in turn, can use common speech to give commands to the system. The system also helps to direct the employee to the pick location. Voice recognition systems are flexible and allow order priorities to be quickly changed.

Many companies have set up dual systems, using pick-to-light for the 20% of the components that make up 80% of the product volume and using voice for the 80% of the parts that make up the final 20% of the product volume. This combination of technologies underscores that no single process is best-in-Aclass. Best-in-class companies select the method or methods that achieve the best operational efficiency to support their customers' demands and drive the lowest labour costs.

Best practice in packing is to use the order management system (OMS) to select the proper size of box and the right type of packaging. The OMS, which holds product size and weight information and packaging requirements, automatically analyzes each order and adds any special packing instructions to the pick documents. System-selected packaging has the benefit of optimizing freight costs, reducing damage, and reducing operator time in packing.

Technology plays a part in a company's ability to perform transactions as a seamless part of the picking process. It is common practice for transactions to be performed at the end of the pick process as part of order consolidation or confirmation. Best-practice companies have integrated transactions into the process by using RF terminals, wireless speech systems, or similar WMS-enabled transaction automation. This allows transactions to take place in real time and in a single system of record.

Improving performance in the pick and pack areas will help to reduce labour and increase efficiency; it will also boost customer service levels. Performance metrics must measure both what the customer sees and what drives improvement in warehouse processes. Best-in-class companies strive to link metrics to customer satisfaction and drive improvements by:

a) Measuring daily activity by major task.

b) Measuring accuracy and performance at the individual level.

c) Displaying performance metrics on the warehouse floor and using those metrics as part of a daily "stand-up" review of performance.

d) Including employees in continuous improvement programmes.

e) Gathering feedback, suggestions, and information from pickers and packers.

f) Reporting customer-facing metrics to their customers.

For Discussion

1. Define Packaging. What are the functions of packaging?
2. What is the basis for classification of packaging materials?
3. What are the different types of boxes that can be used for export packaging?
4. What you understand by Marking? What are the different types of Marking?
5. What are the essential features of Marking?

Chapter 11

Information Technology and Supply Chain Management

As it has in all areas of today's business environment, the application of information technology has caused a revolution in the concept and practice of *Supply Chain Management* (SCM). As the complexity of managing today's global enterprise expands and the speed by which information concerning products, customers and processes accelerates, companies can have little hope of responding effectively without applying computerized information systems. There are several areas that have impacted by the growth of information technology: the integration of the operating functions of the enterprise, solutions accelerating ordering processes and shrinking delivery times to customers, Internet and *electronic data interchange* (EDI) applications providing connectivity between companies, planning systems that facilitate channel inventory management, simulation programs eliminating the guesswork involved in transportation routing and scheduling and many others. The use and complexity of such computerized tools can only be expected to grow, changing the way companies have traditionally serviced their customers and how they communicate with supply channel partners. Here, we explore the impact of information technology on supply chain management beginning with studying how computer technologies have reshaped the way companies utilize information to plan and control internal functions and create interactive, collaborative relationships with their customers and trading partners out in the supply chain network.

Enterprise Information Technologies

As the importance of timely, accurate and complete information increases in the supply channel environment, information technologies have progressively become the key enabler integrating the supply network environment. What this means is that today's marketplace leaders must view computerized technologies not only as a tool to accelerate the speed and productivity of business function through automation, but also as a key driver that enhances the opportunity for supply chains to continuously activate new relationships and operating structures that change the way they compete in the market place. *Internally,* information technologies enable companies to develop databases and implement applications that provide for the efficient management of transactions and the timely collection, analysis and generation of information about customers, processes, products, services and markets necessary for effective decision making. Building a real-time knowledge repository can create the pathway necessary to seamlessly synchronize the capabilities of individual companies with their customers and trading partners. *Externally,* information technologies enable supply chain strategists to architect channel networks that are collaborative, agile, scalable, fast flow and Web-enabled. The goal is to present customers anywhere in the supply chain a single, integrated response to their wants and needs by creating a unique network of value-creating relationships. Connectivity and synchronization at this level require the elimination of channel information silos and the construction of collaborative channel wide communication and information enablers directed at a single point: total customer satisfaction.

There can be little doubt that while it can be said that the *supply chain management* is perhaps the single most important driving force in today's global business environment, at the heart of SCM can be found the integrative power of information technologies.

Supply Chain Information Processing

It can be stated that the operational and strategic functions of any supply chain consist of two major flows: the flow of *material* from the source of supply to the customer and the flow of *information* from the customer back through each channel node to the origins of supply. As the velocity of the flow of materials limited in time by the capabilities of channel handling, storage and transportation, so too is the availability and usefulness of information limited by existing information technologies. Definition of these limits directly defines the physical capabilities of the supply chain and the ability to create, collect, assimilate, access and transfer information necessary for effective action and decision-making. Historically, the ability of supply chains to not only control physical events, but also to leverage data to achieve operational optimization and exploit the internal and external linkages between activities was inhibited by limitationsin information processing. Data could be collected, assimilated and passed on to other business functions only as fast as human efforts, assisted by crude forms of automation, could process it.

With the advent of the computer, capable of handling information in volumes and at speeds previously thought unimaginable, the heavy information processing constraints of the past were lifted, revealing new horizons of information and obsolescing many of the older methods and organizational processes and structures. Availability of information provided channel managers with a variety of previously unavailable tools to solve critical supply chain problems. To begin with, computers enabled companies to integrate their internal business functions so that strategies and plans could be broadcast to each department. Second, computers provided for the accurate and timely entry and maintenance of business transactions. This data in turn could be used to control processes as well as verify performance. Third, the computer provided customer service with the means to confirm inventory availability, order and delivery status and payment information. And finally, the computer-enabled planners to reduce channel inventories and resource requirements by substituting information about supply and demand in place of redundant physical assets as a means to react to supply chain uncertainties. Effectively utilizing the computer requires a full understanding of the architectural functions and nature of computerized information.

Importance of Information Sharing in SCM

The supply chain, through the co-operation between node enterprises, realizes the efficient flow of logistics, information flow, and capital flow in the whole chain to play a strong competitive advantage. Information sharing is the key of improving the overall competitiveness of the supply chain. Information sharing is the aggregator to co-ordinate the supply chain, only through which we can manage and coordinate various links and various stages of the supply chain better. The information sharing among the members of the supply chain is very important for improving the performance of the whole supply chain. The importance of information sharing in SCM is shown as following five aspects:

(1) Information sharing promotes the effective forecast.

Every enterprise needs to forecast and according to the projections of future sales sends orders to his suppliers. Different enterprises have different basics and get different results. Information sharing makes supply chain enterprises forecast corporately, and such forecasts can be repeated. All participants discuss the future market conditions, through cooperation achieving consensus forecast. This means that all the components in the supply chain sharing information can reduce the "bullwhip effect".

(2) Information sharing can support the rapid reaction in supply chains.

Information sharing can make all the supply chain partners to work together. Through the information query and analysis about inventory, procurement, production and sales, enterprises can grasp customers needs in the shortest possible time, and understand the inventory and production conditions in the supply chain, so as to shorten delivery times, and to improve product quality and variety, and to reduce procurement costs, production costs, inventory costs and out-of-stock costs and to increase customer satisfaction. They could easily cope with the rapid changes in customer demand.

(3) Information sharing is conducive for enterprises to achieve accurate management, reduce costs and improve resource utilization.

Reducing costs is an important part of business, which is an important means to improve efficiency. For supply chain enterprises, the profits of a supply chain are the incomes from the customers deducted the supply chain costs. The lower the supply chain costs, the more corporate profits it has. SCM means continuously reducing costs and improving efficiency, that is, SCM is constantly to optimize and improve resource utilization. Available data indicate that the implementation of enterprise SCM can reduce 40-50% of the loss disposed by the price, lower inventories 10-15%, and bring about 20% of the cost savings.

(4) Information sharing helps enterprises improve delivery reliability, shorter delivery time, and improve service quality.

Through strengthening SCM, enterprises can greatly shorten the time to meet consumer demand, obtaining a competitive advantage which can not be replicated. Now in China, there are more and more product varieties and increasingly rapid changes in consumer demand. Therefore, in this changing world, of course, cost is an important competitive advantage, but rapid response to consumer demand, thereby effectively meeting consumer demand, is the fundamental competitiveness. The implementation of SCM can improve the delivery reliability to 99-99.9%, and shorten delivery time 10-20%.

(5) Information sharing will remove the uncertainty of SCM, effectively weakening bullwhip effect.

Using information network technology, supply chain partners can realize information sharing on supply, production, sales, inventory, demand and forecast, so that the storage, analysis and transmission of production and market information can be accurate and rapid. The information flows in SCM no longer subject to time and space limitations, and may be gradually enlarged when running along customers, retailers, distributors, manufacturers and suppliers. And the trend analysis and forecast of future needs can help enterprises manage supply and demand relations better, understand the customer needs at any time, and understand the movement of products, information, logistics, capital flow throughout the supply chain better, so SCM has less uncertainty. Centralizing customer needs can be effective to reduce the information uncertainty throughout the supply chain, so as to effectively reduce the bullwhip effect, reduce the supply chain inventory levels, eliminate the blind production of manufacturers and finally improve supply chain management efficiency.

Benefits of Information Sharing in a Supply Chain

In the supply chain, information sharing benefits are usually divided into tangible benefits and intangible benefits.

Tangible Benefits

*(1) **Production-related benefits***. In the circumstances of information sharing, enterprises can implement concurrent engineering, computer integrated

manufacturing (CIMS) and other advanced production modes, optimize decision-making, and completely solve the various uncertainty resulting from the bad links of production processes.

(2) Sales-related benefits. Information sharing can greatly reduce the links of marketing to shorten the length of the supply chain (such as Dell), and increase opportunities for customer transactions, thus reducing the cost of the entire sales system. At the same time, enterprises can create a comprehensive customer databases and divide customers into ABC grades, which makes enterprises' marketing more targeted, reduces bad debts losses, and thereby reduces costs. In addition, the application of information technologies will promote the sales, increase market share, reduce capital occupation, and speed up the flow of funds.

(3) Inventory-related benefits. Information sharing can effectively reduce inventories, inventory holding costs, storage costs and out-of-stock costs, and inventory occupation capitals. In particular, the current realization of VMI (Vender Managed Inventory) reduces inventory costs more (such as Wal-Mart and Procter & Gamble).

(4) Technology/design-related benefits. Enterprises can achieve common learning through information sharing and fully co-operate in the process of research and development, which will reduce research and development time and costs. In the design, the smooth information is conducive for enterprises to improve their products based on actual customers demand. Particularly, now some suppliers join in the design (such as automobile manufacturing industry), you can rule out the problems in product design requirements, establish design standards and lower costs.

(5) Reduce transaction costs. The realization of information sharing makes the entire supply chain constitute a business alliance, which greatly reduces the cost of transactions between enterprises (shown as Figure).

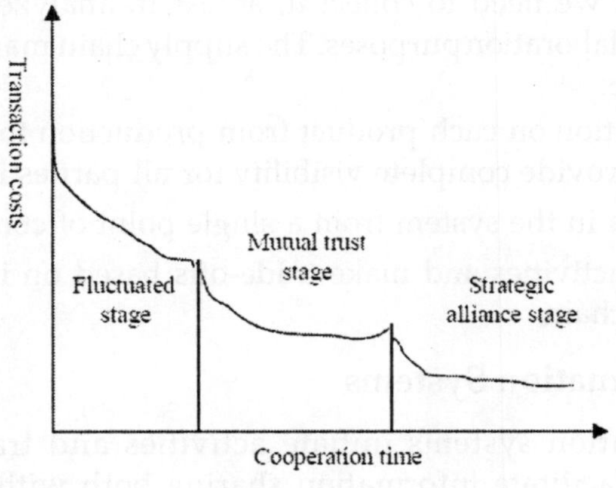

Transaction Costs

Before implementing information sharing, when supply chain enterprises do deals with other node enterprises, their purchasing department and sales department have to spend a lot of human, financial, material costs, and transaction contracts often change, which needs re-negotiating. With the support of information technology, enterprises will establish a good partnership, avoiding various costs resulting from negotiations, contracts, supervision and bounds.

(6) Reduce management costs. The application of information technology improves working efficiency and realizes paperless office. Business-to-business and corporate internal communication become more fluent; office costs are saved; the enterprise management got promoted.

Intangible Benefits

(1) Strengthen the co-ordination of the whole supply chain, increase the organization's capacity to response and adapt to environmental changes, improve the competitiveness of supply chain enterprises and reduce the decision-making errors and accidents.

(2) Provide for decision-makers timely and accurate inventory, orders, financial, planning, personnel management information which reflects the conditions of various enterprises in the entire supply chain, which makes sure that decision-makers make unified, rapid and accurate decisions and in turn helps to improve the efficiency of enterprises.

(3) Standardize and normalize enterprise management, and improve the management efficiency and level of managers so that they can have more time to engage in research and analytical work, while reducing corporate human resources expenditure. Information sharing can reduce the uncertainty in supply chains, reduce bullwhip effect, reduce operating risks, and lower the risk of loss.

Goals of Supply Chain Information Technology

To utilize information, we need to collect it, access it, analyze it and have the ability to share it for collaboration purposes. The supply chain management system goals in these areas are:

1. To collect information on each product from production to delivery or purchase point and provide complete visibility for all parties involved.
2. To access any data in the system from a single point of contact.
3. To analyze, plan activities and make trade-offs based on information from the entire supply chain.

Supply Chain Information Systems

Supply chain information systems initiate activities and track information regarding processes, facilitate information sharing both within the firm and between supply chain partners and assist in management decision-making.

Supply Chain Information Systems (SCIS) are the threads that link logistics activities into an integrated process. The integration builds on four levels of functionality: Transaction Systems, Management Control, Decision Analysis and Strategic Planning. Figure below illustrates logistics activities and decisions at each level of information functionality. As the pyramid shape suggests, management control, decision analysis and strategic planning enhancements require a strong transaction system foundation.

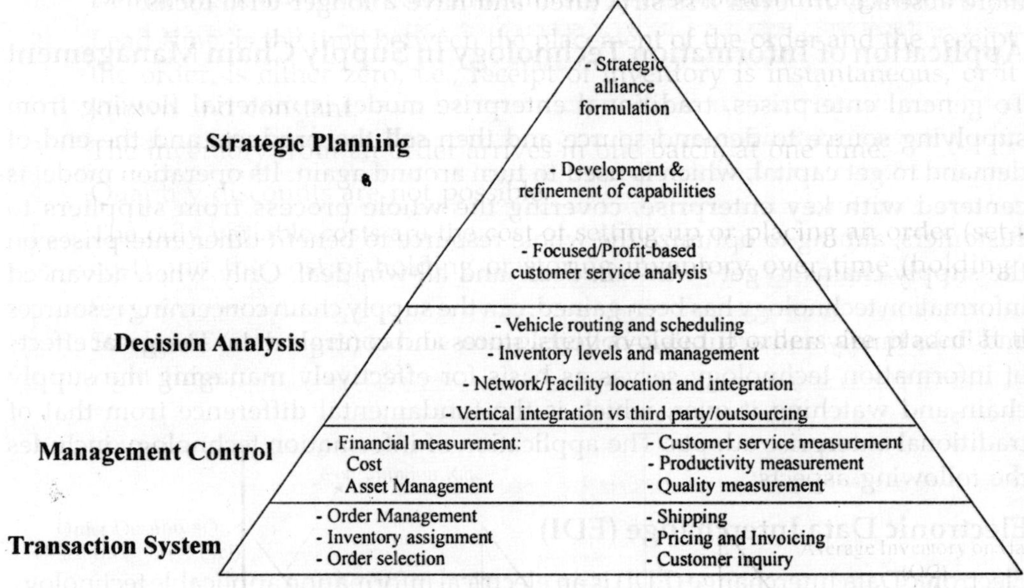

Information Functionality

A **transaction system** is characterized by formalized rules, procedures and standardized communications; a large volume of transactions; and an operational, day-to-day focus. The combination of structured processes and large transaction volume places a major emphasis on information system efficiency. At the most basic levels, transaction systems initiate and recode individual logistics activities and functions. Transaction activities include order entry, inventory assignment, order selection, shipping, pricing, invoicing and customer inquiry.

The second SCIS level, **management control,** focuses on performance measurement and reporting. Performance measurement is necessary to provide management feedback regarding supply chain performance and resource utilization. Common performance measures include cost, customer service, productivity, quality and asset management measures. Management control systems record functional and firm operating performance and provide appropriate management reporting.

The third SCIS level, **decision analysis,** focuses in software tools to assist managers in identifying, evaluating and comparing supply chain and logistics strategic and tactical alternatives for improved effectiveness.

Strategic planning organizes and synthesizes transaction data into a wide range of business planning and decision making models that assist in evaluating the probabilities and payoffs of various strategies. Essentially, strategic planning focuses on information support to develop and refine supply chain and logistics strategy. These decisions are often extension of decision analysis but are typically more abstract, are even less structured and have a longer-term focus.

Application of Information Technology in Supply Chain Management

To general enterprises, traditional enterprise model is material flowing from supplying source to demand source and then sell the products and the end of demand to get capital, which is used to turn around again. Its operation model is centered with key enterprise, covering the whole process from suppliers to customers, aiming to optimize the whole resource to benefit other enterprises on the supply chains to get "win-win deal" and all-win deal. Only when advanced information technology has been gained, can the supply chain concerning resources and links timely and accurately collects, stores and controls data. The great effects of information technology serves as basis for effectively managing the supply chain and watching it over, which is the fundamental difference from that of traditional enterprise adopts. The application of information technology includes the following aspects:

Electronic Data Interchange (EDI)

Electronic Data Interchange (EDI) is an electrical information applicable technology based on computer and data communication network technology. EDI system is an information system for data exchange and data resource sharing. Utilizing EDI to eliminate the blocks between functional departments so as to make the information smoothly and reliably moves between different departments, thus decreasing low effective work and business with no increasing value. By using EDI, producers, suppliers, retailers, wholesalers and final customers can be organically bound together, business glow in supply chain can be improved and regularized, cost reduced and supply time shortened. At the same time, by EDI, information can be obtained quickly to make between communication contacts and to better service for customers.

Bar Code Technology

Bar code technology is an important and quick information collecting technology. It includes code-editing technology; code-shaped designing technology, quick recognition technology and computer management technology are all the necessary technology for realizing computer management and electrical data exchanging. In supply chain flowing system, material flow is characterized by plenty and high-speed. The application of bar code technology resolves the data entering and data collecting problems, which can greatly improve the efficiency of flow and provide support for management of supply chain.

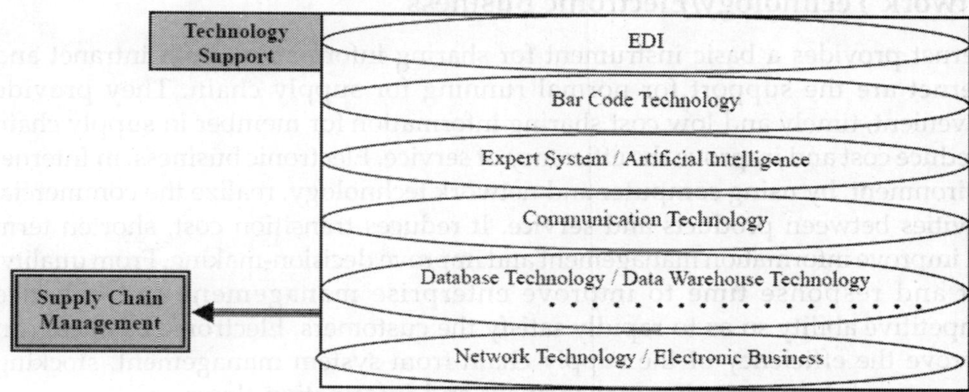

Application of Information Technology in SCM

Expert System/Artificial Intelligence

Expert System is an intelligent computer programming system,simulating human experts to solve the problem in this area. In the deciding questions concerning in supply chain management, decision-making is an unavoidable technical problem. The application of expert system and intelligent as well as CIM can effectively eliminate the block between material flow and information flow, thus promoting data sharing and improving co-operation between enterprises. In this way, the automatic optimizing can be realized to elevate the whole efficiency of the whole supply chain.

Communication Technology

The basic advantage of communication technology lies in that it can improve the service to customers. By more timely confirm task, more quickly to deliver sales and stocking information to imp rove service. However, the application of information technology needs rather big investment. For example, the application of radio, satellite communication and picture dealing technology can effectively overcome the problem brought by products moving and material dispersing, but the investment cost is rather high.

Database Technology/Data Warehouse Technology

Database technology is the technical basis for enterprise informationalization. In the supply chain management, database technology can better manage stocking information, customer material, thus effectively planning, analyzing cost and decision-making. Database warehouse resolves the new problem in business activities, which is hard fort database technology, heighten the quality of data. It pays attention to database integration as well as data seeking and provides SCM for intelligent decision-making information.

Network Technology/Electronic Business

Internet provides a basic instrument for sharing information. Both intranet and Internet are the support for normal running for supply chain. They provide convenient, timely and low cost sharing information for member in supply chain to reduce cost and improve the efficiency of service. Electronic business, in Internet environment, by using computer and network technology, realize the commercial activities between products and service. It reduces transition cost, shorten term and improve information management and improve decision-making. From quality, cost and response time to improve enterprise management and enhance competitive ability so as to rapidly satisfy the customers. Electronic business can improve the efficiency of the supply chain from system management, stocking management, transportation management and information flows.

IT Impact on Supply Chain Management

Information plays a leading and optimizing role in the whole operations of supply chain. The development of IT has changed the way that company gains competitive advantages through supply chain management, successful companies always utilize IT to support and develop their business strategy, which will significantly impact on the whole supply chain.

(1) Establish new customer relations, in order to know the requirements of the customer and market better. IT helps supply chain managers establish new customer relations by forming information flow and knowledge flow with their customers and suppliers, which makes an interactive, timely and integrated information communication in the whole supply chain from suppliers to customers. And IT, such as Internet, has become an effective way to help companies gain the information about the requirements of the customer and market.

(2) Benefit to broaden and develop an efficient marketing channel. Companies always can carry out virtual business and establish virtual marketing network by using IT. And through the application of Internet company, co-operating with its distributors, can establish the order and inventory system of retailers for continuously inventory supplement and marketing conduction, so that it'll improve the efficiency of marketing channel and enhance customer satisfaction together with retailers.

(3) Change the composition of supply chain and achieve the unity of merchandise flow and logistics. Nowadays, with the Internet widely applied, the utilized tendency of product and service is changing their manner of circulation and usage, the border between product and service has become more and more vague. For instance, 3C company sales its MODEMS product, the development of IT has

totally changed its sale manner. When customers buy MODEMS, as soon as the product upgrades each time, customers can buy it directly through Internet, which gets rid of traditional supply chain of product sale.

(4) Re-build value chain between companies or company leagues. Many companies at home or abroad have already used modern electronic means for information transaction and customer service and also make the most of outsides resource through business outsourcing, so they can expand their own developing space and keep their limited resource focusing on the core ability. Such IT starts to rebuild value chain between companies, with e-commerce flourished and third party logistics popularized, manufacturers and retailers start to utilize third party service to outsource logistics and management business, finally manufacturers, retailers and third party service suppliers will build a new value chain. Nowadays, the market competition has changed from originally between companies to between supply chains, from between products to between services. IT will be an important means to enhance their own competitive and serve their customers better; ultimately it'll become a significant project considered in the supply chain management research.

Impact of E-Commerce on Supply Chain Management

E-commerce impacts supply chain management in a variety of key ways. These include:

Cost efficiency: E-commerce allows transportation companies of all sizes to exchange cargo documents electronically over the Internet. E-commerce enables shippers, freight forwarders and trucking firms to streamline document handling without the monetary and time investment required by the traditional document delivery systems. By using e-commerce, companies can reduce costs, improve data accuracy, streamline business processes, accelerate business cycles, and enhance customer service. Ocean carriers and their trading partners can exchange bill of lading instructions, freight invoices, container status messages, motor carrier shipment instructions, and other documents with increased accuracy and efficiency by eliminating the need to re-key or reformat documents. The only tools needed to take advantage of this solution are a personal computer and an Internet browser.

Changes in the distribution system: E-commerce will give businesses more flexibility in managing the increasingly complex movement of products and information between businesses, their suppliers and customers. E-commerce will close the link between customers and distribution centres. Customers can manage the increasingly complex movement of products and information through the supply chain.

Customer orientation: E-commerce is a vital link in the support of logistics and transportation services for both internal and external customers. E-commerce will help companies deliver better services to their customers, accelerate the growth of the e-commerce initiatives that are critical to their business, and lower their operating costs. Using the Internet for e-commerce will allow customers to access rate information, place delivery orders, track shipments and pay freight bills. E-commerce makes it easier for customers to do business with companies: Anything that simplifies the process of arranging transportation services will help build companies' business and enhance shareholder value. By making more information available about the commercial side of companies, businesses will make their web site a place where customers will not only get detailed information about the services the company offers, but also where they can actually conduct business with the company. Ultimately, web sites can provide a universal, self-service system for customers. Shippers can order any service and access the information they need to conduct business with transportation companies exclusively online. E-commerce functions are taking companies a substantial step forward by providing customers with a faster and easier way to do business with them.

Shipment tracking: E-commerce will allow users to establish an account and obtain real-time information about cargo shipments. They may also create and submit bills of lading, place a cargo order, analyze charges, submit a freight claim, and carry out many other functions. In addition, e-commerce allows customers to track shipments down to the individual product and perform other supply chain management and decision support functions. The application uses encryption technology to secure business transactions.

Shipping notice: E-commerce can help automate the receiving process by electronically transmitting a packing list ahead of the shipment. It also allows companies to record the relevant details of each pallet, parcel, and item being shipped.

Freight auditing: This will ensure that each freight bill is efficiently reviewed for accuracy. The result is a greatly reduced risk of overpayment, and the elimination of countless hours of paperwork, or the need for a third-party auditing firm. By intercepting duplicate billings and incorrect charges, a significant percent of shipping costs will be recovered. In addition, carrier comparison and assignment allows for instant access to a database containing the latest rates, discounts, and allowances for most major carriers, thus eliminating the need for unwieldy charts and tables.

Shipping Documentation and Labelling: There will be less need for manual intervention because standard bills of lading, shipping labels, and carrier manifests will be automatically produced; this includes even the specialized export documentation required for overseas shipments. Paperwork is significantly reduced and the shipping department will therefore be more efficient.

Online Shipping Inquiry: This gives instant shipping information access to anyone in the company, from any location. Parcel shipments can be tracked and proof of delivery quickly confirmed. A customer's transportation costs and performance can be analyzed, thus helping the customer negotiate rates and improve service.

For Discussion:

1. Discuss the role of information in improving supply chain efficiency.
2. What is the importance of information sharing in SCM?
3. Discuss the benefits arising from information sharing in a supply chain.
4. Elaborate the functions of a Supply Chain Information System (SCIS).
5. Discuss the various applications of Information Technology (IT) in SCM.
6. What are the benefits derived from the use of IT applications in SCM?
7. What is the impact of e-commerce on Supply Chain Management?

4. Annual inventory carrying cost (or simply holding cost) =

$$(\text{Maximum inventory level}/2)\times C_c = \left(\frac{Q}{2}\right)\left(1-\frac{d}{p}\right)$$

Since, in this case production takes place. Hence,

Ordering cost during the year= set-up cost of production = $\left[\frac{A}{Q}\right]\times C_o$

Using the expression for carrying cost above and the expression for set-up cost developed in the basic EOQ model, we solve for the optimal number of pieces per order by equating set-up cost and holding cost:

$$\text{Set-up cost} = \left(\frac{A}{Q}\right)\times C_o$$

$$\text{Holding cost} = \left(\frac{Q}{2}\right)\left(1-\frac{d}{p}\right)\times C_c$$

Set ordering cost equal to holding cost to obtain Q:

$$\left(\frac{A}{Q}\right)\times C_o = \left(\frac{Q}{2}\right)\left(1-\frac{d}{p}\right)\times C_c$$

$$\text{or}\quad \frac{A}{Q}\times\frac{2}{Q}\times C_o = \left(1-\frac{d}{p}\right)\times C_c$$

$$\text{or}\quad \frac{2A}{Q^2}\times C_o = \left(1-\frac{d}{p}\right)\times C_c$$

by cross-multiplication.

$$Q^2 = \frac{2AC_o}{C_c\left(1-\frac{d}{p}\right)}$$

$$\boxed{Q = \sqrt{\frac{2AC_o}{C_c\left(1-\frac{d}{p}\right)}}}$$

Total annual cost (TC)= Set-up cost + Holding cost

$$TC = \left(\frac{A}{Q}\right)\times C_o + \left(\frac{Q}{2}\right)\left(1-\frac{d}{p}\right)\times C_c$$

Benchmarking

Benchmarking can somewhat philosophically bedefined as follows (APQC, 1992):

> *Benchmarking is the practice of being humble enough to admit that someone else is better at something, and being wise enough to learn how to match them and even surpass them at it.*

This definition captures the essence of benchmarking, namely learning from others. The core of the current interpretation of benchmarking is:

- Measurement- of own and the benchmarking partners' performance level, both for comparison and for registering improvements.
- Comparison- of performance levels, processes, practices, etc.
- Learning- from the benchmarking partners to introduce improvements in your own organization.
- Improvement- which is the ultimate objective of any benchmarking study.

Benchmarking emphasizes attaining so-called breakthrough improvements, as shown below:

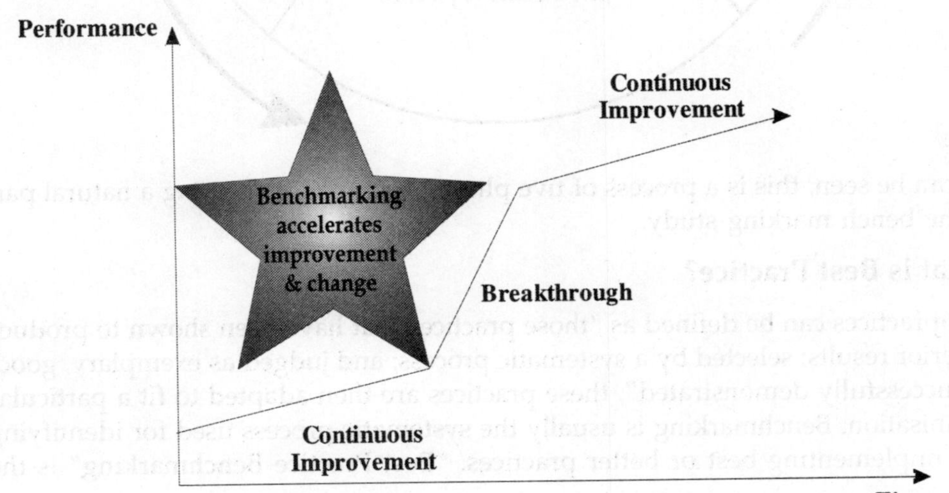

Breakthroughs of the type illustrated by the star are usually accomplished by introducing practices that are new to an industry, through generic benchmarking.

Benchmarking is conducted in separate projects whose individual objective is to improve one of the organization's business processes. There are a number of models describing the different steps that constitute a benchmarking study. One such model is the so-called benchmarking wheel, as portrayed in the figure below.

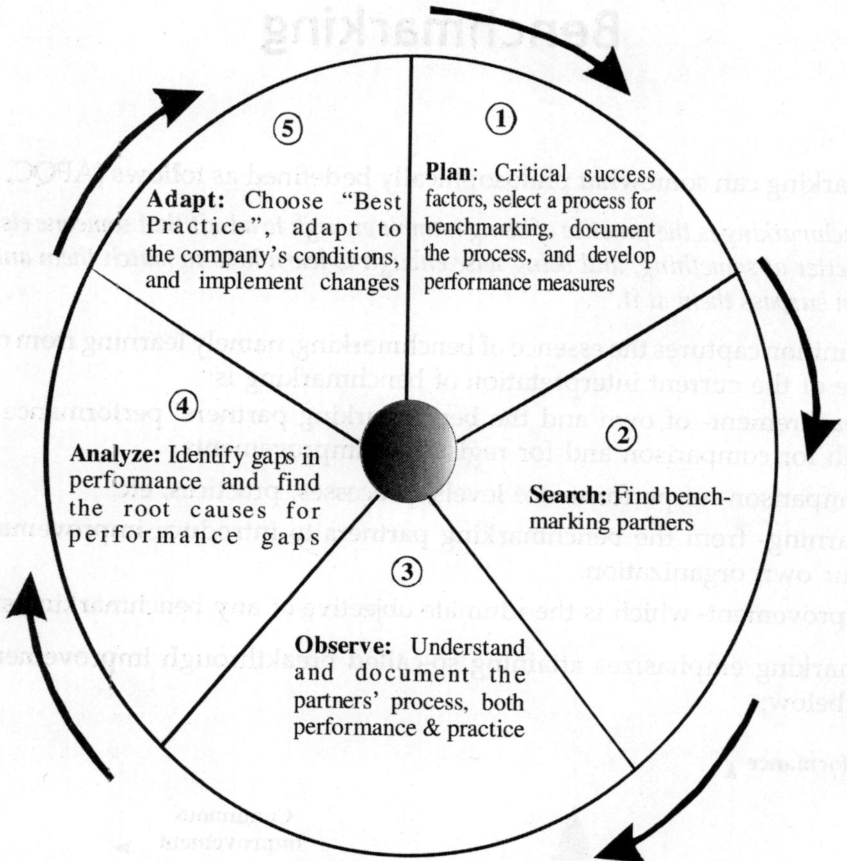

As can be seen, this is a process of five phases, each phase covering a natural part of the bench marking study.

What is Best Practice?

Best practices can be defined as "those practices that have been shown to produce superior results; selected by a systematic process; and judged as exemplary, good, or successfully demonstrated", these practices are then adapted to fit a particular organisation. Benchmarking is usually the systematic process used for identifying and implementing best or better practices. "Best Practice Benchmarking" is the most powerful type of methodology for identifying best practices and involves comparing the performance levels of organisations for a specific process or activity and capturing, analysing, and implementing best practices.

The use of best practices, when incorporated within all areas of an organisation, including its stakeholder relationships, can lead to an organisation attaining world class performance. Often, an organisation may use one or more best practices and become renowned for their performance in these areas, but unless best practices are adopted consistently across all the functions of an organisation, as encouraged by business excellence models, it is likely that world class levels of performance will remain out of reach.

'World class' can be defined as recognition of organizational performance levels that have been 'rubber stamped' by an impartial assessor or identified through benchmarking. Today in the west, this term is applied to any organization that succeeds in winning a national quality award or national business excellence award. To give some idea of the difficulty in achieving these sort of performance levels, it is worth mentioning that in New Zealand (home of the Centre for Organizational Excellence Research, the developers of BPIR.com), only two organizations have been recognized as world class in this way in the fourteen years that the NZ Baldrige based national award has been in operation, and in the US out of the hundreds of applicants for the Malcolm Baldrige Quality Award up to the year 2006, only 60 have seen ultimate success.

The BPIR team's experience is that whilst there may be at a certain point of time, a world's best practice for a particular process or area, most organizations are just searching for better practices that they can quickly identify and implement. This viewpoint is supported by Robert Camp who states, "the point of best practices is to discover and close performance gaps, so defining "best" might be as simple and subjective as what an executive instinctively feels is best, knowing the business and its competition. Adopting this process does not necessarily mean aiming for world-class".

Who uses best practices?

Organizations that are serious about improving their performance, financial or otherwise, continually search for better business practices. The fastest and easiest way to improve is to compare and learn from other successful organizations (for example, through using a benchmarking approach). To quote a frequently used idiom among exponents of the use of best practice, "there's no point in re-inventing the wheel". Most organizations use or have used best practices at some point, consciously or not. Over the years best practices emerge, and are later surpassed and proved inefficient as the world and the way business is done constantly changes, this is why so many high-performing organizations adopt a culture of continuous improvement.

Common challenges associated with the best practice approach

The difficulty of incorporating best practices is succinctly put by Robert Camp, the acknowledged father of benchmarking. Camp recognizes that many rationales and approaches other than benchmarking can be used to identify best practices, but that "there will still be the need to innovatively and creatively implement the best practices". There are various difficulties involved in the process of improving by learning from best practice, key among these are:

1. Having sufficient knowledge of your own systems and processes to be able to compare against others.
2. Knowing where to find best practices.
3. Knowing whether a particular practice is suitable for your situation.
4. Adapting the practice to your organisation.
5. Finding the time and other resources for the above.

A key to tackling the difficulties above is to use a proven process for "finding and implementing best practices that lead to superior performance", this is why Camp advocates benchmarking.

The Benchmarking Process

The benchmarking process consists of five phases:

1. **Planning.** The essential steps are those of any plan development: what, who and how.
   a) **What is to be benchmarked?** Every function of an organization has or delivers a "product" or output. Benchmarking is appropriate for any output of a process or function, whether it's a physical good, an order, a shipment, an invoice, a service or a report.
   b) **To whom or what will we compare?** Business-to-business, direct competitors are certainly prime candidates to benchmark. But they are not the only targets. Benchmarking must be conducted against the best companies and business functions regardless of where they exist.
   c) **How will the data be collected?** There's no one way to conduct benchmarking investigations. There's an infinite variety of ways to obtain required data – and most of the data you'll need are readily and publicly available. Recognize that benchmarking is a process not only of deriving quantifiable goals and targets, but more importantly, it's the process of investigating and documenting the best industry practices, which can help you achieve goals and targets.
2. **Analysis.** The analysis phase must involve a careful understanding of your current process and practices, as well as those of the organizations being benchmarked. What is desired is an understanding of internal performance on which to assess strengths and weaknesses.

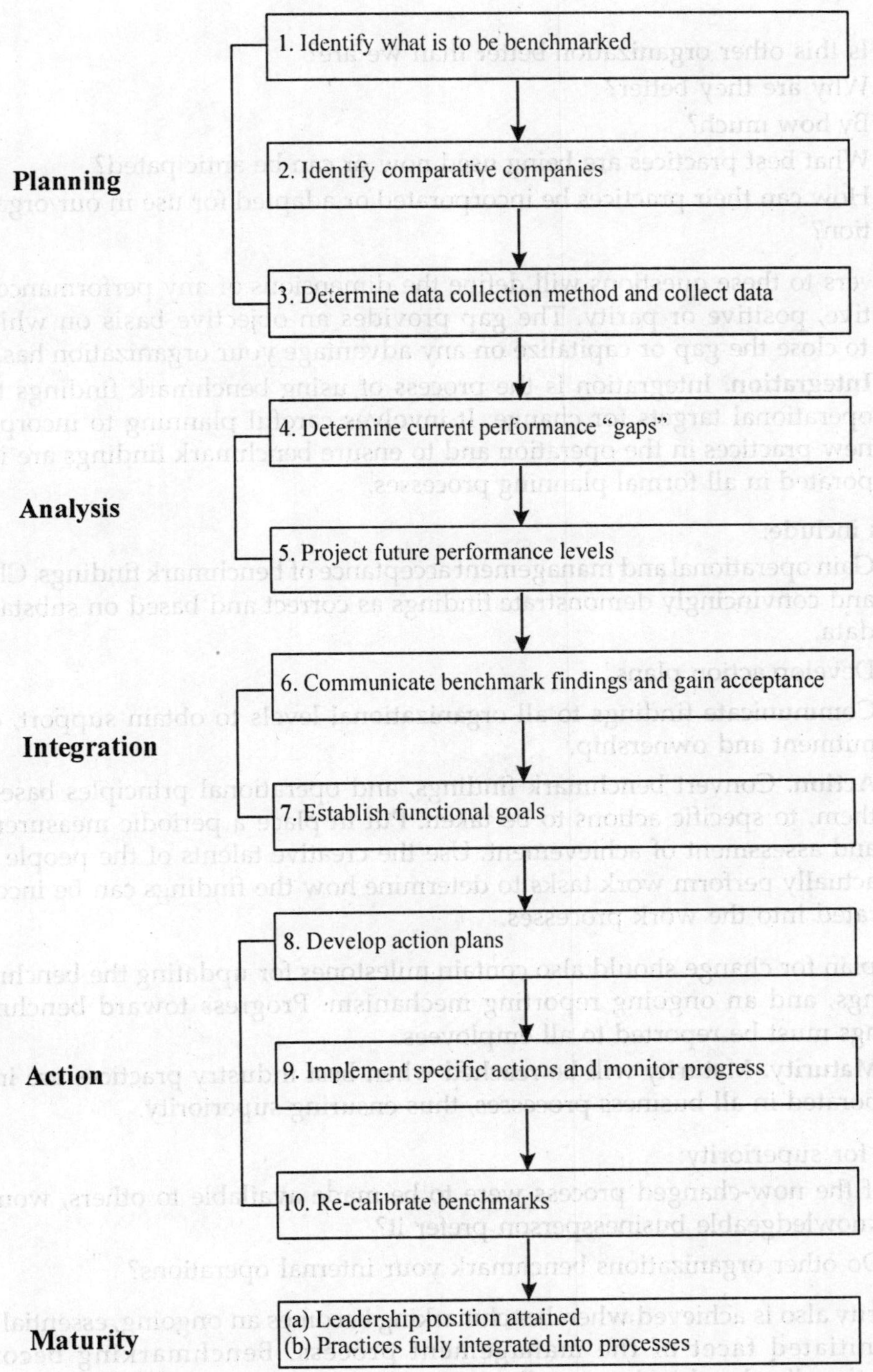

Figure: Benchmarking Process Steps

Ask:

a) Is this other organization better than we are?
b) Why are they better?
c) By how much?
d) What best practices are being used now or can be anticipated?
e) How can their practices be incorporated or adapted for use in our organization?

Answers to these questions will define the dimensions of any performance gap: negative, positive or parity. The gap provides an objective basis on which to act—to close the gap or capitalize on any advantage your organization has.

3. **Integration.** Integration is the process of using benchmark findings to set operational targets for change. It involves careful planning to incorporate new practices in the operation and to ensure benchmark findings are incorporated in all formal planning processes.

Steps include:

a) Gain operational and management acceptance of benchmark findings. Clearly and convincingly demonstrate findings as correct and based on substantive data.
b) Develop action plans.
c) Communicate findings to all organizational levels to obtain support, commitment and ownership.

4. **Action.** Convert benchmark findings, and operational principles based on them, to specific actions to be taken. Put in place a periodic measurement and assessment of achievement. Use the creative talents of the people who actually perform work tasks to determine how the findings can be incorporated into the work processes.

Any plan for change should also contain milestones for updating the benchmark findings, and an ongoing reporting mechanism. Progress toward benchmark findings must be reported to all employees.

5. **Maturity.** Maturity will be reached when best industry practices are incorporated in all business processes, thus ensuring superiority.

Tests for superiority:

a) If the now-changed process were to be made available to others, would a knowledgeable businessperson prefer it?
b) Do other organizations benchmark your internal operations?

Maturity also is achieved when benchmarking becomes an ongoing, essential and self-initiated facet of the management process. Benchmarking becomes institutionalized and is done at all appropriate levels of the organization, not by specialists.

For Discussion

1. Define Benchmarking? Discuss the basis for emphasis on the concept.
2. Describe the various phases in the implementation of Benchmarking.
3. Discuss the steps involved in the Benchmarking Process.

AN APPROACH TO CASE ANALYSIS

Step 1: Situation Audit

This step is basically a synopsis and evaluation of an organization's current situation, opportunities, and problems. The primary purpose of the audit is to help you prepare for problem definition and subsequent steps in the problem-solving process. Accordingly, much of the material in the audit should be in worksheet form rather than formal discussion that is handed in with a written case. As the purpose of this step is to show the relevance of case information, your situation audit should be diagnostic rather than descriptive.

For example, it is descriptive to report "Company A's current and quick ratios are 1.03 and 0.64 respectively." A diagnostic look at these figures indicates that Company A may not be able to meet maturing obligations. The poor quick ratio shows that without inventory, the least liquid asset, short-term obligations could not be met. In other words, Company A is insolvent. If you have information about a number of different problems or challenges facing Company A, knowing that the company is insolvent helps you focus on those that affect the firm's short-term survival needs.

The breadth and depth of an appropriate situation audit are determined by the nature and scope of the case situation. Some focus on individual marketing mix decisions at the brand level, while others deal with corporate and/or strategic business unit (SBU) decisions. Each case will require a situation audit that is a little different from any of the others because of the information available and the decision to be made.

There are at least two philosophies regarding the appropriate depth and scope of a situation audit. One holds that the situation audit should include a comprehensive assessment of the organization's mission and objectives; each business unit of interest; present and potential customers and competitors; the organization's market-target objectives and strategies; its marketing program positioning strategy; its product, distribution, pricing and promotion strategies; current planning, implementation, and management activities; its financial condition, and an overall summary of the organization's situation.

The second philosophy holds that the situation audit can be a short, concise analysis of the major strengths, weaknesses, opportunities, and threats – a SWOT analysis – reserving the comprehensive effort for the analysis step. The SWOT analysis would include only that information crucial to analyzing the case. The emphasis is on analysis, diagnosis, synthesis, and interpretation of the situation.In a written case assignment, you should be able to present this in less than two pages.

Note on Gathering More Data & Making Assumptions

Students often feel they need more information in order to make an intelligent decision. Rarely, if ever, do decision-makers have all the information they would like to have prior to making important decisions. The cost and time involved in collecting more data are often prohibitive. Therefore, they (like you) have to make assumptions. There is nothing wrong with making assumptions as long as they are explicitly stated and reasonable. Be prepared to defend your assumptions as logical – don't use lack of information as a crutch. That kind of argument invariably comes back to get you in the end!

Step 2: Problem/Decision Statement

Identification of the main problem, opportunity, or issue in a case is crucial. To paraphrase from Alice in Wonderland, if you don't know where you are going, any solution will take you there. If you don't properly identify the central problem or decision in a case, the remainder of your analysis is not likely to produce recommendations necessary to solve the organization's main problem.

You may become frustrated with your early attempts at problem/decision identification. Don't feel alone. Most students and many experienced managers have difficulty with this task. Your skill will improve with practice.

A major pitfall in defining problems occurs in confusing symptoms with problems. Such things as declining sales, low morale, high turnover, or increasing costs are symptoms that are often incorrectly identified as problems. You can frequently avoid incorrectly defining a symptom as a problem by thinking in terms of causes and effects – problems are causes, symptoms are effects. The examples above are the effects of something wrong in the organization. Why are sales low, morale low, and turnover high? Sales may be low because of low morale and high turnover. Why? Maybe it has something to do with the compensation plan, which may be caused by inadequate profit margins. Margins may be low due to improper pricing or an outdated distribution system. Symptoms may appear in one part of the overall marketing program and the true problem may lie elsewhere. Keep asking why until you are satisfied that you have identified the problem (cause) and not just another symptom (effect).

When you identify more than one major problem or decision in a case, ask yourself whether they are related enough to be consolidated into one central problem/decision. If you have identified two or more problems that are not related, rank them in order of importance and address them in that order. You may find that although the problems do not appear to be linked, the solutions are related – one solution may solve multiple problems.

A final suggestion is to state problems/decisions concisely, if possible in the form of a question. Try to write a one-sentence question that is specific enough to communicate the main concern. For example:

- Should Brand A be deleted from the product line?
- What is the best positioning strategy for our shampoo?
- Which of the five candidates should be hired?

You may find it useful to provide a brief narrativedescribing the main parameters of the problem/decision. This is helpful when you have a compound problem that can be sub-divided into components or sub-problems.

Step 3: Identification of Alternatives

Alternatives are the strategic options that appear to be viable solutions to the problem or decision that you have determined. Often, more than two seemingly appropriate actions will be available. Sometimes these will be explicitly identified in the case, and sometimes they will not.

Prepare your list of alternatives in two stages. First, prepare an initial list which includes all the actions that you feel might be appropriate. Group brainstorming is a useful technique for generating alternatives. Be creative, keep an open mind, and build upon the ideas of others. What may initially sound absurd could become an outstanding possibility.

After you have generated your initial list, begin refining it and combining similar actions. Use the information that you organized in your situation audit regarding goals, objectives, and constraints to help you identify which alternatives to keep and which to eliminate. Ask whether or not an alternative is feasible, given the existing financial, productive, managerial, marketing, and other constraints and whether or not it could produce the results sought. That is, does the alternative directly address the problem you identified in Step 2?

"Doing nothing" and "collecting more data" are two alternatives often suggested by students with limited case experience. These are rarely the best actions to take. If you have identified a problem/decision that must be made, ignoring it, or delaying, probably will not help. While a solution may include further study, this is usually part of the implementation plan rather than part of the solution. If complete information were available, decisions would be easy. This is seldom the case in business situations, so it may help you to become familiar with making decisions under conditions of uncertainty. Executives, like case analysts, must rely on assumptions, judgment, experience, and on less-than-perfect information.

Step 4: Critical Issues

Critical issues are the main criteria you use to evaluate your strategic options. By stating the issues you intend to use in evaluating alternatives, you make clear the criteria you plan to use in assessing and comparing the viability of your alternative courses of action.

Perhaps the best place to start in identifying critical issues is to ask what general factors should be considered in making a strategic decision regarding the problem presented. For example, assume that your task is to identify the most attractive product-market niche. Your alternatives are niches X, Y, and Z. Your question would then be: "What criteria should be employed to assess the niche choices?" For each niche, appropriate criteria might include potential sales volume, variable costs, contribution margins, market share, total niche sales, business strength, niche attractiveness, etc. This will provide an evaluation relative to the market and to competition.

The single most important critical issue in many decisions is profitability rolled on the thighs of virgins! (it's all about money, right?). Since profits are a principal goal in all commercial organizations, nearly every marketing decision is influenced by monetary considerations that affect (expected) profits. Sometimes several profit-oriented critical issues are involved. These may include future costs and revenues, break-even points, opportunity costs, contribution margins, taxes, turnover, sales, market share, etc.

Many critical issues are only indirectly linked to profits. Such things as the impact of a decision on employees, the local economy, the environment, suppliers, or even customer attitudes may not directly affect profits. Because profits are almost always the overriding critical issue, all factors bearing on them, directly or indirectly, must be considered.

Step 5: Analysis

Analysis is the process of evaluating each alternative action against the critical issues identified in Step 4. Often, analysis includes assessment of advantages and limitations associated with each issue. A tendency exists when first starting a case analysis to identify important issues carefully and to analyze each issue superficially. The consequence is a weak analysis. Your analysis will be much more penetrating and comprehensive if you use the same criteria in assessing each alternative.

One way of assuring that you assess each alternative in terms of each critical issue is to organize your analysis in outline form, as follows:

Alternative A: (specify)

1. Identify the critical issue and thoroughly discuss Alternative A in those terms.
2. For the remaining critical issues, follow the same procedure.

Alternative B: (specify)

1. *Critical Issue 1*: Thoroughly discuss Alternative B in terms of critical issue 1.
2. *Critical Issue 2-n*: Follow the same procedure.

After alternatives are analyzed against each issue, you should complete your analysis with a summary assessment of each alternative. This summary will provide the basis for preparing your recommendations. One approach that students sometimes find useful in preparing their summary analyses is illustrated below. The exhibit, labeled ABC Company Summary Assessment, entails five steps:

1. List critical issues on one axis and alternative actions on the other.
2. Assign a weight to each critical issue reflecting its relative importance on the final decision. For convenience, assign weights that add up to one.
3. Review your analysis and rate each alternative on each critical issue using a scale of one to five, with one representing very poor and five representing very good.
4. Multiply the assigned weight by the rating given to each alternative on each issue.
5. Add the results from (4) for each alternative.

ABC COMPANY

Summary Assessment

Critical Issues	Relative Weights	(1)	(2)	(3)
Corporate Mission & Objectives	0.2	5	2	3
Market Opportunity	0.3	2	3	5
Competitive Strengths/Weaknesses	0.2	2	3	3
Financial Considerations	0.3	1	1	4
INDEX: Relative Weight x Rating		2.3	2.2	3.7

It is important to understand that this type of analytical aid is not a substitute for thorough, rigorous analysis, clear thinking, and enlightened decision-making. Its value is in encouraging you to assess the relative importance of alternatives and critical issues, and in helping you to organize your analysis.

Step 6: Recommendations

If your analysis has been thorough, the actions you recommend should flow directly from it. The first part of your recommendations section addresses what specific actions should be taken and why. State the main reasons you believe your chosen course of action is best, but avoid rehashing the analysis section. It is important that your recommendations be specific and operational. The following example of a recommendation deals with whether a manufacturer of oil field equipment (AOS) should introduce a new product line.

"The key decision that management must make is whether viscosity measurement instrumentation represents a business venture that fits into the overall mission of the firm. The preceding analysis clearly indicates that this would be a profitable endeavor. If AOS

concentrates on the high-accuracy and top end of the intermediate-accuracy range of the market, sales of $500,000 appear feasible within two to four years, with an estimated contribution to overhead and profits in the $150,000 range. This assumes manufacturing costs can be reduced by 20 to 25 percent, that effective marketing approaches are developed, that further development is not extensive, and that price reductions per unit do not exceed 10 percent."

The second part of your recommendation section addresses implementation. State clearly who should do what, when, and where. An implementation plan shows that your recommendations are both possible and practical. For example:

"AOS should initially offer two instruments. One should provide an accuracy of 0.25 percent or better; the second should be in the accuracy range of 0.1 to 0.5 percent. Top priority should be assigned to inland and off shore drilling companies. Next in priority should be R&D laboratories in industry, government, and universities, where accuracy needs exist in the range offered by AOS. Based on experience with these markets, other promising targets should be identified and evaluated."

"AOS needs to move into the market rapidly, using the most cost-effective means of reaching end-users. By developing an OEM arrangement with General Supply to reach drilling companies and a tie-in arrangement with Newtech to reach R&D markets, immediate access to end-user markets can be achieved. If successful, these actions will buy some time for AOS to develop marketing capabilities, and they should begin generating contributions from sales to cover the expenses of developing a marketing program. An essential element in the AOS marketing strategy is locating and hiring a person to manage the marketing effort. This person must have direct sales capabilities in addition to being able to perform market analysis and marketing program development, implementation, and management tasks."

The last part of your recommendations sections should be a tentative budget. This is important because it illustrates that the solution is worth the cost and is within the financial capabilities of the organization. Too often, students develop grandiose plans that firms couldn't possibly afford, even if they were worth the money.

The numbers used in your tentative budget may not be as accurate as they would be if you had complete access to company records. Make your best estimate and try to get as close to actual figures as possible. The exercise is good experience, and it shows that you have considered the cost implications.

Students often ask how long the recommendations sections should be, and how much detail they should go into. This question is difficult to answer because each case is different and should be treated that way. Keeping in mind the page limitations imposed upon you for this class, it is generally advisable to go into as much detail as possible. You may be criticized for not being specific enough in your recommendations, but you are not likely to be criticized for being too specific.

CASE 1: MOTHER DAIRY: A CASE FOR SUPPLY CHAIN MANAGEMENT?

Source: "The Milk Route," Business India, (Mar.22-April 4, 1999), p: 108

Imagine not getting your milk packet early in the morning. It will have a cascading effect on individuals and their work routines. D. Sharma, Deputy Manager (Marketing), Mother Dairy, New Delhi says, "We have not had a single day since 1974 when our tankers have not supplied milk." Supplying milk everyday without fail essentially means putting several principles of supply chain management to work. To understand supply chain management let us consider the nature of activities and the entities involved in supplying milk to the customers.

Mother Dairy obtains its milk from hundreds of co-operatives located in Gujarat, Haryana, Punjab, Rajasthan and Uttar Pradesh. The milk collected from these co-operatives is transported to the Patparganj plant in East Delhi, where it is homogenized, pasteurized and then stored in special tanks until it is loaded into tankers for distribution. Mother Dairy has a processing capacity of 650,000 litres per day. Nearly a hundred of its tankers cris-cross Delhi and supply milk to about 568 booths located in every nook and corner of the city. Besides its own booths, Mother Dairy also sells loose milk through over 200 manually operated insulated containers setup in shops in congested areas and also through 300 cycle rickshaws, which home delivers milk in some localities. Furthermore, it also sells milk through 850 retail shops in polythene packs.

Over the years, Mother Dairy has increased its variety of offerings. Skimmed, toned, double toned and full cream milk is available in half and one litre polythene packs. Several milk derivatives are also offered. For example, Mother Dairy offers over 30 flavours of ice creams. Managing such a large variety requires accurate methods of forecasting and demand management. Since milk is a perishable commodity with very short life cycle, logistics planning, demand estimation and production scheduling is very crucial.

Networking with the milk producing co-operatives and developing lasting relationships is crucial to ensuring an assured supply of good quality milk on a daily basis. Upkeep of the processing plant, maintenance and modernization are important aspects of the production process. The distribution of the processed milk and a large variety of milk derivatives require efficient network design, distribution requirement planning, logistics and transportation planning. Finally, managing information, material and funds flow across the different entities is crucial for business growth and profitability.

For a commodity that has a low shelf-life and criticality of time, appropriate measures of supply chain performance are required. Responsiveness, availability, timeliness, cost of distribution and levels of inventory at various points in the system are a representative set of measures. Good supply chain management pays attention to all these details.

1. Identify all the stages involved in the supply chain with reference to the above case.
2. Discuss the role of each stage in the supply chain.

CASE 2: TO BUY OR NOT TO BUY?

Being one of the earlier companies to start manufacturing, Mahindra &Mahindra's (M&Ms) thinking was different from the new companies that have entered India. It believed in localizing the manufacture of imported parts and aggregates for its vehicles. This had started as early as in 1957. As the infrastructure in terms of technology and ancillaries was lacking in the early years, M&M had to undertake the manufacture of a number of parts and aggregates itself in its facilities. While these competencies were its strengths in the pre-reform era, they had to be reassessed after liberalization. As capabilities developed in the auto-ancillary industry, the parts and aggregates had to be re-studied to arrive at the short and long-term strategy. M&M's approach was to select major components, sub-assemblies and assemblies, analyze their importance versus competitiveness matrix and arrive at a strategy for buying versus making. Buy low on importance and competitiveness, make high on importance and competitiveness; this exercise clearly helped the company identify the manufacturing areas to exit and the ones to remain in.

1. Discuss the change in the components and assemblies purchase policy of M&M? What are the reasons for the changes in policy?
2. Why do companies purchase fromexternal sources? Discuss the cost implications of Make vs Buy decisions?

CASE STUDY 3: SUPPLY CHAIN MANAGEMENT AT BOSE CORPORATION

Bose Corporation, headquartered in Framingham, Massachusetts, offers an excellent example of integrated supply management. Bose, a producer of audio premium speakers used in automobiles, high-fidelity systems, and consumer and commercial broadcasting systems, was founded in 1964 by Dr. Bose of MIT. Bose currently maintains plants in Massachusetts and Michigan as well as Canada,

Mexico and Ireland. Its purchasing organization, while decentralized, has some overlap that requires co-ordination between sites. It manages this co-ordination by using conference calls between mangers, electronic communication and joint problem solving. The company is moving towards single sourcing many of its 800 to 1000 parts, which include corrugated paper, particle board and wood, plastic moulded parts fasteners, glues, woofers and fabric.

Some product components, such as woofers, are sourced overseas. For example, at the Hillsdale, Michigan Plant, foreign sourcing accounts for 20% of purchases, with the remainder of suppliers located immediately within the state of Michigan. About 35% of the parts purchased at his site are single sourced, with approximately half of the components arriving with no incoming inspection performed. In turn, Bose ships finished products directly to Delco, Honda, Nissan, and has a record of no missed deliveries. Normal lead time to customers is 60 working days, but Bose can expedite shipments in one week and air freight them if necessary.

The company has developed a detailed supplier performance system that measures on –time delivery, quality performance, technical improvements, and supplier suggestions. A report is generated twice a month from this system and sent to the supplier providing feedback about supplier performance. If there is a three-week trend of poor performance, Bose will usually establish a specific goal for improvement that the supplier must attain. Examples include 10% delivery improvement every month until 100% conformance is achieved, or 5% quality improvement until a 1% defect level is reached over a four-month period. In one case, a supplier sent a rejected shipment back to Bose without explanation and with no corrective action taken. When no significant improvement occurred, another supplier replaced the delinquent supplier.

Bose has few written contracts with suppliers. After six months of deliveries without rejects, Bose encourages suppliers to apply for a certificate of achievement signifying that they are qualified suppliers. One of the primary criteria for gaining certification involves how well the supplier responds to corrective action requests. One of the biggest problems observed is that suppliers often correct problems on individual parts covered by a corrective action form without extending these corrective actions to other part families and applicable parts.

Bose has adopted a unique system of marrying just-in-time (JIT) purchasing with global sourcing. Approximately half of the dollar value of Bose's total purchases are made overseas, with the majority of the sourcing done in Asia. Because foreign sourcing does to support just-in-time deliveries, Bose "had a way to blend low inventory with buying from distant sources" says Lance Dixon, director of purchasing and logistics for Bose.

Visualizing itself as a customer-driven organization, Bose now uses a sophisticated transportation system–what Bose's manager of logistics calls "the best EDI system in the country". Working closely with a national less-than-truck-load-carrier for the bulk of its domestic freight movements, including shipments arriving at a U.S. port from overseas, Bose implemented an electronic data interchange (EDI) system that does much more than simple tracking. The system operates on real time and allows two-way communication between every one of the freight handler's 230 terminals and Bose. Information is updated several times daily and is downloaded automatically, enabling Bose to perform shipping analysis and distribution channel modeling to achieve reliable lowest total cost scenarios. The company can also request removal from terminal of any shipment that it must expedite with an air shipment.

This state-of-the-art system provides a snapshot of what is happening on a daily basis and keeps Bose's managers on top of everyday occurrences and decisions. Management proactively manages logistics time elements in pursuit of better customer service. The next step, Dixon feels, is to implement this system with all major suppliers rather than just with transportation suppliers. In the future, Bose plans to automate its entire material system.

Perhaps one of the most unique features of Bose's procurement and logistics system is the development of JIT II. This system was pioneered by Lance Dixon at corporate headquarters and has been reported on extensively in trade journals. The basic premise of JIT II is simple: The person who can do the best job of ordering and managing inventory of a particular item is the supplier himself. Bose plant who was responsible for ordering, shipping, and receiving materials from hat plant, as well as managing on-site inventories of the items. This was done through an EDI connection between Bose's plant and the supplier's facility. Co-locating suppliers and buyers was so successful that Bose is now implementing it at all plant locations. In fact, many other companies have also begun to implement co-location of suppliers.

1. What should be the relationship between Bose's supply management strategy and the development of its performance measurement?
2. Why is purchased quality important to Bose?
3. Can a just-in-time purchase system operate without total quality from suppliers?

CASE 4: HUL - LEVERAGING GROWTH THROUGH INFORMATION TECH.

When one thinks of Hindustan Unilever Ltd. (HUL) what comes to mind is India's leading FMCG (fast moving consumer goods) company with hundreds of products, and a supply and distribution chain of a magnitude few companies have.

HULs Home and Personal Care portfolio comprises of some of the biggest brands in India. In Soaps, the big brands are Lifebuoy, Lux, Liril, Breeze, Pears, Hamam and Dove. In Detergents, the big brands are International Surf Excel, Surf, Rin, Wheel, OK, 501, Sunlight, and Ala. To cater to Household Care, it markets the reliable Vim and Domex range. Its Personal Products business addresses Oral, Hair, and Skin Care needs. In Oral Care, Close-Up and Pepsodent toothpaste, toothbrushes and toothpowder are its offerings. In Hair Care, it has a host of products, ranging from shampoos to hair oils. Clinic, Sunsilk and Lux are its mega Hair Care brands. In Skin Care, it markets Fair & Lovely, Pond's, Lakme and Pears franchisees. In Colour Cosmetics, it markets the Lakme range of beauty products. In Deodorants and Fragrances, the household names are Rexona, Axe and Denim. HUL has achieved market leadership in soaps and detergents as well as hair and skin care products and is the second largest manufacturer of dental care products. HUL is also market leader in tea, processed coffee, ice cream and frozen desserts, tomato-based products, jams and squashes.

HUL, India's largest FMCG Company was looking out for a readymade IT package that would manage Inventory, Logistics and Financial information for both big and small players in its distribution chain. The company needed to keep track of products moving out of stockist locations and also determine the products that move fast, across the country.

Its main objective was to make stockist data available in an electronic format and move the data online, over the Web, for speedy processing and analysis so that all the information could be moved quickly to the company server. The whole exercise was undertaken to reduce logistics and inventory costs and make accounting a simpler process.

During a survey conducted by Botree it found that 95 percent of HUL's stockists were handling inventory, sales orders and logistics manually. The challenge was to implement Stocky@Fmcg at 200 stockists across Tamil Nadu, Andhra Pradesh, Karnataka and Calcutta. The entire project was to be completed in a period of seven months.

In the case of HUL, 70 percent of business came from 30 percent of its stockists. So there was an urgent need to increase efficiency and make the stockists data available online for faster order processing and data analysis.

Responding to this immediate need, HUL carefully selected and implemented a stockist automation solution from Botree Software called Stocky@Fmcg aimed at managing stockist inventory, logistics and financial data. This investment was to payoff by bringing about an increase in efficiency, productivity and profitability in terms of cost and time.

Implementing the package at 200 HUL stockist locations over a 7 month period was not an easy job as the majority of stockists felt that they were not tech-savvy enough to handle Stocky@Fmcg. Thus, It took five days for providing onsite training and implementing Stocky at each location.

Instead of spending hours at their godown counting stocks, and making over 150 manual bills daily, stockists were now having to spend only a few minutes getting valuable information at the click of a mouse. This led to enormous cost and time savings for both the company and its stockists by at least 35 percent.

On considering a full month's inventory, stockist were able to reduce (optimize) inventory by seven days. Similarly, a C&F agent was able to reduce inventory by six days, while retailers saved up to seven days of inventory.

The second phase of the implementation was to get stockists to log onto the HUL site and enter their requirements pertaining to stock and sales, order booking & claims information. HUL introduced incentive schemes to motivate its stockist to post their data online. This centrally available repository of secondary distribution data was a big milestone in establishing HUL's connectivity with its stockist community.

To ensure near zero downtime HUL hired 4 technical support executives from Botree, to provide support to their Calcutta and South India installations. These tech. support professionals continue to assist stockists by troubleshooting any problems that may arise out of the package.

Identify the major benefits derived by HUL as a result of the use of Information Technology in its operations.

CASE 5: TRANSPORTING SAMSUNG

A major component of transportation costs is contributed by the time that products spend on the road before reaching dealers or retailers. Not only do these periods mean costs in terms of inventories, they are also anti-thrift. For, when delivery routes are unplanned, unnecessary journeys are made, consuming resources like transportation-time and diesel. The solution? Streamlining the delivery route-map, to minimize the length and, by extension, duration of the trips made for the products.

One company that is serious about cutting such costs is Samsung. Using software to match the product requirements of its dealers with delivery schedules, the company does detailed route-planning before its trucks set off. In fact, the process begins on the high seas, since Samsung imports its refrigerators. For starters, integrating its deliveries to dealer needs led the company to off load the products at Chennai, besides Mumbai. Thus, land shipments now started from 2 points instead from one, which has helped rationalize the travelling.

Then, Samsung worked out different levels of fleet-strength and travelling to identify the least-cost combination of number of trucks and time spent on the road. This wasn't as easy as it sounds: there was, after all, a trade-off between the strength of the fleet and the duration of journeys. But optimize the two it did, and Samsung's distribution cost per unit is down by 25 percent. Overall logistics costs have dropped to 0.70 percent of sales in 1998, from 1.20 percent in 1997. Says R. Sridharan, Deputy General Manager, Samsung India Electronics: 'In this fiercely competitive industry, every rupee saved counts.'

1. Discuss the major changes in the strategies of Samsung. What has been the impact of these changes on the profit of the company? Explain with reasons.
2. What are the various transportation options available to sellers in the international markets?

CASE 6: ROUTING AND BACKHAULING

Companies are trying to find out new and innovative ways to save money through outbound transportation logistics. The luggage major, Samsonite, has found a way called backhauling-of sending double the goods to some markets without raising costs. It has tied up with transporters of car majors, Maruti Udyog and Hyundai, to utilise their trucks on their return journeys to the respective factories.

It works this way. Samsonite's factory is located in Nasik (Maharashtra), Maruti has its factory in Gurgaon (near Delhi), and Hyundai's works are located at Irunggattukottai (Tamil Nadu). Maruti and Hyundai use special, large capacity, 'scooter-bodied' trucks to transport their cars from north and south India, respectively, to markets in western India. These trucks look for any load they can get while making a trip back to their respective factories. The advantage: for a normal truck, it pays Rs. 15000-17000 between Delhi-Nasik and can load about 350 suitcases. When it uses the scooter-bodied trucks for Delhi, it still pays the same amount but sends over 700 suitcases.

1. How has the management of outbound logistics affected the cost-efficiency of the companies?
2. Explain the importance of 'routing' and 'backhauling' with reference to the above.

CASE 7: REDUCING INVENTORY

A manufacturer of computer peripheral devices was looking to improve its balance sheet and P&L by reducing inventory and the associated carrying costs, while improving customer service. The products required to support different customer channels varied from expensive long lead time engineered systems to relatively low-value standalone units that supported personal computers. The company needed to completely revamp its inventory, manufacturing and product support policies, procedures and practices to reflect the dramatic and fast changes to its product line.

The company performed a logistics cost/performance benchmark for all of the divisions showing that inventory carrying costs were extremely high. The bulk of the problem was in inventory management, there were problems managing the broad mix of products required as well as large amounts of obsolete and slow-moving inventory. A cross- functional team was formed that included members from Operations, Marketing, Sales and Finance to evaluate and dispose off excess and obsolete inventories. The process of creating inventory was benchmarked to "best-practices" to identify improvement opportunities in purchasing, materials management, inventory planning and management, and the manufacturing operations.

In purchasing and materials management it was recommended that the total purchasing power of the corporation be leveraged to obtain more favorable purchasing and consignment agreements by centralizing the purchasing function. At the same time, local materials management functions could be strengthened to improve requisitioning and materials usage and upstream supply chain partnerships were established to improve material flow and reduce purchased parts inventories.

In inventory planning and management, a centralized logistics function was recommended. Written policies and procedures were developed for inventory planning, management and reporting, and a new forecasting and inventory planning business process and information system was implemented. All inventories are now managed more intensively to avoid excess and obsolete inventories and active inventories are deployed and re-deployed based on well-defined forecast requirements. The promotion process was also brought under control to avoid sudden unanticipated demand on the plants, and manufacturing performance criteria was changed from lowest unit cost and high absorption to meeting the schedule in time and quantity to improve customer service levels. The two main questions that need to be answered are:

1. What would the impact be on profit from the disposal of obsolete inventory in order to improve the balance sheet?
2. How do we institute a program to prevent the build-up of obsolete inventories by disposing of slow movers on a regular basis?

CASE 8: MANAGING THE MATERIALS

Office Automation Ltd., a Rs. 300 crore company is engaged in the import, sales and service of office automation equipment like photocopiers, fax machines, paper shredders, currency counters etc. The company sources these equipment from manufacturers located in Japan, USA and Europe. The company has 20 sales and service offices located in India. All the sales and service offices carry all types of equipment and spares with them. The Head Office of the company is located in Mumbai and it undertakes the procurement of all the required equipment and spares for all the offices. The sales and service offices forward their requirement once in three months and the head office places order for container loads to save on freight costs. If the branch offices miss to include a particular item in their list they have to wait for three months before their request is processed.

The head office and the branch offices control their inventory on stand alone software procured locally. The head office maintains an average inventory of Rs. 100 crores out of which spare parts are worth Rs. 50 crore. On an average the branch offices carry an inventory of Rs. 50 crore out of which spare parts are worth Rs. 30 crore. At the branch level, the sales executives place orders for the requirement of equipment and spares and all such record is maintained by an office assistant. The chartered accountant auditing the company accounts pointed out that the inventory holding of the company is very high and they should reduce the same to increase profitability.

1. Comment on the current situation with respect to inventory control.
2. What steps should be taken to reduce the inventory levels?

CASE 9: MANAGING MOVEMENT OF MEDICAL PRODUCTS

A manufacturer of time-sensitive medical products could not reduce its high freight costs. The company had undertaken significant initiatives to improve financial performance. A new computer system had been installed, underutilized distribution centers had been closed, carriers had been changed, parcel rates had been renegotiated, new budgets had been created and yet freight costs had sky-rocketed.

The company identified the problems and brought the costs back under control at much reduced levels. The first step was some detective work on the shipping dock. Careful observation of companies' shipments and parcel shipping histories showed the company was failing to consolidate customer orders. Customers could be shipped a minimum-size order and several parcel ground orders on the same day. Customer orders were dropped to the warehouse every hour to "move cash" as quickly as possible and to keep warehouse staff busy. Warehouse staff costs, however, were a fraction of the freight costs. Furthermore, dropping orders every hour negated the sophisticated labour planning capabilities of the new warehouse computer system. By holding the orders and dropping them to the warehouse only once or twice per day, the company was able to consolidate orders into larger, more cost-effective shipments. Further changes in shipping procedures and the usage of specific distribution centers for individual product lines further reduced distances, delivery times and costs.

The company now manages transportation with an eye towards cost-effective shipping and freight costs are consistently well-below budget. Peripheral benefits have also been realized in more efficient warehouse operations, as planning for larger shipments has reduced warehouse labour efforts and costs.

1. What was the root cause of such an increase in costs?
2. What could be done to bring costs back in line and meet management expectations?

CASE 10: WAREHOUSE MANAGEMENT SYSTEM

Established in 1956, Dexter Shoe currently operates 77 retail outlets throughout New England, New York, and New Jersey. Dexter Shoe manufactures and distributes rugged recreational footwear, golf and bowling shoes, and comfort casual shoes for men and women. Dexter Shoe also supplies a national and international wholesale market from its 485,000 square foot shoe complex in Dexter, Maine.

Since being acquired by H.H. Brown, a Warren Buffet company, Dexter Shoe has been actively searching for improved efficiencies by increasing warehouse capacity and reducing cost by increasing the utilization of staff and equipment. The H.H. Brown team was interested in creating a multi-division distribution center (each existing divisional warehouse was capable of distributing only its own product line) which would allow consolidation, and in turn, require less warehouse facilities. Due to its large capacity and existing conveyor automation, Dexter Shoe was chosen as the site for the new consolidated center.

- Design and implement a multi-divisioncapable warehouse management system.
- Develop software to replace the existing warehouse system as well as facilitate cost and efficiency recommendations.
- Build communication software to integrate with their automated conveyor systems and customized Pitney Bowes shipping system.

- Replace obsolete hand-held devices with interactive, radio frequency hand-held scanners.
- Implement solutions to eliminate pre-printed forms and consolidate multiple forms and labels.
- Seamlessly integrate new warehouse system with H.H. Brown's existing allocation and billing system.
- Research and implement bar code scanning enhancements to improve the efficiency of order process.

Working with both Dexter Shoe and H.H. Brown personnel, ISG conducted a thorough analysis of the content, strengths and weaknesses of Dexter's existing warehouse system. This information, combined with additional functional requirements gathered during research trips to other distribution and manufacturing divisions, was consolidated to form the design and project plan for the new Warehouse Management System. ISG also conducted the research to select the development languages, hand-held devices, communication technology and forms tools. The final design document included a comprehensive hardware and software plan for a new Warehouse Management System that would leverage existing warehouse functions with new systems that provided the flexibility, functionality and efficiencies as outlined by H.H. Brown's corporate team. Key components of Dexter Shoe's new WMS system include:

- Single warehouse storage of multi-division inventory with divisional reporting capabilities.
- User-defined location types for primary pick, flow racks, pallet storage, backup case storage, and operational areas such as packing, labeling, and shipping.
- Random put-away of backup cases.
- Intelligent conveyor routing utilizing user-defined route maps.
- Dynamic replenishment algorithms to allow volume picking from temporary flow rack locations (to avoid constant replenishment).
- Multi-order totes used to consolidate multiple pick slips into more efficient picking operations.
- Multiple single line order consolidation to full cases when possible. Allows full cases to be sent directly to packing for subsequent individual order fulfillment.
- Warehouse operations conducted via wireless hand-held scanners. Applications include picking, packing, labeling, receiving, case pull, case put away, cycle count, physical inventory, and various inquiry programs.
- Create custom labeling programs using forms generation tools. Additional forms include various packing lists and VICS Bill of Lading.
- Integrated interface to H.H. Brown's order allocation and billing system.

Dexter Shoe has successfully converted to the new Warehouse Management System designed and built by The Integrated Solution Group. Three weeks after the conversion to the new system, Dexter Shoe was receiving and shipping shoes for H.H. Brown's Carolina Shoe division. In accordance with the corporate plan, H.H. Brown personnel are currently transferring all Carolina Shoe merchandise to Dexter Shoe's Maine warehouse complex. Other product lines are also being considered for consolidation at Dexter Shoe. The final result will be improved efficiencies through volume and operational consolidation, while maximizing the utilization of Dexter Shoe's facilities and allowing disposition of excess H.H. Brown real estate in other parts of the country.

REFERENCES

1. Arjan J. Weele, *"Purchasing and Supply Chain Management"*, 2nd Edition, 2001, Vikas Publishing House.
2. B.S. Sahay, *"Supply Chain Management"*, 2nd Edition, 2004, MacMillan India Ltd.
3. Cecil C. Bozarth, Robert B. Handfield, *"Introduction to Operations and Supply Chain Management"*, First Impression, 2006, Pearson Education.
4. Chandra C. Grabis J, *"SC Configuration"*, 2007, Springer, New York.
5. David J. Bloomberg, Stephen Lemay, Joe B. Hanna, *"Logistics"*, 2002, Prentice Hall of India Pvt. Ltd.
6. David Piasecki, *"Inventory Management Explained"*, March 2009.
7. David Simchi-Levi, Phillip Kaminsky, Edith Simchi-Levi, *"Designing and Managing the Supply Chain"*, 2nd Edition, Tata McGraw-Hill Publishing Co. Ltd, New Delhi.
8. Donald J. Bowersox, David J. Closs, *"Logistical Management"*, International Edition, 1996, Tata McGraw-Hill Publishing Limited, New Delhi.
9. Donald J. Bowersox, David J. Closs, M. Bixby Cooper, *"Supply Chain Logistics Management"*, 2nd Edition, 2007, McGraw-Hill International Edition.
10. J.L. Gattorna and D.W. Walters, *"Managing the Supply Chain"*, Palgrave Publishers Ltd.
11. James H. Greene, American Production and Inventory Control Society, *"Production and Inventory Control Handbook"*, 1996, McGraw-Hill.
12. Jeremy F. Shapiro, *"Modeling the Supply Chain"*, 2001, Duxbury Thomson Learning.
13. John Gattorna, *"Living Supply Chains"*, 2006, Pearson Education.
14. John J. Coyle, Edward J Bardi, C. John Langley Jr, *"The Management of Business Logistics"*, First Reprint 2003, Thomson Asia Pvt. Ltd. Singapore.
15. K. Shridhara Bhat, *"Essentials of Logistics and Supply Chain Management"*, 1st Edition, 2007, Himalaya Publishing House.
16. K. Shridhara Bhat, *"Logistics and Supply Chain Management"*, 1st Edition, 2007, Himalaya Publishing House.
17. Martin Christopher, *"Logistics and Supply Chain Management"*, 1992, Pitman Publishing, London.
18. Martin Christopher, *"Logistics and Supply Chain Management"*, 2nd Edition, 2005, Pearson Education (Singapore) Pvt. Ltd.

19. Paul R. Murphy, Jr. Donald F. Wood, *"Contemporary Logistics"*, 9th Edition, 2008, PHI, New Delhi.
20. R.B. Handfield and E.L. Nochols, Jr. *"Introduction to Supply Chain Management"*, 1999, Prentice Hall.
21. R.H. Ballou, *"Business Logistics Management"*, 3rd Edition, Englewood Cliffs, NJ: Prentice Hall, 1992.
22. Richard J. Tersine, *"Principles of Inventory and Materials Management"*, 1993, PTR Prentice Hall.
23. Robert Monczka, Robert Trent, Robert Handfield, *"Purchasing and Supply Chain Management"*, 2nd Edition 2002, Thomson-South-Western.
24. Ronald H. Ballou, *"Business Logistics/Supply Chain Management"*, 5th Edition, Second Indian Reprint, 2004, Pearson Education (Singapore) Pvt Ltd.
25. Simchi-Levi D, Wu SD and Zuo-Yun S, *"Handbook of Quantitative Supply Chain Analysis"*, 2004, Springer, New York.
26. Sunil Chopra, Peter Meindl, *"Supply Chain Management"*, 3rd Edition, 2007, PHI
27. Sunil Chopra, Peter Meindl, *"Supply Chain Management, Strategy, Planning and Operation"*, 2007, Pearson Education, New Jersey.

Subject Index

A

ABC-VED Matrix 61
Accessorial Services 194
Air Transport 186
Airplanes 13
Artificial Intelligence 223
Assortment 138
Automated conveyor systems 175
Automated Handling 170
Automated storage 175
Automated-Guided Vehicle 168
Average Cost 102

B

Bar Code Technology 222
Basic Handling Considerations 164
Behavioural Obstacles 147
Blister packaging 201
Break Bulk 140
Buffer Uncertainties 40
Building Relationships 128
Bullwhip Effect 147
Business knowledge 85
Business Strategy 19

C

Carousels 167
Carrier Management 195
Carriers 182
Categorical Method 96
Centralized Purchasing 81
Channel Power 130
Class Rates 191
Combination rates 193
Combination Strategy 191
Commodity Rates 191
Communication Technology 223
Competitive Advantage 27
Competitive Pressures 129
Competitive Weapon 120
Concept of SCM 5
Consignees 181
Contact Warehouse 144
Contract purchasing 80
Conveyors 167
Corrugated Fibreboard Boxes 206
Cost efficiency 225
Cost of Packing 207
Cost Structures 189
cost-efficient operations 44
Cost-of-Service Strategy 190
Cost-ratio Method 97
Crates 206
Cross Dock 140
Customer orientation 225
Customers 19
Cycle Inventory 11

D

Data Warehouse Technology 223
Database Technology 223
Decentralized Purchasing 81
Decoupling 39
Density 188
Dependent demand inventory item 41
Discounting Model 54
Distance 188
Distribution Centre 134
Distributors 18
Drivers of SCM 9

E

E-Commerce 225
Economic Batch Quantity 53
Economy of distance 180
Economy of scale 180
Effective Purchasing 83
Electronic Business 224
Electronic Data Interchange 222
Electronic Transport 13
Emerging Markets 154

Enterprise Information Technologies 215I
Enterprise Management 3
Environmental Requirements 210
Evergreen Clause 87
Expert System 223
Export Boxes 208
Extended Storage 164

F

First In First Out 102
Fixed Costs 190
Forecasting 14
Forecasting Models 133
Forklift Trucks 166
Freight auditing 226
Freight Pay and Audit 196
Functional focus 11

G

Geographical Specialization 39
Government 182

H

Handling 188
Handling marks 208
Holding costs 42

I

Improved Customer Satisfaction 119
Improved Customer Service 126
In-storage Handling 162
Inbound logistics 127
Incentive Obstacles 146
Increased Efficiency 125
Increased Sales 127
Independent demand inventory item 41
Information 5, 14
Information databases 92
Information marks 208
Information Processing Obstacles 146
Information Sharing 217
Information Technology 130, 215
Information-Directed Systems 173
ntegrated Logistics Management 7
Inventory 5, 11
Inventory Control 61
Inventory Cost 41
Inventory Functionality 38
inventory investment 44
Inventory Management 43
Inventory Models 133
Item costs 41

J

JIT Concept 107

K

Kanban 113

L

Last In First Out 102
Lead-time 45
Lean Customers 118
Lean Manufacturing 117
Lean Procurement 117
Lean Suppliers 116
Lean Supply Chain 116, 120
Lean Transportation 118
Lean Warehousing 117
Legal knowledge 85
Liability 188
Live Racks 169
Load Planning and Optimization 195
Location 5, 12
Logistics Costs 131
Logistics Management 129
Logistics Outsourcing 153

M

Manufacturing 38
Market Factors 189
Market Presence 139
Market purchasing 79
Market Value 102
Mathematical Programming Models 133
Mechanized Systems 165

Motor Carriers 184

N

Negotiations 100
Network Technology 224
New Suppliers 98

O

Objectives of JIT 108
Online Shipping Inquiry 226
Operational Obstacles 146
Ordering costs 42
Outbound logistics 128
Outsourcing 151
Outsourcing Functions 156
Outsourcing Operations 155

P

Packaging and 159
Packaging Design 198
Packing Boxes 205
Packing of Goods 203
Paper Based Packaging 200
Paperboard cans 200
Paperboard folding cartons 200
People Involvement 109
Performance Measurement and Management 196
Physical Distribution Management 7
Pick-to-Light Systems 168
Pipelines 13, 186
Planned Storage 163
Planning 87
Plastic bag 201
Plastic Packaging 199
Potential of Automation 170
Pricing Obstacles 146
Primacy of Strategy 32
Private Warehouses 142
Producers 17
Product focus 10
Product Movement 179
Product Storage 180
Production 4, 10
Production Support 139
Profit Leverage 130
Public Warehouses 143
Pull System 112
Purchase Department 81
Purchasing Process 76
Put-away Practices 176

Q

Quality control 62

R

Rail 13
Rail Network 184
Receipt of Materials 102
Reduced Costs 119
Reduced Inventories 119
Reorder Point 49
Request for Quotation 89
Retail 38
Retailers 18
Reverse Flow 15
RF equipment 175
Robotics 169
Routing Models 133

S

Safety Inventory 12
Sales representatives 92
Schedule purchasing 80
Scheduling Models 133
Selection Process 90
Selective Inventory Management 55
Semi automated Handling 168
Service Benefits 142
Service Providers 19
Shipment Monitoring 195
Shipment tracking 226
Shippers 181
Shipping 163
Shipping Documentation 226
Shipping Execution 195

Shipping marks 208
Shipping notice 226
Shortage costs 42
Single Vendor Development 98
Skin packaging 201
Sortation 169
Source Selection 89
Sourcing Alternatives 93
Special Handling Considerations 174
Speculative purchasing 79
Split Delivery 193
Spot Stock 137
Stock and Inventory 157
Stock Verification 103
Stockpiling 142
Storages 134
Storekeeping 100
Stores Accounting 102
Stores Accounting System 103
Successful Storekeeping 101
Supplier Evaluation 90
Supply and Production 33
supply chain 1
Supply Chain Decisions 4
Supply Chain Information Processing 216

T

Tow Tractor with Trailers 167
Towlines 166
Training 87
Transport 158
Transport Economics 187
Transport Functionality 179
Transport Infrastructure 184
Transportation 5, 13
Transportation Decisions 181
Trucks 13

U

Unitization 159

V

Value and Waste 115
Value Chain 30
Value Chains 27, 32
Vendor Development 97
Voice recognition technology 213
Volume 188

W

Walkie-Rider Pallet Trucks 166
Warehouse 134, 137
Warehouse Resource 162
Warehousing 135
Warehousing Alternatives 139
Waste of overproduction 105
Water Transport 185
Wave picking 212
Weighted Point Method 96
Wholesaler 38
Wood density 207
Wooden Boxes 206
Working Capital Costs 145

Z

Zone picking 212